SPIES, INFORMERS AN
'ANTI-SINN FÉIN SOG

SPIES, INFORMERS
AND THE
'ANTI-SINN FÉIN SOCIETY'

The Intelligence War in Cork City
1920–1921

John Borgonovo

Foreword by
Eunan O'Halpin

IRISH ACADEMIC PRESS
DUBLIN • PORTLAND, OR

First published in 2007 by
IRISH ACADEMIC PRESS
44, Northumberland Road, Dublin 4, Ireland
and in the United States of America by
IRISH ACADEMIC PRESS
c/o ISBS, Suite 300, 920 NE 58th Avenue
Portland, Oregon 97213-3786

WEBSITE: www.iap.ie

British Library Cataloguing in Publication Data
An entry can be found on request

ISBN 0 7165 2832 0 (cloth)
ISBN 978 0 7165 2832 6 (cloth)
ISBN 0 7165 2833 9 (paper)
ISBN 978 0 7165 2833 3 (paper)

Library of Congress Cataloging-in-Publication Data
An entry can be found on request

Typeset by FiSH Books, Enfield, Middx.
Printed by Antony Rowe Ltd., Chippenham, Wiltshire

Contents

Acknowledgements

This book was originally undertaken in 1997 as a Master of Arts thesis at University College Cork. Since then, that work has collected dust on a shelf at UCC's Boole Library. While editing Florence O'Donoghue's memoir (*Florence and Josephine O'Donoghue's War of Independence, 'A Destiny that Shapes Our Ends'*), I received some research assistance from Jack Lane of the Aubane Historical Society. Much to my surprise, Jack asked me if I had any plans to publish my thesis. It still seems remarkable to me that someone actually found the work, and read it. That conversation led to the release of this book by Irish Academic Press. Much thanks is due to Jack for his initial encouragement, and to my editor Lisa Hyde, who proved equally enthusiastic when I proposed the project to her.

I received a tremendous amount of assistance while researching this book. I would like to thank the staffs at the National Library of Ireland, the Military Archives at Cathal Brugha Barracks; the University College Dublin Archives Department; the Cardiff City Library; the Imperial War Museum in London; Boole Library at University College Cork; the Cork Public Museum; the Cork City Library; the Cork Archives Institute; the Cork YMCA; and the Irish Cultural Center in San Francisco. Along the way a number of people helped with my research, including Meda Ryan, Tom O'Neil, Sgt. Gerry White, the late Dr Margaret O'Donoghue, and Donal Donovan.

My year at University College Cork was a remarkable learning experience. During my studies, Professor Gabriel Doherty shepherded me through UCC's academic maze, and served as an excellent thesis advisor. In the past year, he has also graciously provided his advice during my two book projects. I am grateful for his assistance over the years.

While living in Cork, I was fortunate for the friendship of Kevin Keily, Chris Murray, Ray Walsh, Barry Coleman, and Niall de Barra. They made my stay entertaining, and have since provided me with comfortable bases of operations during my return trips to Ireland.

My associates in San Francisco and Oregon have proved supportive of my continued study of this period. Many an evening they have listened to my thoughts about the Irish Revolution. Their patience with my perceived historic eccentricity is much appreciated.

Since I dedicated my first book to my parents, I feel free to dedicate this work to the rest of my family. They have always offered their love and encouragement, even when it has not been asked. Thanks to my sister Nora, sister Ann, new brother-in-law Mike, brother Dan, sister-in-law Brenda, and my nephews Aidan and Casey who always make me laugh.

Foreword

John Borgonovo's book is essential reading for anyone who wishes to understand the Irish revolution. It cannot answer every question which arises about the nature and the ethics of political violence in Cork city during the War of Independence, but it addresses the grim matter of premeditated death in a disciplined and dispassionate manner, drawing on a range of sources, many of which, such as the Bureau of Military History statements, have only recently become available. These give IRA perspectives on individual acts of violence, where previously historians had had to rely largely on the British military and police accounts, supplemented by newspapers and local memory.

As Peter Hart, Meda Ryan and others have shown, Cork county was an exceptionally violent place during the War of Independence. This book makes a comparable contribution in respect of Cork city, not only in charting that violence, but in advancing explanations of it. This is particularly so in respect of IRA motivations for the shooting of alleged informers, an especially difficult area which cannot be considered and understood in isolation from the actions of the British government and of Crown forces, and from the IRA's understanding of how those forces secured information from the local population, which included many Protestant loyalists and a very large number of ex-servicemen, some of them unemployed and in desperate straits.

Borgonovo makes excellent use of the recollections of IRA men involved in some particularly ghastly killings. Mick Murphy, later to captain Cork to All Ireland hurling glory, recalled the exceptional talkativeness of one fifteen-year-old, the son of an Englishman, caught while attempting to track the movements of a group of volunteers. The child was imprisoned for a time while interrogated; then he was shot. Was age not considered a mitigating factor in Cork city, as it was during the considerable campaign in Ireland and Britain to secure clemency for Kevin Barry ('Just a lad of eighteen summers', and my grandmother's brother), who did not even contest the charges of killing British soldiers for which he was condemned? Again, Borgonovo deals in detail with the fate of James Blemens and his son Frederick. James Blemens was believed to be at the centre of a group of loyalists who met secretly in the city to collate information of possible use to the authorities – a so-called 'Anti-Sinn Féin Society'. Whether such a group existed, and whether Blemens was part of it, and whether that necessitated his abduction, interrogation and death, why did his son, whose executioners themselves thought insignificant, also have to die? Would the example of the father's death not have served just as well as a warning to others minded to give information to the authorities?

   John Borgonovo's exploration of the organization and conduct of the intelligence war in Cork city in 1920/1, and especially his dissection of premeditated civilian deaths, makes for shocking though fascinating reading. The narrative and analysis are too unsettling for a casual or whimsical glance; this valuable book needs to be read from start to finish.

Professor Eunan O'Halpin
Dublin
August 2006

Introduction

Cork city offers an excellent case study of the Irish Republican Army (IRA) campaign of 1919–21. In many ways, the city was a microcosm of the larger struggle in Ireland. Hunger strikes, assassinations, ambushes, espionage, executions, and reprisals occurred in Cork with a dizzying frequency. Led by officers regarded by the British Army as 'probably the best in Ireland,'[1] the city Volunteers were an elite within the IRA. For two years the Cork city IRA proved bold, resourceful, and unyielding in its fight for Irish independence from Britain.

During the guerrilla conflict, the Cork city IRA also distinguished itself through a brutal campaign against local civilians suspected of providing information to the Crown forces. In 1920–21, the IRA executed at least twenty-six Cork citizens for 'spying'. This study attempts to answer four essential questions about those events. (1) Who were the Cork city civilians shot by the IRA in 1920–21? (2) Were they informers? (3) What was the context of the killings? (4) Was the IRA intelligence network capable of identifying civilian spies operating in the city?

The activities of the shadowy 'Anti-Sinn Féin Society' also play a prominent role in this history. Employed by Crown forces as a cover for unofficial reprisals in the city during late 1920, the 'Anti-Sinn Féin Society' moniker was also used by IRA veterans to describe a presumed circle of Cork loyalists accused of providing information to the British. Determining the existence of such a group is essential to deconstructing the IRA's actions against Cork's perceived informers amid the confusion and turmoil of 1920–21.

This work is essentially an updated version of my MA thesis completed at University College Cork in 1997.[2] Since then, a debate has arisen in the Irish historical community concerning the IRA's execution of alleged civilian informers during the Irish War of Independence. Much of that discussion centres on Dr Peter Hart's *The IRA and Its Enemies, Violence and Community in Cork, 1916–1923.*[3] When I originally completed this study in 1997, Dr Hart's book had not yet been published, though I did review his PhD thesis of the same title and briefly addressed his central themes. I have since expanded my own response, strictly in terms of

1

interpreting events in Cork city in 1920–21. New material has also been added, including the Bureau of Military History statements of Cork IRA veterans, and a memoir written by the IRA intelligence officer Florence O'Donoghue and his wife Josephine Brown O'Donoghue, one of the top Republican spies of the conflict. That memoir, *Florence and Josephine O'Donoghue's War of Independence, 'A Destiny that Shapes Our Ends'* was published by Irish Academic Press in March 2006. (I am the editor of that work.)

This book focuses exclusively on events in Cork city during 1920–21. My study does not address the larger issue of civilian informants during the Irish War of Independence, or explain IRA attitudes towards its perceived civilian enemies throughout Ireland. However, it is hoped that when studying the example of Cork city, the reader will consider its wider implications in the Anglo-Irish conflict of 1919–21.

NOTES

1 Peter Hart (ed.), *British Intelligence in Ireland, 1920–21, The Final Reports* (Cork: Cork University Press, 2002), p. 39.
2 The thesis can be found in the Boole Library, University College Cork, under its original title, *Informers, Intelligence and the 'Anti Sinn Féin Society': The Anglo-Irish Conflict in Cork City, 1920–21.*
3 Peter Hart *The IRA and Its Enemies, Violence and Community in Cork, 1916–1923* (Oxford: Oxford University Press, 1998).

CHAPTER ONE

The 'Anti-Sinn Féin Society'

The Anglo-Irish war in Cork city reached its crescendo on the night of 11 December 1920. Following an IRA ambush of a police patrol (Auxiliary Cadets) in Cork's suburbs, enraged British forces burned down sections of the city centre, destroying civic landmarks and scores of local businesses, causing millions of pounds in damage and throwing between 1,500 and 2,000 people out of work. The reprisal shocked Ireland and brought international attention to the conflict in Cork. A sympathetic observer wrote: 'Cork is heroic, noble, immortal; its ruins are a monument to her love for liberty and humanity.'[1] The events of that evening were the culmination of a year-long escalation of violence in the city.[2]

The Irish Volunteer movement first gained headway in Cork city in early 1914. Founded by Tomás MacCurtain, with the assistance of Terence MacSwiney and Seán O'Hegarty, by 1916 the city had developed into one of the strongest centres of Volunteer activity in the country. During the Easter Rising, however, confusion over orders and events in Dublin prevented the Cork Volunteers from joining the rebellion and resulted in the surrender of their weapons, much to the disgust of rank-and-file Volunteers.[3] Both the Irish Volunteers and Irish Republican Brotherhood [IRB] organisations court-martialled MacCurtain and MacSwiney for their role in the fiasco.[4] Although the leaders were eventually exonerated, many Cork Republicans felt dishonoured by their inaction. Four years later, as Terence MacSwiney lay dying at the end of his fabled hunger strike, he wrote to IRA leader Cathal Brugha: 'Ah Cathal, the pain of Easter Week is dead at last.'[5]

BEGINNING OF THE IRA CAMPAIGN IN CORK CITY

Cork's Volunteer organization [hereafter used interchangeably with the term Irish Republican Army or IRA] remained intact after the

Rising, though younger and more militant officers soon rose into its leadership ranks. By late 1918 the city boasted two Volunteer battalions (The First and Second), and served as the headquarters and operations base for the newly organized Cork No. 1 Brigade, commanded by Tomás MacCurtain. (Three Cork brigades represented the following areas: Cork No. 1 Brigade, Cork city and Mid-Cork; Cork No. 2 Brigade, North Cork; and Cork No. 3 Brigade, West Cork.) By the end of 1919, city Volunteers were impatient to take the field against British forces.[6] According to Cork No. 1 Brigade Adjutant Florence O'Donoghue:

> A fair state of training, organization and discipline had been obtained; training was beginning to pall; police aggressions, raids, searches, espionage and arrests were likely to increase where no effective resistance was offered; the prospect of obtaining arms, except by capture from the occupation forces was extremely poor; and the political field did not appear to offer any reasonable hope that freedom would be achieved without fighting for it.[7]

On the evening of 2 January 1920, Cork No. 1 Brigade units stormed Carrigtwohill Royal Irish Constabulary (RIC) Barracks, the first British post captured in Ireland since 1916.[8] IRA Chief of Staff Richard Mulcahy wrote: 'the actions in Cork may be considered to be the beginning of the nation-wide offensive in reply to the suppression of Dáil Éireann.'[9]

Three months later, the Anglo-Irish conflict accelerated in Cork city. On 19 March 1920, IRA gunmen assassinated Constable Murtagh near the city centre. Hours later, local Royal Irish Constabulary (RIC) officers burst into the home of Brigade Commander Tomás MacCurtain (the recently elected Lord Mayor of Cork) and shot him down at his bedroom door.[10] The MacCurtain assassination galvanized Republicans throughout Ireland and became a focus of Brigade operations during the next five months. Terence MacSwiney succeeded MacCurtain as both Lord Mayor and Commander of the Cork No. 1 Brigade. MacCurtain's death also returned Seán O'Hegarty to the IRA leadership, a year after he resigned as Brigade Vice-Commander during a feud with MacCurtain over IRB activity in the city (O'Hegarty led the city IRB).[11] Throughout the spring and summer, IRA attacks against police and British soldiers became more common throughout Cork. In response, RIC reinforcements (British recruits known as 'Black and Tans'), Auxiliary Cadets (a specially raised police division composed of former British military officers),[12] and the British Army moved into the city.

Cork's next crisis began on the evening of 12 August 1920. British troops raided Cork City Hall and arrested thirteen IRA Volunteers, including Lord Mayor Terence MacSwiney.[13] The British Army had uncovered a Cork No. 1 Brigade Council meeting and captured the unit's senior leaders. Brigade Commander MacSwiney, Vice-Commander Seán O'Hegarty, Quartermaster Joe O'Connor, Fourth Battalion Commander Michael Leahy, and city First Battalion Commander Dan Donovan were arrested. For good measure, the soldiers also netted Cork No. 2 Commander Liam Lynch, present for an IRB meeting later that evening. Brigade Adjutant Florence O'Donoghue (who escaped arrest) called the City Hall raid 'the most important capture of the war in Munster'.[14]

Remarkably, the British military snatched defeat from the jaws of victory. A few days after the raid, with the exception of Terence MacSwiney, the City Hall prisoners were released apparently without being identified. The British Army's inability to recognize Cork's senior Volunteer leadership illustrates its poor intelligence standing in the summer of 1920. Meanwhile, Terence MacSwiney began a hunger strike that eventually captured the world's attention and turned him into the conflict's most celebrated martyr. Although the Cork No. 1 Brigade lost its second commanding officer in six months, the Volunteers were lucky to have escaped the City Hall raid so lightly. Florence O'Donoghue believed: 'what is certain is that if all the officers captured had been recognized and detained, it would have been a staggering blow to two of the Cork Brigades.'[15]

After considering the precise timing of the British Army's City Hall operation, IRA leaders suspected the involvement of a civilian informer. In fact, the British discovered the ill-fated Brigade Council meeting through Republican indiscretion rather than civilian exposure. O'Donoghue, who also served as the Brigade Intelligence Officer, was at the centre of a subsequent IRA investigation into the source of the raid. He wrote:

A British raid on local mails at one point on 9 August gave them an indication of the possibility that some of the officers would meet in the City Hall three days later. There was not in the manner in which this information fell into the British hands any question of treachery, or even culpable negligence, on the part of anybody concerned; it was an accident of war which gave the astute Intelligence officer of the British Sixth Division at Cork a slight lead which he fully utilized. He had a stroke of luck, and he made the most of it.[16]

The British Army's Sixth Division Official History supports O'Donoghue's version. 'Crown forces, disguised as civilians ... raided mails in several districts ... On one occasion, a dispatch captured in this way resulted in the arrest of a number of rebels, including Terence MacSwiney.'[17] (When this account was written in 1922, the Army recognized that it had captured 'a number' of rebels in the raid. It is unclear if the military was so aware in 1920.)

This explanation was not evident to the IRA immediately follow-ing the City Hall raid. Seán O'Hegarty, MacSwiney's successor as Brigade Commander, testified to the Volunteers' alarm about possi-ble civilian informers in their midst.

> With regard to that night, we made the closest enquiries through every channel to find out if the raid was a chance shot or whether they had been specifically summoned by some spy who saw us all enter the City Hall. We [*the Brigade Staff*] had also been speculating the point, and we all had our individual suspicions at different times, all of which came to nothing.[18]

The City Hall raid was a watershed in Cork's Anglo-Irish conflict. The loss of Terence MacSwiney brought into prominence the fierce Seán O'Hegarty. Under his leadership the Cork No. 1 Brigade's guerrilla campaign grew in volume and violence. MacSwiney's long and painful hunger strike also seemed to have embittered Cork Volunteers and generated widespread Republican sympathy in the city, contributing to a volatile local environment. Describing that 'grim month,' Florence O'Donoghue would later recall: 'the whole world was black about us.'[19] Finally, the City Hall raid underlined the Volunteers' vulnerability when the British possessed accurate information about IRA movements. Civilian spies could be the Crown forces most effective weapon against the growing insurgency. The City Hall raid showed IRA leaders that in the wrong hands, one piece of information could undo them all.

THE ANTI-SINN FÉIN SOCIETY

It was during these late summer months of 1920 that threats first appeared in Cork newspapers from a group calling itself the 'Anti-Sinn Féin Society'. Rumours of such an organization were initially heard in April 1920, following the killing of Tomás MacCurtain.

> A theory is gradually gaining ground ... that Mr MacCurtain, the Lord Mayor, fell victim to a new secret Anti Sinn Féin organization modelled and run upon the exact same lines as the famous Ku-Klux-Klan, the secret society founded in America after the Civil War to keep Negroes in check. The similarity is startling. It is quite obvious that the tragedy was perfectly rehearsed beforehand, all the details corresponding exactly to Ku-Klux-Klan methods. The crime followed a fiery speech made by Mr MacCurtain in the Cork Corporation on the week before, when he denounced strongly the methods pursued by police against Sinn Féin. The fact which ... matters is the entirely new orientation given to the Irish situation. In the opinion of men best fitted to judge, the murder of Mr MacCurtain may be followed by a sort of ugly triangular duel between the forces of the Crown, Sinn Féin, and private bands of avengers.[20]

Nothing more was heard of such a group until the evening of 14 July 1920, when a schoolteacher named Murphy was attacked in the West Cork village of Timoleague.[21] Disguised men claiming to be members of 'The Anti-Sinn Féin organization' dragged Murphy from his home, and interrogated, beat, and threatened him.[22]

Around the same time, the *Daily Mail* reported: 'A new secret society has arisen in the south, anti-Sinn Féin, and styled 'The Brotherhood of Irish Avengers.'[23] No more news of this 'Brotherhood' appeared in the local press, but as the Irish Rebellion spread, stories of other 'Anti-Sinn Féin Societies' emerged from around the country.

In August 1920, four IRA officers in Boyle, Co. Roscommon, received death threats signed by 'The All Ireland Anti-Sinn Féin Society'. A few nights later, masked men wearing RIC overcoats attacked three of the Volunteers, beating two officers and firing shots at a third.[24] Two months later, the 'Anti-Sinn Féin Society, Wexford Branch' mailed a notice to the Mayor of Wexford. The letter warned of severe reprisals against Sinn Féin supporters in the event of the shooting or wounding of 'Government officials'.[25] At the end of October, a bulletin from a Lisburn (Co. Antrim) branch of the Anti-Sinn Féin Society claimed: 'A fair warning to Sinn Féiners and sympathizers: Lisburn will not claim an eye for an eye but three or more lives for either the murder of or injury to any local members of the Royal Irish Constabulary or Auxiliary Forces.'[26] On 30 November, a notice was posted around the village of Beaufort, County Kerry:

Warning
Any trees or roads found cut must be filled in at once. Take note, you rebels, unless this is done at once, four houses will be burned out and blown up.
Signed,
Anti-Sinn Féin League
Two Thousand. Growing stronger every day, and no waiting.[27]

County Kerry experienced a more ambitious and terrifying threat in December 1920, days after the abduction of three British Army officers at Waterfall, just outside Cork city. The following notice was posted throughout counties Kerry and Cork.

NOTICE AND WARNING
Take notice all you rebels, who are on the run throughout County Kerry, take this as the last and solemn warning. Unless the three missing officers, Capt. Chambers, Capt. Green, and Lieut. Watt are released within ten days of this order, 17 December, the following individuals and houses will be blown to the Devil. No mercy given. Remember the Macroom Mutilators. Not a tooth for a tooth, but 50 to 1. Bantry, 12 houses and 29 known men; Glengariff, 4 picked houses and 7 known men; Kenmare, 12 houses and 17 men; Killarney, no houses but 5 certs; Tralee District, 29 located men; Killorglin, 15 men; Kilgarvan, 5 men; Caherciveen, 11 men, 17 houses; Clonakilty, 7 men, 11 houses; Drimoleague, 9 men (certs), 5 houses; Kilkeel, 7 men and the whole village; every newspaper in the county, not forgetting the staff by any means; Listowel, 16 men, 14 houses; Dingle Peninsula, 75 men, 97 houses. We have declared war. The military has been too lenient. This is our fourth day in Ireland, so get ready. Which is it?
We work mysteriously but deliberately.
From ANTI SINN FEIN SOCIETY.[28]

Two Kerry newspapers heard from the society three months later. While a local court investigated the RIC's killing of a local man, the *Liberator* and the *Kerryman* were warned against publishing any details. The order was signed: 'President, Anti-Sinn Féin Society.'[29] A month later in County Clare, masked men cut off the hair of a dressmaker in her Kilmihil home. They left a note reading: 'Anti Sinn Féin Gang. Beware.' She identified her assailants as police, claiming they had threatened her three times previously.[30]

The city of Cork, however, remained a special target for 'Anti-Sinn Féin Society' communiqués. In late 1920, local residents received repeated and explicit warnings from this supposed group. On 13 October, Cork newspapers published what Sinn Féin TD Liam de Róiste called 'one of the latest developments in terror here'.[31]

Anti-Sinn Féin Society
Circle Headquarters,
Grand Parade, Cork
Gentlemen,
I am instructed by the Supreme Council of the All Ireland Anti-Sinn Féin Society (Cork Circle) to request that you will be good enough to give publicity to the following decision which this organisation has reluctantly come to as a result of the present campaign of assassination being waged against member of His Majesty's forces in this county. My society desires it to be known that their object is to stop murders and not in any way to interfere with the aspirations of the people. By publishing this letter numerous lives may be saved.
DECISION
At a specially convened meeting of the All Ireland Anti-Sinn Féin Society, held in Cork on this 11th day of October, we, the Supreme Council of the Cork Circle, have reluctantly decided that – If in the future any members of his Majesty's forces be murdered TWO members of the Sinn Féin Party in the County of Cork will be killed, and in the event of a member of the Sinn Féin Party not being available THREE sympathizers will be killed. This will apply equally to laity and clergy of all denominations. In the event of a member of his Majesty's forces being wounded or an attempt being made to wound him, ONE member of the Sinn Féin Party will be killed, or if a member of Sinn Féin is not available TWO sympathizers will be killed.
I have the honour to subscribe myself,
Yours truly,
The Assistant Secretary
The Editor 'Cork Constitution', 'Examiner', and 'Evening Echo'
Copy to Canon Cohalan, Bandon.[32]

A month later city IRA forces kidnapped three British Army officers at Waterfall, Cork. The next day a poster appeared around the city:

ANTI-SINN FEIN SOCIETY NOTICE

If Capt. Green, Capt. Chambers, Lieut. Watts are not released unharmed within 48 hours, leading members of the IRA will be suitably dealt with. Ignore this at your peril.
Vengeance may be slow, but it's sure.[33]

Another warning was published in Cork newspapers the following week, on 1 December.

ANTI-SINN FEIN SOCIETY
CORK AND DISTRICT CIRCLE
Membership 2000 and Still Growing
TO ALL CORK CITIZENS
TAKE NOTICE that any householders known to shelter any rebel, or who is known to subscribe to any rebel funds, or to assist in any way the murderous gang of assassins known as Sinn Féin, had better increase his or her FIRE AND LIFE INSURANCE, as it will be needed. It will be wiser than buying spurious Dáil Éireann Bonds.
REMEMBER 1641
REMEMBER 1798
By Order of the Committee
J.P.H.D.
Secretary.[34]

The texts of the three Cork city messages are noteworthy. The authors seemed to go out of their way to reveal a formal organization of local citizens loyal to Britain. The October announcement was signed by an 'assistant secretary' of the 'Cork circle' of the 'All Ireland Anti-Sinn Féin Society.' A 'secretary' also signed the December notice, issuing it on behalf of the 'committee' of the society's 'Cork and District Circle' claiming a membership of 2000. It reminded readers of 1641 and 1798, pivotal victories by Protestant Unionist planters over Catholic Gaelic natives. While the notices warned Cork citizens of possible reprisals for IRA attacks, they also seemingly revealed a loyal, Unionist secret society operating in the city.

Taken at face value, the announcements presented a Unionist counterpart to the secretive Irish Republican Brotherhood. The Anti-Sinn Féin Society appeared structured along IRB lines, with local circles commanded by a Supreme Council. Like the IRB, the Anti-Sinn Féin Society espoused the use of assassination and terror against its political opponents. It would seem local Irish Unionists, fed up with the Irish Volunteers' campaign against public order, had finally decided to answer assault with assault, arson with arson, and murder with murder.

BRITISH REPRISALS IN THE CITY

The Anti-Sinn Féin Society warnings were published after a period of sustained IRA activity against British forces around the city. On 2 October, Cork No. 1 Brigade members assassinated RIC Constable Cheve near his city home.[35] Two days later, Volunteers were interrupted while preparing an elaborate ambush outside the city at the Cork Viaduct.[36] The same day, Volunteers killed one Auxiliary Cadet and wounded another in the city centre.[37] One 8 October, Brigade forces attacked a British Army lorry on Barrack Street, killing one soldier and wounding three more.[38] Five days later, the Anti-Sinn Féin Society issued its first proclamation to the city of Cork.

The first Anti-Sinn Féin Society announcement coincided with the increase of unofficial Crown force reprisals in Cork city. Armed assaults and arson attacks on local Republicans accompanied reprisal threats from unidentified Crown forces, published in local newspapers and posted in flyers around town. It is important to place Cork city's Anti-Sinn Féin Society threats into this unofficial reprisal context.

On 24 November, following the kidnapping of a suspected police spy named Tom Downing, a notice signed by 'Black and Tans' threatened violent reprisals if the man was not released.[39] The warning was posted around the city and appeared in local newspapers. Liam de Róiste wrote: 'the office of the *Cork Examiner* I hear, is in continual danger. Armed police entered the premises the other night and compelled the editors to print the notice relating to Mr Downey [sic].'[40] Two days later, two shops were burned down during evening curfew, after the owners received a 'Final Warning' from 'Black and Tans'.[41] The arson occurred days after the Anti-Sinn Féin Society threatened reprisals for the kidnapping of the three British Army officers taken at Waterfall. Two weeks later, on 10 December, another threat from 'B and T's' appeared in the *Cork Examiner*, vowing 'one man and one shop will disappear each hour' if the IRA did not release a second suspected police informer kidnapped the previous afternoon.[42] On the same day, the *Examiner* published a warning from the 'Death or Victory League'. It threatened to shoot any of the 'male sex of Cork' seen 'loitering on street corners or on the pathways without reasonable excuse', and to fire on 'any man or boy found to be standing or walking with one or both hands in his pocket'.[43]

The Anti-Sinn Féin Society and 'Black and Tan' reprisal notices appear to be the work of the same parties. Both warned of violent arson and shooting reprisals in response to IRA assaults on Crown force personnel and civilian supporters. Each was apparently published in local newspapers at gunpoint. Indeed, this was the information received by Liberal MP T. McKinnon Wood. In the House of Commons he asked Irish Secretary Hamar Greenwood whether, 'on the night of 30 November, an officer and two men in uniform entered the offices of the *Cork Examiner* in Patrick Street, Cork, and forced three of the staff, at the point of a bayonet, to insert a notice of that journal for 1st December, drawn up by the Anti-Sinn Féin Society'?[44] Though Greenwood denied the charge, the publication of general reprisal warnings (such as the Anti-Sinn Féin Society's promise of killing two Sinn Féiners for every Crown force casualty, or the 'Death or Victory League' vow to shoot anyone seen with their hands in their pockets) seemed designed to curtail IRA activity through the threat of drastic reprisals.

While the promised assassinations of Sinn Féin officials never materialized, an arson campaign had already begun in the city. In September 1920, several Sinn Féin leaders received arson threats from unidentified parties.[45] The first significant assault on Cork's commercial sector occurred later that month. On the evening of 27 September, a large bomb wrecked the Castle & Co. shop near the Cork Arcade.[46] Ten other businesses were damaged in the blast, and windows were shattered over a block away. A mixed patrol of police and military claimed the IRA tossed a bomb and fired on them, but witnesses disputed the version and denied seeing any other civilians nearby. Circumstantial evidence implicates the Crown forces in the bombing.

In November, following the initial Anti-Sinn Féin Society warnings, arson attacks against Republicans started in earnest in Cork. The burnings occurred at night, when the city streets were clear except for police and military patrols enforcing an evening curfew (in place since July). Police officials blamed the Anti-Sinn Féin Society. Cork's Royal Irish Constabulary County Inspector reported:

> During the last month there is such a revulsion of feeling and abhorrence at the atrocities committed by Sinn Féin that a new

organization known as the Anti Sinn Féin Society has sprung into existence. This organization is also secret and its personnel is unknown to police. It is believed that many of the recent burnings in Cork are attributed to it.[47]

During the night of 21 November, the premises of Dwyer's and Company was bombed and set afire. The business suffered £10,000 damage. At 3 am the same night, arsonists struck the main Sinn Féin Hall at 56 Grand Parade. Police claimed: 'the building was set on fire by four armed and masked men who are believed to belong to the Anti-Sinn Féin League whose personnel and organization are as secret as those of the Sinn Féin Society.'[48]

On 23 November at 1 am, the Cork Brewery Workman's Club was set alight. According to police the building was used as a Sinn Féin meeting hall. 'The destruction of it would appear to be due to recent opposition amongst a section of the people towards Sinn Féin.' The Shandon Sinn Féin Hall was burned down the following night and another city Sinn Féin club was torched the evening after that.[49]

The arson peaked on 27–28 November. At 1 am on the 27th, Blackrock Parish Hall was burned to the ground. Police claimed: 'it is believed to be attributable to the Anti Sinn Féin.' An hour later, the Douglas Parish Hall was similarly destroyed. At 4 am the business premises of Herbert Forrest on Patrick Street was set ablaze, causing £15,000 damage. The following evening at 11:30 pm, the Irish Transport and General Workers Union Hall burned down. Later that night three more businesses were set afire. The police reported: 'the motive for the fire is not apparent, but possibly it is the work of the Anti Sinn Féin Society.' At 2 am, two houses on North Main Street were burned to the ground. Police theorized: 'it seems possible that the burning was caused by the Anti Sinn Féin Society.'[50]

There was little letup during the next few days. In the early hours of 30 November, unknown assailants bombed and tried to set fire to Cork City Hall.[51] The next night three more shops were burned down. The Thomas Ashe Sinn Féin Club was also destroyed by fire. The following evening on 2 December, the National Insurance Company on Tuckey Street was set ablaze. The County Inspector claimed: 'it is thought the outrage is attributed to the Anti Sinn Féin Society.'[52] Despite police protestations, these attacks were almost certainly carried out by local Crown forces.

SUSPECTED BRITISH INVOLVEMENT IN THE ANTI-SINN FÉIN SOCIETY

While the Cork RIC seemed happy to blame the fires on the Anti-Sinn Féin Society, contemporary observers were unsure if such an organization really existed. Sinn Féin TD de Róiste could not determine if the Anti-Sinn Féin Society notice of 13 October was 'real or false'.[53] The Unionist *Cork Constitution* questioned 'whether this new "Anti-Sinn Féin Society" is a military, constabulary, or civilian organization'.[54] A British newspaper reported the opinion of an unnamed Irish government official. 'Though at first he was disposed to regard the "Society" as a joke, he is now inclining to the opinion that it is seriously meant.'[55] Munster's RIC District Commissioner Major Holmes, however, assured a doubtful senior civil servant in Dublin Castle. '"The Anti-Sinn Féin League," he told me, *does* exist, and is not a myth to cover the Armed forces of the Crown.'[56]

Republican propagandists saw a connection between the Anti-Sinn Féin Society and Dublin Castle's *Weekly Summary,* a government newspaper distributed to the Irish police. The *Weekly Summary* prominently reprinted newspaper reports of the Anti-Sinn Féin Society, under headlines such as: 'The Aftermath of Murder – Sinn Féin Reaps the Whirlwind.'[57] To the editor of Sinn Féin's underground newspaper the *Irish Bulletin*, the story 'puts an end to the doubts as to the composition of the "Anti-Sinn Féin Society"'.[58] The encouragement of reprisals in a government publication indicates the British Administration's tacit approval of the campaign.

Irish independence sympathizers in Westminster expressed similar suspicions. On 25 November, Lt Commander Joseph Kenworthy questioned Irish Chief Secretary Sir Hamar Greenwood:

> Whether the Government have any knowledge of the so-called Anti-Sinn Féin Society; whether he is aware that this society boasts of being engaged in an active murder campaign; whether there are any relations between the Intelligence Service in Ireland and this society; and whether any steps have been taken to suppress this organisation. Greenwood denied any government connection to the group.[59]

Liberal T. McKinnon Wood asked the Irish Secretary if the Anti-Sinn Féin notice of 1 December in the *Cork Examiner* had been published at gunpoint by British forces. Greenwood answered: 'I am informed that the allegation of this question is entirely false. So far as can be ascertained, no members of the Crown forces were responsible for the drawing up or the sending of the notices in question, which I understand were received by the *Cork Examiner* through the ordinary post, and not in the manner described.'[60]

Commander Kenworthy seemed confident of the culprits. He told the House of Commons on 13 December:

> He had another letter in which it was stated that Forest's draper shop was burned in front of the *Cork Examiner* office, in full view of the staff, by Black and Tans. They threatened the editor's life if an advertisement was not printed that day. The advertisement said that they had been requested to publish a statement by the Anti-Sinn Féin Society of the Cork District ... The suspicion in Cork and in all parts of Ireland was that they were Auxiliary police.[61]

Republicans echoed these charges. Sinn Féin Lord Mayor Donal 'Óg' O'Callaghan, told an American audience: 'The *Cork Examiner* and *Evening Echo* have been forced at the point of a revolver to insert threatening notices to the citizens ... The paper has to insert them, but is afraid to refer, and never has referred in any of its columns, to the manner in which these notices are handed to them and they are forced to put them in.'[62]

On 16 December, Kenworthy again questioned Greenwood: 'whether he is now aware of a body who call themselves the Anti-Sinn Féin Society; if he has seen the threatening notices issued by this society to all the citizens of Cork, and whether his Majesty's Government is aware of the composition of the committee who issued this notice?' Greenwood responded: 'I have no information regarding this so-called society or as to the persons responsible for the threatening notices which purported to have been issued by it.'[63] This was not true. The RIC Inspector-General's November report to the Irish Secretary contained specific references to the appearance of the Anti-Sinn Féin Society in Cork. [64]

British Prime Minister David Lloyd George shared the Anti-Sinn Féin Society's reprisal mentality. Army Chief of Staff Sir Henry Wilson wrote: 'Lloyd George is under the ridiculous belief that for every one of our people murdered two Sinn Féiners were murdered, and he was gloating over this and hugging it to his heart as a remedy for the present disgraceful state of Ireland.'[65] At a Cabinet meeting in September 1920, Lloyd George suggested something sounding very similar to the Anti-Sinn Féin Society. Sir Henry Wilson, a participant at the meeting, wrote that the Prime Minister 'seemed satisfied that a counter murder association was the best answer to Sinn Féin murders'.[66]

Of the three 'Anti-Sinn Féin Society' threats, there is only direct evidence of one (published on 1 December 1920) inserted in newspapers by uniformed members of the police. However, strong circumstantial evidence points to Crown forces, probably Auxiliary Police, as the authors. (Auxiliary Company K was stationed in the city at this time.) The Cork notices were posted around town after curfew, when British forces controlled the city streets. They were published simultaneously with similar newspaper warnings written by 'Black and Tans'. Most importantly, the appearance of the bulletins coincided with a dramatic rise in unofficial British reprisals. Starting in November, the city convulsed through a sustained unofficial reprisal campaign against commercial targets and Republican homes and businesses. At the same time a Crown force 'murder gang' attempted to assassinate Republicans throughout Cork (See Chapter Five for details.) Placed in this context, it seems highly likely the Anti-Sinn Féin Society warnings were written by members of the British forces as a cover for their reprisals, and to convey a sense that they were supported by active 'loyalists' in Cork.

SUMMARY

Facing growing guerrilla resistance in Cork, British forces began an unofficial reprisal campaign. Numerous city Sinn Féin halls, businesses, and homes were burned in November and December. At the same time, the 'Anti-Sinn Féin Society' promised more severe reprisals in Cork. It is probable that local Crown forces published these threats.

It is difficult to ascertain the Cork city IRA's response to the Anti-Sinn Féin warnings. Certainly notices written by a supposed group of Unionist gunmen did nothing to alleviate the Brigade's anxiety following the disastrous raid on Cork City Hall. Here was evidence of the Volunteers' worst nightmare: a secret society of Cork loyalists intent on wreaking violence on Cork Republicans. It is unclear if the Brigade leaders believed such a group existed, or if they thought the threats were produced by the Crown forces. There does seem some connection, however, between the Anti-Sinn Féin Society warnings and a dreadful new chapter about to unfold in Cork's intelligence war. Shortly after the first Anti-Sinn Féin Society threats, the IRA kidnapped and secretly killed a number of Cork city civilians. Two months later, city IRA forces shot eight suspected civilian informers in a two-week span. A number of IRA veterans later referred to these victims as members of an 'Anti-Sinn Féin Society'.

NOTES

1 *The Sinn Féiner*, 25 December 1920.
2 Throughout this text the terms 'city' and 'Cork' are used interchangeably. In order to avoid any confusion with the county of the same name, I refer to the county as 'county Cork'.
3 Florence O'Donoghue *Tomás MacCurtain, Soldier, Patriot* (Tralee: Anvil Books, 1958), pp. 94–117. Numerous city Volunteers emphasized their individual efforts to save weapons during the Rising, which, though true, glosses over the larger failings of the Cork Volunteers in 1916. For examples, see Pa Murray's and Mick Murphy's Bureau of Military History statements, Military Archives, Cathal Brugha Barracks, Dublin.
4 O'Donoghue, *Tomás MacCurtain*, p. 116.
5 MacSwiney to Brugha, 30 September 1920, I 1955:59, MacSwiney Papers, Cork Public Museum. See also P.S. O'Hegarty, *A Short Memoir of Terence MacSwiney* (Dublin: Talbot Press, 1922), p. 68; and Geraldine Neeson's Letter to the Editor, *Cork Examiner*, 25 September 1995.
6 Seamus Fitzgerald 'East Cork Activities – 1920,' *Capuchin Annual*, 1970, p. 360; O'Donoghue, *Tomás MacCurtain*, pp. 155–6.
7 O'Donoghue, *Tomás MacCurtain*, p. 156.
8 Richard Mulcahy, 'Chief of Staff 1919', *Capuchin Annual*, 1969, p. 351.
9 Ibid.
10 The Cork Coroner's Jury Inquest provided convincing evidence of police responsibility for MacCurtain's killing. See the Tomás MacCurtain Inquest in the Public Records Office CO 904/47.
11 O'Donoghue, *Tomás MacCurtain*, p. 153.
12 RIC Chief General Tudor wrote a notice in the *Times of London*, requesting recruits for the Auxiliary Cadet division. 'I appeal to all who have held his Majesty's commission and feel as I do – that the paramount need of the moment is the overthow of the gang of assassins known as the Irish Republican Army – to offer themselves for service in this corps d'elite.' *Times of London*, 14 December 1920.
13 Florence O'Donoghue *No Other Law* (Dublin: Anvil Books, 1986), p. 91.
14 Ibid, p. 90.
15 Ibid, p. 92.
16 Ibid, p 89.
17 See the division's official history, *A History of the 6th Division in Ireland*, p. 46, a copy of which can be found in the Strickland Papers, Imperial War Museum.
18 O'Hegarty's written testimony in the 1922 IRB court-martial of Donal 'óg' O'Callaghan, Ms. 31,237, NLI.
19 See Patrick 'Pa' Murray's letter of 6 January 1959 to Florrie O'Donoghue regarding the extreme distress of a subordinate during the later stage of the strike, Ms. 31,296, NLI. O'Donoghue's quote comes in his memoir *Florence and*

Josephine O'Donoghue's War of Independence, A Destiny that Shapes Our Ends (Dublin: Irish Academic Press, 2006), p. 34.

20 *Daily Mail*'s Ireland correspondent, reprinted in the *Cork Weekly News*, 3 April 1920.

21 *Cork Constitution*, 17 July 1920.

22 Liam de Róiste Diary, 17 July 1920, Cork Archives Institute.

23 Reprinted in the *Weekly Summary*, 13 August 1920.

24 Niall Harrington *Kerry Landing* (Dublin: Anvil Books, 1992), pp. 53–5. Harrington was one of the beaten Roscommon Volunteers, and believed his youth saved him from being shot. Earlier, the four Volunteer officers had unwisely visited Boyle shops patronized by the police, and ordered the owners to obey an IRA boycott of the RIC. The indiscretion resulted in their identification as Volunteer leaders.

25 *Cork Constitution*, 22 October 1920.

26 *Weekly Summary*, 29 October 1920.

27 *Cork Constitution*, 30 November 1920.

28 *Cork County Eagle and Munster Advertiser*, 25 December 1920.

29 *Cork Examiner*, 11 March 1921.

30 *Cork Examiner*, 11 April 1921.

31 De Róiste Diary, 13 October 1920, CAI.

32 *Cork Constitution*, 13 October 1920; *Cork Examiner*, 13 October 1920.

33 *Cork Constitution*, 24 November 1920.

34 *Cork Constitution*, 1 December 1920; *Cork Examiner*, 1 December 1920.

35 *Cork Examiner*, 3 October 1920; 'British Casualties – Military', IRA records, A/0437, Military Archives.

36 County Inspector's Confidential Report for Cork (City and East Riding), October 1920, CO 904/113; *Cork Constitution*, 5 October 1920.

37 CI Report for Cork, October 1920.

38 *Cork Constitution*, 9 October 1920; 'British Casualties – Military', MA.

39 *Cork Examiner*, 27 November 1920.

40 De Róiste Diary, 28 November 1920.

41 *Cork Constitution*, 29 November 1920.

42 *Cork Examiner*, 10 December 1920. The informer was George Horgan, described in Chapter Two.

43 Ibid.

44 House of Commons Debates [HCD], 25/11/20, Vol. 135, c. 645.

45 *Cork Weekly News*, 18 September 1920.

46 *Cork Constitution*, 28 September 1920.

47 County Inspector's Report for Cork (City and East Riding), November 1920, CO 904/113.

48 *Cork Examiner*, 23 November 1920; CI Report for Cork, November 1920.

49 CI Report for Cork, November 1920; *Cork Constitution*, 25–28 November 1920.

50 *Cork Examiner*, 28 November 1920, 29 November 1920; CI Report for Cork, November 1920.

51 County Inspector's Report for Cork (City and East Riding), December 1920, CO 904/113.

52 Ibid.

53 De Róiste diary, 12 October 1920.

54 *Cork Constitution*, 13 October 1920.

55 *Daily Chronicle* reprinted in the *Weekly Summary*, 13 September 1920.

56 Mark Sturgis *The Last Days of Dublin Castle* (Dublin: Irish Academic Press, 1999), p. 91.

57 *Weekly Summary,* 12 November 1920, reprinted in the *Irish Bulletin* 30 November 1920, Vol. 3. No. 63.
58 *Irish Bulletin,* 9 November 1920, Vol. 3, No. 41.
59 House of Commons Debates, 25 November 1920, Vol. 135, c. 645.
60 HCD, 13 December 1920, Vol. 136, c. 1136.
61 Debates reported in *Irish Times,* 14 December 1920.
62 Statement of Lord Mayor O'Callaghan to the American Commission on Conditions in Ireland, 13/1/21. See *Evidence on Conditions in Ireland* (Washington DC: American Commission on Conditions in Ireland, 1921), p. 788.
63 HCD, 16 December 1920, Vol. 136, c. 721.
64 RIC Inspector-General's Confidential Monthly Report for November 1920, CO 904/113.
65 C.E. Calwell *Field Marshal Sir Henry Wilson: His Life and Diaries* (London: Cassell, 1927), p. 223.
66 Ibid., p. 247.

CHAPTER TWO

The November Disappearances

The Cork No. 1 Brigade acted decisively on its intelligence front during November and December. In roughly six weeks, Brigade Volunteers killed six suspected British Army intelligence officers, two Auxiliary Cadet intelligence specialists, and four Cork city civilians accused of 'espionage'.

ASSASSINATIONS OF BRITISH ARMY OFFICERS

On 29 October, two Royal Artillery officers named Brown and Rutherford were secretly shot by Cork No. 1 Brigade Volunteers while they travelled by motorcycle in the Macroom area.[1] Charlie Brown, Adjutant of the Brigade's Seventh Battalion, claimed the two officers were found in the country disguised as tourists and carrying a camera.[2] The British Army later stated, 'Brown and Rutherford had been employed from time to time on intelligence work.'[3]

About two weeks later, on 16 November, city Volunteers pulled Captain N.W. Green, Captain S. Chambers, and Lieutenant W.S. Watts off a train at Waterfall, near Cork. The officers were driven to a nearby field, shot, and secretly buried.[4] Much publicity followed the abductions, but the Cork No. 1 Brigade never announced its execution of the British officers. Anti-Sinn Féin notices posted around Cork and Kerry threatened massive reprisals if the missing officers were harmed (see Chapter One, p. 8). While the warning did not help the abducted men, it may explain the IRA's efforts to hide the killings. Mick Murphy, a tough commander of the Cork city IRA's Second Battalion, placed the Waterfall killings in a wider context. He later explained:

> Captain Kelly was in charge of the British Intelligence system here and
> he had six intelligence officers on his staff, and each of them was

wiped out one after the other. There were three caught at Waterfall outside the city by some lads from my Battalion ... They pulled the three of them off a train on their way to Macroom and shot them.[5]

The same day of the Waterfall abductions, city Volunteers kidnapped two Auxiliary Cadets assigned to intelligence duties. On 16 November 1920, the IRA intercepted Cadets Agnew and Mitchell inside Cork city's Johnson and Perrott Motor Garage, and took them to a secret location for execution.[6] The IRA never announced the killings, and the dead constables remained listed as missing.

On 23 November, IRA Volunteers from the Brigade's Third Battalion intercepted Captain Thompson of the Manchester Regiment while he motorcycled from Ballincollig to British Army headquarters in Cork. They stretched a rope across the road, pulled Thompson from his machine, then shot him in a turnip field on the city outskirts.[7] The British military recorded: 'Thompson was an intelligence officer.'[8]

Two days earlier, the Cork No. 1 Brigade attempted to abduct another unidentified Army intelligence officer while he attended mass in Cork.[9] According to city IRA intelligence operative Dan Healy, this British officer regularly attended Sunday services with RIC Constable Carroll. IRA gunmen intercepted Carroll and kidnapped his companion, whom they assumed was the implicated military intelligence officer. Unfortunately for the IRA, the victim turned out to be RIC Detective Thomas Ryan. The Volunteers released Ryan a few days later, following a published threat by 'Black and Tans' to burn part of the city if he was harmed.[10]

In a little over three weeks, the Cork No. 1 Brigade killed eight suspected British intelligence officers, and attempted to shoot a ninth. British officials acknowledged the covert assignment of the two Auxiliary Cadets and three of the dead Army officers (Thompson, Brown, and Rutherford). The case of the three military officers taken at Waterfall is shrouded in mystery.

THE WATERFALL OFFICERS

At least three senior IRA leaders identified the Waterfall victims (Green, Chambers, and Watt) as intelligence operatives, but the British Government denied such a link. One officer, Captain Green, did have a military intelligence connection. In July 1920, Cork No.

3 Brigade commander Tom Hales was captured and subsequently tortured by British Army interrogators. In a letter smuggled from prison, Hales identified his assailants as Captain Kelly (head of Sixth Division Intelligence), Lt. Keogh (a member of Kelly's intelligence staff), Lt. Richardson, and Lt. Green.[11] (Green's official posting was Lieutenant, but he held a temporary rank of Captain from his First World War service. Military protocol used the senior rank.) In a letter written about the officer abductions on 26 November, Cork No. 1 Brigade Chaplain Father Dominic O'Connor seemed to implicate Captain Green. 'There were six officers in all taken and court-martialled and sent to a better land. One of them was the Tom Hales torturer, and he squealed like a rat when he was caught.'[12]

British officials offered different versions of the Waterfall victims' regiments and assignments. The British Army placed Green and Chambers within the Army Education Corps.[13] The Sixth Division official history reported: 'None of these officers were in any way connected with the Intelligence Branch, nor with the suppression of the rebellion. As Education Officers, they were non-combatants.'[14] However, the *Times of London* provided different unit designations for the two men, listing Chambers with the First Battalion, Liverpool Regiment, and Green with the Third Battalion, Lincoln Regiment.[15] In the House of Commons, Winston Churchill claimed: 'Captain Green and Lieutenant Watts might have been witnesses to the murder of a police sergeant, and Captain Chambers was the principal witness against Father O'Donnell who was arrested in October 1918. Presumably these were the reasons they were kidnapped.'[16] Surprisingly, Churchill neglected to mention the two officers' Education Corps postings or standings as non-combatants. (Churchill's information apparently came from an Army inquiry into the episode.)[17] The Sixth Division's official history offers a slightly different explanation, especially relating to Lt Watts. 'Green and Chambers had witnessed a murder a few days previously in County Kerry, and the latter had also been connected with the arrest of an Australian RC [Roman Catholic] Chaplain ... There could have been no possible motive for the murder of Lt Watts.'[18] Watts' wife confirmed he was an electrical engineer, and his commanding officer, Colonel Faber of the Royal Engineers, testified that Watts was 'in charge of the electrical establishments in the city'.[19]

Earlier that month, two RIC constables were assassinated on a train in Ballybrack, County Kerry, but there is no mention from IRA sources of any connection between that episode and the Waterfall abductions.[20]

Lt Chambers did testify at the court-martial of the Australian Army Chaplain Captain (Reverend) Thomas O'Donnell in November 1919.[21] The case is mysterious. It seemed the priest made some anti-British comments at dinner in a Killarney hotel and Chambers reported the incident to military authorities. In his testimony, Chambers said he was in Kerry, 'inspecting the education of the Cork Brigade'. This would be consistent with Education Corps duties. Chambers' travelling companion was a reticent commercial traveller who refused to provide authorities with any information and only reluctantly testified at Father O'Donnell's court-martial. Chambers took notes of the priest's compromising statements at dinner and subsequently produced them at the trial. He also questioned hotel staff as to any local company the priest may have kept. Father O'Donnell reported that when he went to Cork later, 'in the hotel I met some interesting strangers, some of whom wanted to converse with me. One told me that he had seen me last week in the Gresham Hotel. I did not doubt him. I found another diligently inquiring from the hall porter my name, etc.'[22] During O'Donnell's court-martial, Chambers took the priest's comments out of context and added emphasis to rather innocuous Irish nationalist sentiments. The weakness of the case was apparent to an Australian military court that quickly acquitted Fr O'Donnell.

Chambers' role in the Fr O'Donnell case leaves many questions. Although a vocal Irish nationalist, O'Donnell was vacationing in Ireland after two years of combat on the Western Front. He owned a good war record and had spoken at Army recruitment meetings in Australia. Nevertheless, despite Irish and Australian protests, he spent two weeks in solitary confinement awaiting trial.[23] Lt Chambers had apparently investigated O'Donnell personally. Chambers' behaviour in the affair can be read through either of the two military functions attributed to him. He could have been a conscientious education officer, or a covert intelligence operative. Despite Winston Churchill's claims to the contrary, it is clear that the IRA had little motivation to shoot one British officer for the harassment of another.

It is difficult to prove the three Waterfall officers were involved with British Army intelligence. Green and Chambers frequently moved between military posts in Munster. Official reports referred to their presence 'a few days previously in County Kerry', where they supposedly witnessed the killing of two police. When they were abducted, Green and Chambers were again travelling, this time to Macroom. Suspicion over their duties remains. While the Army's official version claimed the two officers were unarmed, a fourth officer travelling with the men testified that Green, 'might have been armed'.[24] This would contradict military reports that he was a non-combatant, and is curious since the men were wearing civilian clothes when abducted. It should also be noted that historian David Fitzpatrick suspects the British Army used Education officers for intelligence duties during this period, as their posting offered excellent cover for covert operatives.[25] Regardless of the officers' true intentions, disguised British officers travelling around Munster inspecting Sixth Division military posts would likely have drawn IRA suspicion. It is impossible to confirm if these men were intelligence officers. It is certain, however, that the IRA thought they were and acted on that assumption.

The Waterfall killings were neither random nor spontaneous. Before their killing, the three British officers were trailed and monitored by city IRA Volunteers. The IRA abduction party was informed of an 'altered time of their departure by train from Cork'.[26] A fourth British officer, Lt Good, also travelled with the three Waterfall victims. Although he was held up while sitting in the same carriage as Green and Chambers, the kidnappers left Good unharmed.[27] That would indicate the Volunteers' familiarity with their quarry, and a disinclination to shoot random British officers. The Waterfall operation required excellent scouting and precise information about the officers' movements, both indicative of the high quality of IRA military intelligence during this time.

The abductions were premeditated. These were the IRA's first widespread killing of off-duty British Army officers in Munster. In those months, military officers could still safely travel around Ireland in uniform or mufti. That assumption ended abruptly after 'Bloody Sunday', which occurred the same week as the Waterfall killings. There, Michael Collins' gunmen killed a dozen suspected British intelligence officers in Dublin, indicating a common concern among IRA leadership in Dublin and Cork of growing British military intelligence efforts in Ireland. The ease with which the gunmen of the Dublin Brigade assassinated members of the 'Cairo Gang' and the shock and outrage to the killings in Ireland and Britain, illustrates the non-belligerent status still enjoyed by British Army officers during this period. Soldiers could be shot while they were on-duty, but after hours they were protected by presumed rules of war.

In Cork, at least thirty staff officers assigned to Cork's Victoria Barracks lodged in unprotected homes around the city.[28] Off-duty British troops moved about town unmolested until 28 February 1921, when IRA Volunteers killed six unarmed soldiers in the Cork city centre following the execution of IRA prisoners at Victoria Barracks.[29] In November 1920, the assassination of unarmed British officers by the Cork No. 1 Brigade was a drastic step. It seems likely that some perceived external threat compelled the IRA to employ such measures.

The Cork No. 1 Brigade ruthlessly dealt with suspected British Army intelligence officers. Volunteer leaders then shifted their attention to perceived civilian agents in Cork city. Days after the last military officer abduction, civilians began to disappear around the city of Cork. The IRA claimed at least two of these citizens were members of a pro-British civilian spy ring operating in the city.

LOYAL CIVILIANS AS INTELLIGENCE AGENTS?

There are many questions regarding the existence of a civilian loyalist intelligence ring in Cork city. Such an organization cannot be ruled out. We know that Crown forces in Cork received information throughout the War of Independence. The British Army's Sixth Division (headquartered in Cork) recorded: 'Intelligence officers had, in many cases, gained touch with friendly disposed civilians.'[30] The IRA's Cork No. 2 and Cork No. 3 Brigades claimed loyalist civilian spy rings operated in their territories. Cork No. 3's commander Liam Deasy claimed: 'We discovered an organization which called itself the Anti-Sinn Féin Society in the area of the Bandon Valley.'[31] (Deasy's story remains mired in a highly charged historical debate at the present time.)[32] George Power, the Vice-Commander of the Cork No. 2 Brigade, told of a similar group operating in North Cork, organized by British military intelligence officer Lt Vincent. Power said when his brigade captured Vincent, they found on him a notebook with the names of forty Cork Protestant collaborators.[33] Although historian Florence O'Donoghue (Adjutant and Intelligence officer of both the Cork No. 1 Brigade and later the IRA's First Southern Division) repeated Power's tale in his biography of Cork No. 2 Brigadier Liam Lynch, the allegations remain unproved.[34] However, there is definite evidence that at least one loyalist civilian intelligence organization operated in county Cork during the same period.

During the War of Independence, the Cork No. 1 Brigade received information from an IRA Volunteer working as a clerk in the British Admiralty Headquarters at the Haulbowline Naval Base in Queenstown (Cobh).[35] Florence O'Donoghue's papers in the National Library contain a section titled 'Captured Documents'. This collection includes a typewritten transcript of three telegraph exchanges, 'From Admiral, Queenstown ... to Captain Hall, Admiralty', probably dated about July 1920.[36] Captain Reginald 'Blinker' Hall was a British spymaster who served as Director of Royal Naval Intelligence, and maintained an intelligence network focused on Irish ports. The Queenstown (Cobh) commander asked Hall: 'Persons are going around the coast stating they belong to the "Irish Coast Intelligence Corps". Please inform me if there is such a Corps and is it acting under your orders?' Captain Hall responded: 'I do understand there is a private organization round the coast, but it is not under my orders and has not official status.' Hall reported in a later communiqué: 'You may feel assured that I have started no official group in Ireland and am only making use of the offer of their services thro' a third party ... In the counties of Cork and Waterford there are several agents who write me thro' the Governor of the Bank of Ireland, and do not wish their names disclosed.'

There is no evidence that the 'Irish Coast Intelligence Corps' produced effective information against IRA efforts in Munster. Though Florence O'Donoghue held a list of Corps members, it does not appear the IRA shot any as informers. However, the importance of this group is its mere existence. It shows that loyal citizens in Cork were organized to provide information to the Crown forces.

If the Irish Coast Intelligence Corps assisted the British, then it is reasonable to assume similar groups of loyalists formed during the conflict. City IRA veteran Stan Barry recalled the problem of pro-British spies around the city. 'A fair Redmondite support, Cork a garrison town and Queenstown a naval town, naval pensioners at Cork, dock yards at Haulbowline and Passage West. There was great snobbery there and some pro-British then.'[37] In this environment, one can assume that when Cork No. 1 Brigade officers heard of some very suspicious civilian meetings taking place, they would have investigated the possible presence of another pro-British spy formation.

On 18 October 1918, Tomás MacCurtain received an anonymous letter from someone claiming to be the daughter of a schoolmate of his mother. The author appeared to work as a domestic servant in a manor house near Cork, and felt compelled to write MacCurtain because: 'I fear some foul deeds coming off.' Her story is bizarre and almost unbelievable.

> A strange gentleman half Indian and half American who was a night scout in the wars in France and South Africa came here three times in the last two months ... and had a meeting with seven other men in a room upstairs. The other men were all wearing masks on their faces. I found your name on a slip of paper under the fender after the first meeting. At the last two meetings a masked man stood outside the room on the landing all the time and two others were outside on the ground around the house and there was eight chairs used each time in the room and a lot of papers burned in the grate ... The men I am sure were all in the war and are all Britishers ... There is something ugly in the whole thing. I am nine years in this place and never saw anything this way before ... I have nothing more to say but wish you well.[38]

It seems easy to dismiss the MacCurtain letter. The described meeting of plotting, masked men appears melodramatic and improbable. The story may have been the work of a prankster or an eccentric. British authorities could have penned the note to intimidate MacCurtain. However, the tale cannot be completely ruled out. One could speculate that the information was factually based and then embellished by an imaginative writer eager to add gravity to his or her intelligence. The envelope postmark matches the date of the letter, and Florence O'Donoghue, an experienced intelligence operative,[39] kept the document in his personal papers for fifty years. Enclosed with it is a scrap of paper supposedly found in the fireplace, along with O'Donoghue's notes from his attempt to decipher it. The documents likely came into O'Donoghue's possession after the fact, possibly during an IRA investigation into MacCurtain's death.[40]

While ultimately it is impossible to confirm the veracity or author of the MacCurtain letter, officers of the Cork No. 1 Brigade appear to have seen the document and taken it seriously. The warning would have alerted the Brigade leadership to the possibility of a covert civilian group operating against them in Cork. It may have also aroused unnecessary Republican suspicions and driven the IRA to see enemies where they did not exist. In any event, the MacCurtain letter provides a plausible starting point for the IRA's apparent obsessions with a civilian spy ring in Cork city.

SECRET KILLINGS OF CORK CIVILIANS IN NOVEMBER

On the evening of 24 November 1920, an ex-soldier named Tom Downing was kidnapped on his way to a meeting at the Cork branch of the Federation of Demobilized Sailors and Soldiers.[41] He was never heard from again. A notice was posted around the city of Cork and printed in the *Cork Examiner* on 26 November.

KIDNAPPING IN CORK
NOTICE
If Mr Downey [*sic*] is not returned to his home within 56 hours
Cork citizens prepare especially Sinn Féiners.
(signed)
BLACK AND TANS

Writing the next day, Liam de Róiste recorded: 'I do not exactly know who Mr Downey is, but he is probably a man that common reports say is in some way attached to the detective force, and the presumption is that he has been captured by some of the Volunteers.'[42] De Róiste also reported an after-hours visit to the *Cork Examiner*. 'Armed police entered the premises the other night and compelled the editors to print the notice relating to Mr Downey [*sic*].'[43]

The IRA did not heed the police threat. A year later, Florence O'Donoghue reported to the IRA Adjutant-General, 'This man was convicted and shot as a spy in Cork on 28 November 1920.'[44]

On 29 November, the *Cork Constitution* reported that: 'James Blemens, Inspector in Horticulture and Bee-keeping under the Department of Agriculture and Technical Instruction for Ireland, was removed from his home on the Blackrock Road, and taken to an unknown destination.'[45] Earlier that afternoon, a group of men in a motor car abducted his son Frederick Blemens. According to the *Cork Examiner*, the elder Blemens was 'popular with many citizens as well as residents in various parts of the county'.[46] Added the *Constitution*: 'The affair has caused quite a sensation.'[47] Neither James Blemens nor his son Frederick were ever seen again. Cork No. 1 Brigade Commander Seán O'Hegarty later reported to IRA General Headquarters (GHQ): 'These men were both executed as spies after trial and conviction here ... the date of execution was December 2.'[48]

On 9 December, a group of armed men invaded George Horgan's

Cork home and took him away.[49] The next day, another ominous bulletin appeared in the *Cork Examiner*:

NOTICE

IF G. Horgan is not returned by 4 o'clock on Today (Friday), 10th December, Rebels of Cork, Beware, as one man and one shop shall disappear for each hour after the given time.

(Signed)

'B's and T's'[50]

Like the threat regarding Tom Downing, the IRA ignored this warning. IRA Commandant J. McCarthy later reported: 'George Horgan was executed on 12 December 1920 and buried.'[51]

In roughly two weeks, four men went missing in Cork city. IRA leaders later confirmed that city Volunteers kidnapped the four victims, took them to a secret destination, and executed them.

Tom Downing and George Horgan were obviously important to the Cork police. While many other civilians disappeared during the Anglo-Irish conflict in Cork city, Horgan and Downing were the only ones to rate a reprisal threat. It should be noted that the same month a similar 'Black and Tans' warning appeared in Cork news-papers following the abduction of RIC Detective Ryan. (The IRA released Ryan, who had been mistaken for a British Army intelli-gence officer.)[52] The reprisal threats raise another question. In this period, IRA 'police' regularly arrested Cork citizens prosecuted by the underground Dáil Courts.[53] Locals likely assumed Horgan and Downing were detained in a similar proceeding. However, the Crown forces immediately recognized the IRA's intention to execute the two men (hence the reprisal threat). That prompt conclusion would be easily explained if Horgan and Downing were assisting police. The mere fact that 'Black and Tans' threatened reprisals in both cases implicates the two men and ties them to Crown forces in the city. With George Horgan, the police connection could be innocuous since it was reported: 'He was on friendly terms with the military and police, and used frequently to speak with them.'[54] Regardless, while the Crown forces valued Horgan and Downing, the two men proved equally important to the IRA. Despite potential reprisals, the Volunteers deliberately disregarded police warnings and shot both of them.

James Blemens was of a different social class than Downing and Hogan. His kidnapping merited the *Cork Examiner* headline: 'Well

Known Official Removed.'[55] Newspapers reported that Blemens was a respected member of the community without apparent political connections. His son Frederick, likewise, had no obvious links to the British Administration.[56]

EXPLAINING THE NOVEMBER DISAPPEARANCES

The observer must ask why these Cork citizens were killed. Brigade Intelligence Officer Florrie O'Donoghue, who was at the centre of most of the IRA's execution decisions, explained the Volunteers' dilemma with civilian informers.

> The absence of any facilities for the detention of prisoners over a long period made it impossible to deal effectively with the doubtful cases. In practice there was no alternative between execution and complete immunity. That made it imperative to obtain the clearest proof of guilt before a man was executed ... This was never an easy matter. I felt it to be a personal moral responsibility to secure it in every case before sanction for execution was given. Frequently we deferred action over and over again where there was reasonable doubt; in most of these cases we never took any action at all. In the tense atmosphere of late 1920, when Seán O'Hegarty was Brigade O/C, I remember him on one occasion getting impatient at my careful presentation of the evidence pro and con in one case, and exploding, 'Kill the bastard – what good is he anyway!' I knew of course that was not an order and that particular gentleman went free.[57]

The IRA obviously found reason to 'sanction for execution' the four November victims. In the clouded period of 1920–1, it is difficult to ascertain what exactly occurred in Cork city, but some idea can be gleaned from Mick Murphy. Murphy was a carpenter and a famous hurler who led county Cork to three All-Ireland titles in the 1920s. During the War of Independence period he also commanded the city's Second Battalion, and organized numerous actions and ambushes. Years later, Murphy sat down with well-known IRA leader Ernie O'Malley and gave his version of events.

> There was a young lad Parsons who was 15 years old and he had been watching my house. He was the son of an Englishman. He was captured by Tadg Sullivan who saw him touting around, and he told me where the young lad was, so I questioned him ... This young lad

Parsons, whom I was talking about, he admitted quite freely that he was watching my house and that he was employed by the police. And furthermore he said he'd been tracking Tommy MacCurtain before Tomás was murdered. Swanzy, the District Inspector, made use of him ... He said there was a Junior and a Senior Secret Service attached to the Y.M.C.A. and they held meetings in Marlborough Street, Cork. I wanted to bomb them but Seán Hegarty said, 'No, that's not the way.' Then we killed them one by one. Parsons was shot. He was the most open-spoken young fellow that I ever met in my life. He gave us all their names and he told us their meeting place, the Y.M.C.A. And he told us they used to meet in a house in Rockboro Road and that a Mrs. Brown lived next door. It was Blemens' house they met in. A father, son and daughter lived there. Mrs. Brown was in touch with Florry [sic] O'Donoghue, and she told Florry about them. We got into the back and we saw them and we heard them. And they were shot, one by one, and in groups. Blemens and his son were shot one night ... Every spy who was shot in Cork was buried so that nothing was known about them. They just disappeared.[58]

At this stage, Murphy's statement will be taken at face value, though the credibility of his story will be revisited in Chapter Eight. However, it is Murphy's description of Brigade commander Seán O'Hegarty coldly advising, 'No, that's not the way', which reveals the relevance of four men disappearing seemingly at random during two weeks in Cork city.

The November victims were shot secretly instead of publicly. At this stage, the Cork No. 1 Brigade was not afraid to shoot and label informers or spies. The previous February, Volunteers had attached a warning note to the body of the British agent Timothy Quinlisk, in which the IRA assumed responsibility for his execution.[59] In February 1921, city Volunteers hung similar notes on the bodies of seven suspected informers shot during the month. The Cork No. 1 Brigade often disregarded public opinion when it felt action was called for. In the first half of 1920, city Volunteers assassinated a number of popular police officers, and the following February it killed two respected civic leaders. If the IRA's motive for the November kidnappings was revenge or reprisal, why not state so publicly, as it did when it burned the homes of prominent Cork loyalists the following May?[60] Why were these men secretly killed and buried? Mick Murphy offers a believable explanation: The IRA wanted to first identify and then pick off members of the 'civilian spy ring' operating in the city. It dealt with the initial identifications quietly, to keep other members of the group unaware of the Brigade's intentions and suspicions. This would make later executions easier.

Members of the Cork No. 1 Brigade believed they faced a civilian intelligence organization in Cork city during the War of Independence. In *Rebel Cork's Fighting Story*, IRA veteran Seamus Fitzgerald referred to a 'civilian spy ring' operating in the city.[61] Various city Volunteers informed Ernie O'Malley of an Anti-Sinn Féin spy ring operating in Cork.[62] Frank Busteed, commander of the Brigade's Sixth Battalion, told writer Seán O'Callaghan of the existence of an inner and outer ring of the Anti-Sinn Féin organization in the city.[63] It seems that as far back as the summer of 1920, the IRA suspected a tiered intelligence network in Cork. After the capture of the IRA's Second Battalion commander Connie Neenan, the British Army reported: 'In a notebook found in Neonan's [sic] possession was the name of the Divisional Intelligence officer and beneath it in Irish the words, "in the ring".'[64]

These references, as well as Mick Murphy's startling story of young Parson's confession, show that the IRA thought it had stumbled upon a secret spy organization, a real 'Anti-Sinn Féin Society'. Following Seán O'Hegarty's orders, city IRA forces apparently secretly eliminated four suspected civilian spies, in order to avoid tipping off its other local enemies. Abductions served a further function for the IRA. Unlike an assassination, when the assailant shot his victim and fled the scene, kidnappings gave IRA intelligence officers opportunity to interrogate their prisoners before they were killed.

It cannot be assumed that the British monopolized torture during the Anglo-Irish conflict.[65] While there is no direct evidence of IRA mistreatment of civilian prisoners, the Cork Volunteers frequently removed their intended victims for questioning, which one can assume took place under duress. 'The lad Parsons' apparently revealed an abundance of information during his IRA interrogation. Florrie O'Donoghue told his IRA superiors that, in Cork, 'the men shot have in most cases admitted their guilt before being executed'.[66] He does not say why these prisoners would feel compelled to fatally incriminate themselves. It is possible the Cork No. 1 Brigade kidnapped these four men in order to force them to identify the rest of their 'ring'. It then secretly killed them.

If the IRA's execution dates are accurate, all four victims were held for a few days before their deaths. Tom Downing was not killed until four days after his abduction.[67] George Horgan was shot three days following his kidnapping.[68] The IRA held James and Fredrick

Blemens three days before their execution.[69] These lags would give the Volunteers ample time to question their prisoners before shooting them. Mick Murphy described the Blemens' situation coldly. Fred Blemens told Murphy: 'I don't know anything but the old man might know something.'[70] According to Murphy, the elder James Blemens provided no information. Murphy continued: 'They didn't think they'd be shot. We shot them one by one, and we shot Blemens who was dead drunk.'

The November victims were apparently tried by IRA court-martials, but no transcript of the proceedings survived the conflict. It is unknown if any of the men provided the IRA with any information about an Anti-Sinn Féin spy ring in the city.

SUMMARY

In November, the Cork No. 1 Brigade assassinated eight suspected Crown force intelligence officers. Five of the officers were definitely assigned to intelligence, while the duties of the other three remains open to question. Shortly after these killings, Cork city Volunteers abducted and executed four local citizens accused of providing information to Crown forces. Two of these victims had connections to the RIC. The other two had no superficial ties to local British forces.

City Volunteers were first warned about civilian intelligence operatives in 1919. A group of loyal Cork citizens called 'The Irish Coast Intelligence Corps' worked for British Naval Intelligence during this period, providing a precedent for a civilian spy formation in Cork. City IRA veterans claimed that in 1920–1, loyalists in Cork city were organized into a civilian spy ring they called 'The Anti-Sinn Féin Society'. At least two of the IRA's November victims were accused of belonging to this group. The IRA interrogated the accused, probably to find out more about the supposed Anti-Sinn Féin group. After the victims' execution, their bodies were secretly buried, possibly to avoid tipping off other local spies operating in Cork.

The Cork No. 1 Brigade's intelligence front remained quiet for the next two months. When city Volunteers struck again in February, it was in stunning fashion. During a two-week span, seven suspected spies were killed in the city of Cork. Usually a card reading 'Spies and Informers Beware' was pinned to their bodies. It would seem the Brigade no longer feared scaring away its civilian enemies.

NOTES

1 *Cork Examiner*, 2 November 1920; *Cork Constitution*, 18 November 1920; *Irish Times*, 22 August 1921; List of IRA Executions, Military Archives.
2 Charlie Brown in the O'Malley Notebooks, University College Dublin.
3 *History of the Sixth Division in Ireland*, p. 61.
4 List of IRA Executions 1920, Military Archives; *Cork Examiner*, 17–18 November 1920; Mick Murphy in the O'Malley Notebooks.
5 Mick Murphy in the O'Malley Notebooks.
6 List of IRA Executions 1920, MA; Richard Abbott *Police Casualties in Ireland, 1916–1922* (Cork: Mercier Press, 2000), pp. 311, 313; *Cork Constitution*, 22 November 1920.
7 *Cork Examiner*, 24 November 1920; List of IRA Executions, MA.
8 *History of the Sixth Division in Ireland*, p. 60.
9 Dan Healy, Bureau of Military History Statement.
10 County Inspector's Report for Cork (City and East Riding), November 1920, CO 904/113; *Cork Weekly News* 27 November 1920.
11 Statement of Tom Hales, 27 July 1920, Donal Hales Papers, U64, Cork Archives Institute.
12 Full text of the letter can be found in the Strickland Papers, IWM.
13 Results of Military Inquiry, General Headquarters Ireland, 6 December 1920, A/0341, Department of Defence Archives [DDA]; *History of the Sixth Division in Ireland*, p. 60; Cork Quarterly Sessions, Reported in *Cork Constitution*, 18 October 1921.
14 *History of the Sixth Division in Ireland*, p. 60.
15 *Times of London*, 21 December 1920.
16 House of Commons Debates, 18 November 1920, Vol. 1134, c. 2073.
17 Results of Military Inquiry, DDA.
18 *History of the Sixth Division in Ireland*, p. 60.
19 Cork Quarterly Sessions, *Cork Constitution*, 15 October 1921.
20 T. Ryle Dwyer *Tans, Terror and Troubles, Kerry's Real Fighting Story 1913–23* (Cork: Mercier Press, 2001), pp. 254–5; Abbott, p. 149.
21 *Cork Constitution*, 27 November 1919.
22 *Cork Constitution*, 22 October 1919.
23 *Cork Constitution*, 10 November 1919.
24 Cork Quarterly Session, *Cork Constitution*, 15 October 1921.
25 David Fitzpatrick, '"Unofficial Emissaries", British Army Boxers in the Irish Free State, 1926', *Irish Historical Studies*, XXX, No. 118, November 1996, p. 208.
26 Langford Pension Statement, Robert Langford Papers, U156, Cork Archives Institute.
27 Good's testimony in the Cork Quarterly Sessions, *Cork Constitution*, 15 October 1921.
28 Ms. 31,223, NLI.
29 *Cork Constitution*, 1 March 1921; *Cork Examiner*, 1 March 1921.
30 *History of the 6th Division in Ireland*, p. 22. The official history also mentions 'civilians who had previously given information', p. 29.
31 Liam Deasy *Towards Ireland Free* (Cork: Royal Carbery Books, 1992), p. 200.
32 Meda Ryan and Peter Hart have debated the killing of Protestants in the Bandon Valley area accused of membership in a local 'Anti-Sinn Féin Society'. Ryan has produced evidence that a number of these victims were in fact informers, while Hart believes the motive was sectarian. As these killings took place outside the bounds of this study, I will refrain from comment.

33 George Power in the O'Malley Notebooks.
34 O'Donoghue, *No Other Law*, p. 119.
35 Seamus Fitzgerald, 'East Cork Activities – 1920,' *Capuchin Annual*, 1970, p. 364. The author Fitzgerald was a senior IRA officer in Cobh, and later a historian of the conflict in Cork. See his Bureau of Military History Statement, WS# 1737, National Archives, and the Fitzgerald Papers, Cork Archives Institute.
36 Ms. 31,223, NLI. The messages contain quotations from Divisional Commissioner Smyth's address at the Listowel RIC Barracks in early July. Smyth's speech is quoted in Anthony Gaughan *The Memoir of Constable Jeremiah Mee* (Dublin: Anvil Books, 1975), pp. 103–4.
37 Stan Barry in the O'Malley Notebooks.
38 Ms. 31,157, NLI.
39 While serving as an Irish Army Intelligence officer, O'Donoghue proved effective against Allied and Axis agents operating in Ireland during World War II. See O'Donoghue, *Florence and Josephine O'Donoghue's War of Independence*, p. 206.
40 See also O'Donoghue's notes regarding the aftermath of the MacCurtain killing, Ms. 31,313, NLI.
41 *Cork Examiner,* 26 November 1920; IRA List of Executions 1920, MA; Bride Downing to Dáil Minister of Defence, Cathal Brugha, 13 December 1921, A/0535 VI, MA.
42 De Róiste Diaries, 27 November 1920, CAI.
43 De Róiste Diaries, 28 November 1920.
44 Florence O'Donoghue, Adjutant First Southern Division, to Geroid O'Sullivan, GHQ Adjutant-General, 10 February 1922, A/0535, MA.
45 *Cork Constitution,* 1 December 1920.
46 *Cork Examiner,* 1 December 1920.
47 *Cork Constitution,* 1 December 1920.
48 Seán O'Hegarty, OC Cork No. 1 Brigade to Adjutant-General O'Sullivan, 17 November 1921, A/0535, MA.
49 Anna Horgan to Richard Mulcahy, Minister of Defence, 28 August 1922, A/0535, MA.
50 *Cork Examiner,* 10 December 1920.
51 Intelligence Officer McCarthy to Major-General Emmet Dalton, OC Southern Area, 6 September 1922. Report forwarded to Minister of Defence, Richard Mulcahy, by Dalton, A/0535, MA.
52 *Cork Weekly News*, 27 November 1920;
53 For example, the previous month the RIC reported that the IRA abducted three citizens (Robert McGivery, John Chambers, and Michael Griffith) who were subsequently released. See CI Report for Cork (City and East Riding), October 1920, CO 904/113.
54 *Cork Constitution*, 1 December 1920.
55 *Cork Examiner*, 1 December 1920.
56 *Cork Examiner*, 1 December 1920; *Cork Constitution*, 1 December 1920; Mrs. Sarah Beale (James Blemens' daughter) in the Cork Quarterly Sessions, *Cork Constitution*, 6 June 1921.
57 O'Donoghue, *Florence and Josephine O'Donoghue's War of Independence*, p. 84.
58 Mick Murphy in the O'Malley Notebooks.
59 *Cork Examiner*, 20 February 1920.
60 *Cork Constitution*, 27 May 1921.
61 Seamus Fitzgerald 'Actions in Cork', in *Rebel Cork's Fighting Story, 1916–1921, Told by the Men who Made it* (Tralee: Kerryman, 1947), p. 112.

62 The following IRA veterans described a civilian spy ring in the O'Malley Notebooks: Stan Barry, Martin Corry, Eamonn Enright, Pat Minihan, Mick Murphy, Florrie O'Donoghue, Connie Neenan, and Paddy O'Reilly.
63 Seán O'Callaghan *Execution* (London: Frederick Mueller, 1974), p. 63. O'Callaghan confirmed this in a letter to me, 22 November 1996.
64 '6th Division Weekly Intelligence Summary: 12 December 1920', Strickland Papers, IWM; *Summary of Important Orders to the 17th Infantry Brigade*, booklet published by the Brigade, copy in the Strickland Papers, IWM.
65 Dan 'Sandow' Donovan told his nephew of an argument he had with Seán O'Hegarty in the summer of 1920, over O'Hegarty's desire to kidnap District Inspector Oswald Swanzy instead of killing him outright for his role in the assassination of Tomás MacCurtain. Apparently O'Hegarty wanted the Volunteers to force Swanzy to name MacCurtain's killers before they executed him. Brigade gunmen shot down Swanzy in Lisburn, Northern Ireland in August 1920. Author's interview with Donal O'Donovan, 20 November 1996.
66 Florence O'Donoghue, IO First Southern Division, to Chief of Staff, Richard Mulcahy, 24 June 1921, Mulcahy Papers, P17A/20, UCD.
67 *Cork Examiner*, 26 November 1920; Abduction date from B. Downing (wife of victim) to Richard Mulcahy, 13 December 1921, MA; Execution date from O'Donoghue to G. O'Sullivan, 10 February 1922, A/0535, MA.
68 *Cork Examiner*, 10 December 1920; Department of Defence to A. Hogan, A/0535.
69 *Cork Constitution*, 1 December 1920; *Cork Examiner*, 1 December 1920; Seán O'Hegarty to G. O'Sullivan, 17 November 1921, A/0535, MA.
70 Mick Murphy in the O'Malley Notebooks.

CHAPTER THREE

'Spies and Informers Beware'

George Horgan, the last of four Cork citizens to disappear in 1920, was kidnapped by the IRA on 9 December and executed three days later. During his seventy-two hour detention, three dramatic developments altered the situation in Cork.

MARTIAL LAW AND THE BURNING OF CORK CITY

On 10 December, the British Government declared Martial Law in the city of Cork, along with the rest of county Cork, and counties Kerry, Limerick, and Tipperary. A portion of the Martial Law proclamation read:

> Note well: That a state of armed insurrection exists, that any person taking part therein or harbouring any person who has taken part therein, or procuring, inviting, aiding or abetting any person to take part therein, is guilty of levying war against His Majesty The King, and is liable on conviction by a military court to suffer DEATH.[1]

The day following the Martial Law declaration, city Volunteers ambushed a lorry of Auxiliary Cadets at Dillon's Cross on the outskirts of the city, killing one constable and wounding eleven more.[2] Within two hours, groups of police, unchecked and occasionally assisted by military curfew patrols, began to sack businesses and set buildings alight around Cork. The flames grew until a large section of the city centre was in flames. For the rest of the night, Crown forces looted homes and shops, attacked civilian bystanders, and even shot at firefighters (wounding two). Earlier in the evening, armed men with English accents invaded a Cork home and killed brothers Con and Jeremiah Delaney, members of the First Battalion, Cork No. 1 Brigade. During the disorder, fifty-seven city businesses were destroyed, twenty badly damaged, and a dozen homes and shops wrecked. Cork City Hall and the Carnegie Public Library were also burned to the ground. Damages ran over £3,000,000 and between 1500 and 2000 people were thrown out of work.[3]

Shocked Sinn Féin civic leaders appealed to the ambassadors of Europe and the United States:

> During the present week the people of Cork – men, women, and children – have been held up in the streets of this city and robbed of all they possess, hundreds of shops have been looted, unoffending citizens publicly whipped, shot, and it is to be feared, in some cases burned alive in their homes, the principal business quarter of the city bombed, burned, and destroyed by the Armed Forces of the Crown, rendering thousands of people homeless and workless. In the name of humanity and our tortured people seeking protection from such savage tyranny, we respectfully urge the immediate intervention of your government.[4]

Despite considerable evidence implicating Crown forces in the destruction (specifically Auxiliary Cadet Company K) at Westminster, Irish Secretary Sir Hamar Greenwood denied any involvement by British forces. Dismissing witness reports of police tossing firebombs into Cork City Hall and the Carnegie Library, Greenwood claimed the buildings were destroyed by flames from the city centre, despite the fact that a quarter mile of city and the River Lee separated these two buildings from the Patrick Street fires.[5] Greenwood also implied that IRA Volunteers had set the blazes in order to embarrass the British Government.[6]

City Sinn Féin leaders indignantly wired Greenwood. 'On behalf of the whole citizens, we absolutely and most emphatically repudiate the vile suggestion that the city was burned by any section of the citizens. In the name of truth, justice, and civilization, we demand an impartial inquiry into the circumstances of the city's destruction.'[7] Police and Labour Party investigations found British forces responsible for the Cork burnings, but no official government inquiry findings were ever released. Despite objections by a small but vocal Westminster minority, the events in Cork attracted only brief attention in Britain.

BISHOP COHALAN'S EXCOMMUNICATION ORDER

On 12 December, the Catholic Bishop of Cork, Daniel Cohalan, acted to prevent a repetition of the previous night's violence. He wrote a pastoral letter that illustrates the bishop's outrage at both IRA and British violence in the city. Although Cohalan was a moderate nationalist, he evidently felt compelled to protect his vulnerable diocese from further British reprisals. At masses throughout Cork, parish priests read Bishop Cohalan's message.

> The crimes of the Government in Ireland are on a different plane, and are infinitely greater than the crimes of a private military organisation ... Instead of defending the lives and property of the innocent, the government, by a carefully laid plan, for which not even a clock of legality has been provided, has conducted through its servants a reprisal campaign of murder of the innocent and of destruction of their property, with the view of securing the submission of the Republican Army by terrorism exercised over the innocent and unoffending ... But murder is murder and arson is arson, whether committed by agents of the government or by members of the Irish Republican Army; and it is the duty of an Archbishop to denounce murder and arson, from whatever source they come. In the awful circumstances in which we live, to protect our men and boys from the danger of murder and arson, and to protect the community at large from the evil of reprisals, I notify again to the faithful of this diocese through the different churches the following degree of excommunication which has been already promulgated and which is already in force:
> Besides the sinfulness of the acts from their opposition to the law of God, anyone, be he a subject of this diocese or an extern, who, within the diocese of Cork shall organise or take part in ambushes or kidnappings, or shall otherwise be guilty of murder or attempted murder, shall incur, by that very fact, the censure of excommunication.[8]

Cohalan's excommunication order applied equally to both members of the Crown forces and the IRA, but it obviously had greater impact on the almost exclusively Catholic Volunteers. The Cork No. 1 Brigade Chaplain, Father Dominic O'Connor (brother of Brigade Quartermaster Joe O'Connor), tried to reassure his charges with a unique interpretation of Canon Law. 'These acts performed by the IV [*Irish Volunteers*], the army of the Republic, are not only not sinful but are good and meritorious and therefore the Excommunication does not affect us. There is no need to worry about it. Let the boys keep going to Mass and Confession and Communion as usual.' Father Dominic did suggest using tact with the clergy. 'Just as there is no necessity telling a priest that you went to Mass on Sunday, so there is no necessity to tell him one is in the IRA or that one has taken part in an ambush or kidnapping etc.'[9]

Despite Fr. Dominic's urgings, the excommunication aroused Republican fury and challenged Volunteer morale. On the one hand, city Volunteer leader Connie Neenan dismissed Cohalan, saying he 'was never taken seriously by us'.[10] Ernie O'Malley also recorded the remark of devout North Cork IRA leader Liam Lynch: 'Old Cohalan had dinner with [General] Strickland I suppose, before he took the pen in his fist, but nobody minds him now.'[11] However, in a devout country like Ireland, excommunication must have embittered Cork Volunteers, who were almost entirely Catholic. Writing Ireland's Papal Nuncio ten years later, Brigade leaders Seán O'Hegarty and Florrie O'Donoghue expressed some of that resentment. 'The men are now scattered ... But wherever they are and under whatever conditions they live, over all our heads hovers the nightmare horror of this Decree of Excommunication: tarnishing our honour, besmirching our motives, a challenge to our historical justification, a menace to the salvation of our souls.'[12]

Alienation from the Catholic Church may have contributed to the deteriorating situation in Cork city. In the New Year, Cork Republicans increased their cold-blooded killings of civilians in the city. One can speculate about the timing of Cohalan's excommunication decree and the expansion of violence against local civilians. By this period, IRA leaders had left their work and homes and gone 'on the run' throughout the city. Isolated from family and friends, removed from their Catholic moral framework, and living day-to-day in a vacuum with fellow insurgents, these activists likely took a militant turn. Regardless of their motivation, by the beginning of 1921, the Volunteers showed less reluctance to kill their fellow Cork citizens.

For the remainder of 1920, the IRA refrained from action, allowing the devastated city to catch its breath following the trauma of 11 December. By New Year's Day, according to the Unionist *Cork Constitution*: 'People were beginning to conclude that the day for ambushes in the city had gone, to the great relief of all God-fearing people.'[13] Such optimism proved short-lived. For the next seven months, the city existed in a tense and uneasy routine, punctuated periodically by bloody outbursts. Beneath a relatively normal façade, a bitter and secret Anglo-Irish intelligence war continued unabated.

On 4 January 1921, the Cork No. 1 Brigade struck at police in the centre of Cork. IRA fighters armed with pistols and bombs ambushed an RIC foot patrol crossing Parnell Bridge. The Volunteers killed two constables, wounded the remaining five, and escaped without casualty.[14] This bold strike in the heart of a city garrisoned by approximately 2000 British troops and 260 police, underlined the strength of IRA forces in Cork.[15] Without detection, the Volunteers planned an ambush, deployed their forces, and escaped British reinforcements. The Cork No. 1 Brigade's strong intelligence arm made much of this success possible. For the rest of 1921 the Volunteers struggled to maintain their advantage in this field.

SHOOTING OF DETECTIVE MALIFF

Two IRA attacks in January had repercussions in the intelligence sphere. On 9 January, IRA Volunteers fired on Constable Carroll and his companion Cornelius (Cors) Sheehan near Cork's Good Shepherd Convent. Carroll was wounded in the wrist while Sheehan was hit in the shoulder.[16] Cork's RIC County Inspector reported: 'The motive in this case was to murder the Constable and his friend who was suspected of supplying information.'[17] Cors Sheehan, an attendant at the Cork Lunatic Asylum, was fatally shot by the IRA as a spy two months later. During the January assault, the IRA assailants fired at Sheehan and Constable Carroll from a considerable distance and failed to significantly wound either man. When compared to later IRA assassinations, this attempt seemed clumsy and haphazard. It is not clear if it was a planned operation, or a chance encounter between Volunteers and someone wanted by the Brigade. If the shooting was a case of the latter, it can be taken as evidence of Brigade orders to shoot certain civilian suspects on sight.

A week later, RIC Detective Sergeant John Maliff was seriously wounded outside the Washington Street Courthouse.[18] According to Mick Murphy, Maliff was 'picked out to act at the Cork military barracks, where he was interviewing prisoners and terrifying them. He knew our men. Word came out to us about him but he was not to be found'.[19] Murphy received information that Maliff, a highly regarded rugby player, would attend the Munster–Leinster rugby match at Cork's Mardyke grounds. Accompanying Maliff that day was Detective Constable Thomas Ryan, the same RIC detective kidnapped and released by the IRA in November.[20] Mick Murphy and two members of the Cork No. 1 Brigade's 'Intelligence Squad' (Denis Hegarty and Frank Mahoney) attacked the police officers after they left the rugby grounds. The detectives, dressed in mufti, were shot numerous times and 'dangerously wounded.' Both eventually recovered from the attack, though the RIC transferred the two men out of the city. Maliff later testified to clear an innocent farmer tried for the assault.

The attempted Maliff assassination reveals the IRA's tendency to selectively eliminate threats to its organisation in the city. As will be discussed in Chapter Six, by this time few Irish policemen in Cork were willing to identify IRA Volunteers. According to the RIC, only a small number of Cork's active Volunteers were 'known personally to police, and these only to a few men'.[21] Apparently, Detective Maliff was one of these men and used his knowledge to assist the military. As a result, the IRA marked him for death.

It is interesting to contrast Maliff with his companion Detective Ryan. As previously noted, the IRA had kidnapped Ryan in November, confusing him with a military intelligence officer. The Volunteers released Ryan a few days later, despite the fact that he served as a political detective with the RIC. This would indicate that the city Volunteers did not shoot local RIC constables randomly. Further evidence comes from Detective Ryan's abduction. During his November kidnapping, Ryan was accompanied by Constable Carroll (the same man who was shot with Cors Sheehan in January). While Volunteer gunmen had the drop on Constable Carroll, they declined to shoot him. IRA leaders knew Carroll's identity and had been tracking him for some time, yet they did not authorize his killing. Both Ryan and Carroll, though police officers, were apparently not dangerous enough enemies to warrant an IRA execution. Detective Maliff was judged a more serious threat to the Cork No. 1 Brigade, and was selected for assassination.

THE FEBRUARY KILLINGS

The Brigade's next shooting shocked Cork. On the evening of 9 February, a well-known city businessman named Alfred Reilly was killed while returning to his home in the Cork suburb of Douglas. The 58-year-old was taken from his pony and trap, placed against a wall and shot twice in the face. A card pinned to his coat read: 'Spy. By Order IRA. Take warning.'[22]

According to the *Cork Constitution*: 'One of the most horrifying deeds recently recorded in Cork city or county was the shooting dead of Mr Alfred Reilly, JP.' Reilly was a member of Cork's business establishment and served on the Cork Chamber of Commerce

Executive Council.[23] His assailants had no obvious motive, wrote the *Constitution*. 'The shooting of such a gentleman for apparently no conceivable reason is regarded as a most terrible crime, and the circumstances of the awful tragedy are wrapped in mystery.'[24]

Three days after the killing of Alfred Reilly, on the evening of 12 February, armed men held up an ex-soldier named John O'Leary near his city home. O'Leary, 33-years-old, worked as a clerk in the British Army's Victoria Barracks. His assailants took O'Leary's barrack pass, then shot him three times. He died in hospital three days later. O'Leary lost a leg in the First World War, and used an artificial limb.[25] According to the *Cork Constitution*: 'He was regarded as a quiet, inoffensive young man, who performed his duties efficiently and was generally popular.'[26]

On 14 February, two days after O'Leary's assault, another shooting occurred in Cork city. Unidentified men entered a pub and walked out patron William Sullivan, a Munster Fusiliers war veteran. Hours later, Sullivan's body was found in Tory Top Lane, in the city's southern suburbs. A card pinned to Sullivan's vest read: 'Spy. Penalty Death. Let all spies and traitors beware.' Sullivan was 35-years-old and unemployed at the time of his death.[27]

The following evening, on Tuesday 15 February, the body of another member of Cork's business establishment was found, this time in a Wilton pasture on the city's outskirts. Charles Beale, a manager with Woodford and Bourne Wine Merchants, disappeared the day before. He was English, Protestant, and moved to Cork eight years earlier to join Woodford and Bourne. Like Alfred Reilly, Beale served on the Cork Chamber of Commerce Executive Council, and had also signed a petition calling for Irish Dominion Home Rule.[28] Beale had been shot three times in the abdomen and once in the temple. A piece of cardboard tied around his neck read:

Convicted spy.
The penalty for all who associate with the Aux. Cadets, the Black and Tans, and the RIC.
IRA.
P.S. Beware.[29]

On Friday, 18 February, an especially brutal incident took place. At 8 pm, six armed and masked men entered the Cork Workhouse and asked for directions to the St Michael's Ward. There they found an unemployed building labourer named Michael Walsh. The 45-

year-old Boer War veteran was 'undergoing treatment for a functional disorder'. The raiders ordered Walsh out of his bed in front of 'a large number of patients who were somewhat perturbed by the presence of the disguised visitors'. Wearing only his slippers and pyjamas, Walsh 'was not able to walk, and had to be assisted down the stairs from the ward'.[30] After carrying Walsh through the Workhouse gate, the assailants stopped along the road. Walsh was then 'riddled with bullets', suffering wounds to his heart, shoulder, lung, abdomen, jaw and temple. Attached to the dead man's pyjamas was a card reading: 'Caught at last. Spies and informers beware. IRA.'[31]

Two days following Walsh's assassination, on Sunday afternoon 20 February, an ex-soldier and night watchman named William Mohally was discovered critically wounded on Cork's Lower Glanmire Street. Mohally had been shot once near the right ear and once under his left eye. An ambulance conveyed Mohally to the South Infirmary Hospital, but 'his recovery was not expected'.[32] A few hours later, four men arrived at the infirmary. They produced revolvers, disabled telephones, and ushered the night staff into the surgical ward. 'Here Mohally was recognised.' They ordered staff members to place the unconscious man onto a stretcher and carry him outside to the hospital's Blackrock Road gate.

> One of them bent down over him, placed a revolver to his mouth and fired. An interval of a second or two elapsed before any remark was made. Then one of the assailants said: 'Give him another.' The man who shot Mohally again bent over him, and sent a second bullet through his cheek. They then walked away and Mohally was dead.[33]

Hours before Mohally's killing, a corpse was fished out of the River Lee near the Douglas Road. Michael Finbarr O'Sullivan was found blindfolded, with four bullet wounds in his body. He was a tailor residing in Douglas and had been missing for three weeks. The coroner guessed O'Sullivan had been in the water for about that time, but an IRA intelligence officer involved in the killing said it occurred on 21 February (though his body was found on the 20th).[34] O'Sullivan served with the Royal Army Medical Corps during the First World War.[35]

Yet another remarkable incident took place the same day, on an English train connecting the Cork ferry to London. A railway worker at Paddington Station discovered Cork businessman George Tilson locked in the train lavatory with his throat slit and a bloody razor at his side. The man was still alive, and when a police officer asked him if he had done the deed himself, Tilson nodded affirmatively. Police found a note in Tilson's pocket reading: 'I have been shadowed from Cork, not to be done in by them. George F. Tilson.' When the policeman told Tilson 'he was very foolish', Tilson shook his head negatively. He died shortly afterwards. According to the deceased's brother Henry, George Tilson had received a letter threatening his life on 15 February. Henry Tilson told an inquest that the letter 'made him [George] feel greatly nervous'. Two days later George Tilson told his brother he was 'too nervous for words', and left for England. 'When he was saying good-bye to me on the steamer,' continued Henry Tilson, 'he was under the impression that he was being pursued, because he stated so to me. He was nervous of what he termed "the overshadowing danger".' A London Coroner's Jury returned a verdict of, 'suicide whilst temporarily insane as the result of receiving the letter'.[36]

Two days later, on 22 February, 25-year-old barber Daniel McDonnell was walking to his father's house a few minutes before evening curfew. Near his home, four armed men held up McDonnell and emptied his pockets. Then, according to McDonnell, one of them said: 'We have got you at last, you spy.'[37] Taking his chances, McDonnell dashed up the street under fire from his assailants. He was wounded seven times but survived, probably due to faulty pistol ammunition used by his attackers. McDonnell served with the Royal Air Corps during the First World War.[38]

It had been a dramatic and traumatic two weeks in Cork city. The killing spree was extraordinary, even in the violent context of Cork's Anglo-Irish conflict. During that brief span, IRA forces assassinated seven Cork civilians, wounded an eighth, and drove a ninth to suicide. At first glance, there seems to be a tenuous correlation between the victims. Six of the nine were former British soldiers, and the remaining three were members of Cork's Protestant, Unionist business community. However, in order to avoid spurious connections about the February killings, each case will be examined individually and placed within the larger context of the Anglo-Irish conflict in the city.

BRITISH PRESSURE IN JANUARY

The IRA shot four suspected civilian informers in November and December, but had done so secretly. In January, only one attempted civilian shooting occurred, and that seemed a spontaneous, or at least poorly planned, assassination. In the ensuing months, no other period would match the civilian executions of February. So what prompted the Cork No. 1 Brigade to take such violent actions in such a short span?

At the time of the February killings, Cork's inhabitants were under strong pressure to provide Crown forces with information about IRA activities. The city had experienced official and unofficial reprisals during the previous months. These culminated in the terrifying assault on Cork city centre on 11 December, which destroyed scores of businesses and threw hundreds out of work. Cork residents would have expected even more destruction in the wake of additional IRA activity in the city. Fear of Crown force reprisals could have motivated some Cork citizens to offer information about the IRA, in order to prevent another cycle of violence and destruction in the city.

Martial Law, declared on 10 December, curtailed the city's commercial and civic welfare. Residents suffered through censored newspapers and correspondence, restricted travel, banned public gatherings, and a strict dusk-to-dawn curfew. However, British authorities made it clear that cooperative Cork citizens could weaken the severities of Martial Law. On 17 January, Cork's Military Governor General E.P. Strickland wrote a public letter to Cork's acting Lord Mayor, Barry Egan:

> I wish to let the inhabitants of Cork City, through you, its Chief Magistrate, know that I am ready to give them any possible consideration, and to let the restrictions of martial law rest as lightly as possible on law-abiding people if I can see any signs that they themselves are taking steps to assist me to that end. It surely must be to their advantage to further the cause of peace, and this cannot be done by a passive attitude.[39]

A Cork loyalist offered an interesting response to General Strickland's appeal in a letter to the *Cork Weekly News*.

> Sir – General Strickland's letter in the *Constitution* addressed to the Deputy Mayor is good, but its appeal to Loyalists and threat to disaffected persons would be more useful if it were a little more explicit. What exactly does the Military Governor suggest that Loyal citizens do? They cannot give information for they have none. They cannot fight either for or against the king for they have no arms. They cannot

put up lists of the occupants of their houses behind their door [*a Martial Law regulation*] for the 'Republican Army' has proved itself strong enough to take them down again. If Loyalists (and their number is larger than is generally believed) give any exhibition of their loyalty, can and will the Military Governor assure them of protection from the consequences? I mean no disrespect but at present he probably cannot do so. This is really the crux of the whole question. Nothing succeeds like success (especially in Ireland) and when the Government shows that it can really both govern and protect it will have no lack of adherents to its rule. But, in the meantime, if General Strickland will privately or publicly advise Loyalists what they can reasonably do to help towards peace, I am certain they will do it to the best of their ability.[40]

General Strickland clarified what he desired from Cork's loyal population during an interview with the *Manchester Guardian* published on 24 January.

General Strickland said what he had in mind was the sort of organisation that the people of an English town would probably set up if they found their district being made the scene of operations like those of the 'murder gang'. He imagined that they would hold a meeting and form some sort of vigilance committee to police their town. Under the present conditions, of course, any force formed for such a purpose would be unarmed, but that would not prevent it from assisting in the intelligence work – the collection of information – which was the first condition of any success in putting down crime.[41]

An anonymous letter to Strickland from a Cork loyalist called for a 'firm hand', but recognized the impracticality of the general's suggestion. The writer pointed out: 'If a public meeting were called and denounced the murder of police and military, why, sir, our lives would not be worth a week's purchase ... Sinn Féin have the people terrorised.'[42]

It is difficult to ascertain the effect of General Strickland's request in Cork, but the Crown forces did profess increased assistance from civilians during January. According to the RIC County Inspector's January Report: 'Hardly a day passes by that information of contemplated ambushes comes to hand ... Six cases have been reported of parties of armed men (30 to 100) lying in ambush in the City and suburbs. Each case has been investigated, and in at least three cases the information was definitely found to have been correct.'[43] On 27 January, General Strickland told the *Evening Standard*: 'Recently as a result of the official reprisals a good deal of information about preparations of ambushes was reaching the military authorities. Much of it was of an unreliable character and faulty in facts, but there were also cases where reported ambushes were found in the course of preparation.'[44] The British Army's Sixth Division claimed of this period: 'the organisation of the Intelligence branch had by now been considerably developed ... and at the same time the Proclamation of Marital Law had undoubtedly frightened a large number of civilians and made them more willing to give information to the Crown forces.'[45]

Events in Cork city in January support British claims. Crown forces uncovered a series of Cork No. 1 Brigade weapons dumps during this period. The most spectacular seizure occurred on 13 January in Clogheen, just outside Cork. While raiding the Bowles family farm, British soldiers came across 15-year-old Mary Bowles, as she discreetly tried to leave the property wearing a bulky dress. Beneath Bowles' clothes, the soldiers found an armoured vest, two loaded pistols, and a Lewis machine gun. Nearby, the raiding party discovered three rifles, ammunition, revolvers, IRA documents, and four suspected Volunteers.[46] On 20 January, British forces uncovered Volunteer uniforms and ammunition on Washington Street, Cork, while preparing to blow up two businesses as a reprisal for the IRA's attempted assassination of RIC Detectives Maliff and Ryan.[47] On the same day in Carrigrohane, a few miles west of the city, the British reported the capture of four rifles and a dozen shotguns.[48] On 24 January, back in Clogheen, the military claimed to have seized ten IRA revolvers and a dozen rifles.[49] On 28 January, a 'quantity of ammunition' was reported discovered in a home on Paul Street, Cork.[50]

During the Anglo-Irish conflict, probably the greatest difficulty facing the IRA was its shortage of arms. The Volunteers as a whole possessed only a few thousand rifles and pistols, and their operations were severely hampered by a lack of ammunition.[51] The IRA's arsenal was mainly captured in attacks on the police and military, and the seizure of arms was the prime motive behind most IRA ambushes. Any loss to the limited weapons supply was a body blow to the organisation.

The Cork IRA disputed some of these reported weapons seizures. Writing in the Volunteer magazine, An tÓglach, in February 1921, Florrie O'Donoghue complained: '... These reports have become a daily occurrence of late, and they seem to be a regular policy in the 6th Division area at least, arising I think out of a circular issued by the Intelligence Department of that Division ...' While some of the British claims may have been false, January did seem a poor month for the Cork city IRA.[52]

Crown forces believed the month's arms seizures hampered IRA operations in Cork. The RIC County Inspector reported in January: 'Owing to the recent activities of the police in securing quantities of arms and ammunition, as well as a Lewis Gun, the organisation as far as the city is concerned is more or less weakened. The Cork police have been congratulated by Divisional and Brigade commanders for their work in this direction.'[53]

Crown force success continued into the first days of February. On the morning of 8 February, British troops raided an IRA sanctuary called Rahanisky House, in the Cork suburb of Whitechurch.[54] A number of pistols and some rifle ammunition were discovered, and the eleven men found in the home were subsequently convicted of levying war against the Crown. The captured included Brigade staff officer Seán MacSwiney (brother of the late Lord Mayor Terence) and Con Conroy, an IRA intelligence officer who had recently worked in Victoria Barracks. The British raiding party searched no other location in the neighbourhood that day, which indicates they acted on specific information. The next day the IRA executed Alfred Reilly.

IRA EXPLANATIONS

IRA sources offer limited guidance about the February killings. Ballyvourney Volunteer James Minighan told Ernie O'Malley: 'Word came out to the Joker [the nickname of Brigade commander Seán O'Hegarty] that certain members of the Anti-Sinn Féin Society were implicated in tracking down our men and Seán sent my sister Mary to Cork with a verbal message, for he wouldn't write anything down on paper if he could avoid it. She was told to tell Florrie O'Donoghue that Beale, Baker, and Wight were to be shot at once.'[55] Baker and Wight appear to have been J.H. White of Baltimore Stores on King Street, and R.S. Baker of Baker and Wright Importers on Academy Street.[56] Like Alfred Reilly and Charles Beale, both White and Baker were members of the Cork Chamber of Commerce.[57] If Minighan's testimony is accurate, it would indicate that Florrie

O'Donoghue (who resided in the city, while Seán O'Hegarty moved about West Cork with the Cork No. 1 Brigade flying column[58]) either failed or chose not to shoot Baker and White.

It seems that instead of shooting all the city's accused spies, the IRA warned a few suspects to leave the country or face execution. Liam de Róiste wrote on 19 Februrary: 'there is a rumour that three prominent businessmen have been ordered by the IRA to leave Cork.'[59] Since Alfred Reilly and Charles Beale were already dead by the time De Róiste wrote this entry, it appears the Sinn Féin T.D. was referring to other prominent businessmen. One of the threat-recipients was probably the unfortunate George Tilson. As reported earlier, he received an anonymous letter on 16 February, warning: 'your time is nearly up'.[60] In Youghal, IRA leader Paddy O'Reilly issued similar expulsion orders in March, to two members of 'the ring of spies called Anti-Sinn Féin'.[61] The Cork RIC reported: 'Some Loyalists have left the country, it is believed, on receipt of a warning notice from the IRA.'[62]

It is next to impossible to determine the recipients of the IRA expulsion orders. The only leads are speculative. As mentioned above, IRA veteran James Minighan claimed the two Cork businessmen Baker and White had been implicated. Cork No. 1 Brigade officer Frank Busteed told historian Seán O'Callaghan that 'Nicholson', the manager of Woodford and Bourne Wine Merchants, was shot for leading the 'Anti-Sinn Féin Society.'[63] This interesting information is undermined by the significant detail that no one named Nicholson died or disappeared in Cork during this period. However, a Fred Nicholson did run Woodford and Bourne in 1920–1, and was the superior of Charles Beale.[64] It is possible that Busteed was informed of Nicholson's involvement with civilian spying and confused him with his Woodford and Bourne colleague Charles Beale.

Cork No. 1 Brigade leader Connie Neenan provides an easy order to the February killings. Neenan, a commander of the city's Second Battalion, told author Uinseann MacEoin:

> Information on our lads was passed along from certain business people and Loyalists living a low profile existence. It was not until September 1920 ... that we laid a trap and caught this clerk in the main post office. He was the main channel through which the notes were passed. He confessed everything. We now had twelve names, some of them very prominent people. One by one they were shot

dead, except one fellow who made off to London, but he, we were told, committed suicide on the train.[65]

Circumstantial evidence supports Neenan's story. In September 1920, the IRA abducted and secretly executed an ex-soldier named Seán O'Callaghan.[66] He, plus the four secretly killed in November, combined with the seven February victims, adds up to Connie Neenan's 'twelve names'. Neenan even accurately described George Tilson's suicide on the Cork–London train. All the pieces seem to fit. Unfortunately, Connie Neenan had no first-hand knowledge of these alleged events. From July 1920 through to the end of February 1921, Neenan served a six-month jail sentence for possession of ammunition and incriminating documents.[67] He did not return to Cork city until after the final February killing.[68] While Neenan offers a plausible explanation of the February killings, his story cannot be judged without a closer examination of the IRA's nine victims.

REILLY AND BEALE

The most controversial assassination during February was the shooting of Alfred Reilly. Although part of Cork's Protestant establishment, Reilly was neither an outspoken Unionist nor a prominent anti-Republican activist. Olga Pyne Clarke, a member of Cork's Unionist elite living near Reilly, claimed: 'there was no reason for the killing of Mr Reilly.'[69] Sinn Féin's Liam de Róiste was likewise perplexed: 'In the case of a Mr Reilly, managing director of a large bakery place, there seems to be a grave doubt as to who shot the man, and the motive for it.'[70] According to the *Constitution*: 'Mr Reilly was connected with no political organisation, and his time was devoted to the interests of the business firms with which he was associated.'[71]

Reilly did not publicly express any animosity towards the Republican movement, and as a city business leader he marched in the funeral corteges of both Tomás MacCurtain and Terence MacSwiney. Reilly supported Irish Dominion Home Rule and organised a Methodist Church petition calling for Lord Mayor MacSwiney's release from prison during his hunger strike.[72] Reilly's only previous contact with the IRA apparently occurred when Republican Police offered to protect his apple orchard from nocturnal thieves. His wife claimed (obviously incorrectly) that her husband 'did not have an enemy in the world'.[73] Numerous civic organisations condemned his killing, and Reilly's advanced age (58-years-old) likely added to local resentment of the act.[74] Throughout the Anglo-Irish conflict, the IRA killed only one other city citizen of Alfred Reilly's stature. There seemed to be no obvious motive for Reilly's assassination. He was a Justice of the Peace, but since numerous local JPs supported the British Judiciary during the conflict and survived unscathed, Reilly's legal position seems unrelated to his execution.[75] However, the IRA did indeed kill Reilly publicly and label him a 'spy'. IRA leader Mick Murphy placed Reilly within a civilian Unionist intelligence group operating out of the Cork Y.M.C.A. 'This man was a member of the senior secret service of the Y.M.C.A.' Murphy's accusation provides the most likely motivation for the IRA's killing of Reilly, as it had no other rationale for the assassination.

The case of Charles Beale is similar to Reilly's (Beale coincidentally attended Reilly's funeral). According to Mick Murphy, Beale was a 'Y.M.C.A. senior secret service agent'.[76] Beale had an obvious connection to this alleged spy network, as the IRA executed his father-in-law James Blemens two months earlier. It is possible the Volunteers suspected Beale solely because of his relationship to James Blemens. This theory is supported by the IRA's execution of James Blemens' seemingly inoffensive son Frederick, killed with his father in December. However, the Volunteers did not blame the entire Blemens family for the alleged activity of James Blemens. The Brigade apparently did not bother Blemens' other son James Jr during the conflict.[77] His daughter Sarah (Charles Beale's wife) and Beale's brother Henry (a prominent Unionist) likewise remained in the city throughout 1921. The Volunteers were probably aware of the potential propaganda damage they would incur for persecution of a single family. Yet they shot Charles Beale anyway.

Beale's correspondence with a British military officer could have caused his execution. According to Beale's widow, the couple had housed a British Army officer attached to the military police in Cork. When the officer returned to England, Beale continued to correspond with him.[78] If anything incriminating passed in those letters, the IRA likely would have been aware of it, since they closely monitored mail in the city. (See Chapter Seven for details.) The testimony of city Volunteer Eamonn Enright seems to support this explanation. Enright recalled: 'Some of the big businessmen had managed the Anti-Sinn Féin Society. They were Unionists and Protestants. Three of them were shot after a raid on the mails. A manager of Woodford Bourne was shot.'[79] Beale was indeed a manager of Woodford and Bourne.

For Mrs Beale, the only warning of trouble came two weeks earlier when two unknown men called at their home for her husband. The men '... did not answer her straight ... they muttered something and went away. They would not be the sort of men her husband would mix with. They wore moustaches.'[80] These mous- tached visitors could have been IRA gunmen hunting Beale. They may also have been jobseekers, 'looking for an appointment in the shop', as Mrs Beale originally assumed. It is even possible the visi- tors were British intelligence operatives. The available evidence does not permit any conclusion about the visit.

Like Alfred Reilly, the IRA must have believed James Beale supplied the British with information. There was no other explana- tion for his assassination.

The other February victims had no obvious connection to Reilly and Beale. Indeed, they were of a different religion and social strata. Speaking of Cork's civilian informers, Florence O'Dongohue later wrote of a class of 'mercenary touts and pimps, usually local and native ... The second class, contemptible and unprincipled were men of such limited range and ability that their value to the enemy must have been slight. We put some of them out of action for their proven guilt, as a stern warning to others and to let their paymasters know that we were aware of their activities'.[81] At least two of the February victims fit into this 'second class' category.

MOHALLY AND WALSH

The IRA had hunted William Mohally for some time before his death. He was remembered locally as a recruiting sergeant for the British Army in Cork during the First World War, and later worked as a night watchman for shopkeepers on King Street (now MacCurtain Street).[82] While on patrol on 9 September, Mohally was beaten with crowbars by four men who had broken into a shop.[83] Curiously, nothing in the shop had been touched or stolen. On the night of 28 November, armed civilians opened fire on Mohally and chased him down King Street, but he found refuge outside a nearby police station.[84] He likely left Cork for some time afterwards. IRA officer Bob Langford later recalled: 'After another raid by the mili- tary, I reported the re-appearance of a spy named Mohally.'[85] Irish

Secretary Sir Hamar Greenwood provided a motive for Mohally's assassination. 'There appeared to be no doubt that he was cruelly done to death because of his friendly association with the police and military authorities.'[86]

A curious, though unsubstantiated story should be mentioned. City IRA Volunteer Eamonn Enright later recalled: 'Around Douglas St a chap was shot and left for dead. He was removed to the South Infirmary where he regained consciousness and talked. The doctor in charge was all right so he gave him a whiff of chloroform which kept him under, and he reported that if this spy lived he would talk. He was removed on a stretcher and shot.'[87] Although Mohally was shot on Lower Glanmire Street, some distance from Douglas Street, his case strongly resembles Enright's description. This would explain the Brigade's decision to attack the wounded victim in the hospital, which had not occurred in its prior failed assassinations.

Like Mohally, Michael Walsh aroused the IRA's attention long before his assassination. Sir Hamar Greenwood told the House of Commons: 'It was stated in evidence that Walsh ... had been previously kidnapped by Sinn Féiners, and that as soon as released attempts had been made upon his life.'[88] His sister later testified that Walsh left his job at the Ford Factory the previous year.

> He was not at Ford's for the past six or eight months, as he was taken out of it by Sinn Féiners one day. They dragged him here and there since then ... Some time ago he was arrested by the military and taken to the Bridewell. In his pocket was found three Sinn Féin summonses ... He was deported by Sinn Féiners and taken across the water, but he came home again, thinking he was alright. There were 14 shots fired into her house at him a month ago. They chased him into the house and trampled a child she had been nursing, and the child died. Her brother escaped over a wall.[89]

(Her horrifying story about the baby is inconclusive, as Cork newspapers, British records and IRA sources reported no such episode.)

However, British Sixth Division Intelligence officer Captain Kelly offered a definite British connection to Walsh, stating that Walsh had been arrested by the IRA and detained in Cork Union Hall, until his rescue by British soldiers during a raid on the place. 'We sent him to England but he returned and was shot by the rebels.'[90] The assistance of Walsh by British military intelligence raises considerable suspicion that he was in fact a British informant.

Additional information in the Walsh case comes from IRA intelligence officer Siobhan Creedon Lankford. A worker in the Mallow Post Office, Creedon served as an intelligence officer in the Cork No. 2 Brigade (making her one of the few women officers in the IRA).[91] Later she married Cork Sinn Féin activist Seamus Lankford, then a Vice-Guardian at the Cork Workhouse. She told Michael Walsh's story in her book *The Hope and the Sadness*:

> One evening a man was brought into the workhouse hospital; he had been removed from the North Infirmary because he was a spy. The hospital ward would not keep him, because they couldn't be responsible for his safety. He was called 'Mickeroo', and it was said that his wife, who was illiterate, had given him away. She had taken a letter of his to a neighbour to read; enclosed was a money order for information he had given. This information was passed on to the IRA and 'Mickeroo', being really ill, sought refuge in the North Infirmary. He was removed by order of the police to the workhouse hospital. Spies didn't get far in those days, and one night an IRA squad removed 'Mickeroo' from the ward. He was taken outside the back gate of the institution. The matter was quickly referred to Seamus and Mr Barry, the workhouse master, as they were talking in the latter's office. Quickly they phoned the South Infirmary to ask for an ambulance – 'A man was unconscious on the road outside the workhouse gate.' The ambulance arrived, and the wounded man was rushed to the South Infirmary. He was dead on arrival. It took a few days for the British to sort out what had happened. Frank O'Connor's story 'Jumbo's Wife', is taken from this happening.[92]

(Frank O'Connor's short story tells essentially the same tale as Lankford. As a Cork resident and a rank-and-file Volunteer during this period, O'Connor was in a position to have heard the details of the Walsh killing. Though many of O'Connor's IRA stories were based on true events, it is dangerous to put too much stock in his version.)

IRA leader Mick Murphy offers a different version of the case against Walsh, though an intercepted message likewise appears in his recollection. 'Information about this spy was discovered by us in captured mails. He was also observed by some of our intelligence men going into police barracks.'[93] No additional information corroborates Murphy's account.

GEORGE TILSON

Among the nine victims, the strange case of George Tilson includes the only published motivation for an IRA assault.[94] The *London Star* claimed: 'The deceased is reported to have said he was a secret service agent.'[95] Unfortunately, there appears to be no source for the *Star's* report. None of the inquest witnesses claimed to have heard such a confession. Henry Tilson asked the railway worker who found his brother: 'you are certain he did not make a statement to the effect that he was a secret service agent?' The man replied: 'perfectly certain.' A second railway worker also attended to the dying Tilson. 'Answering the Coroner, the witness said the deceased did not say anything to him about being in the secret service.'[96] Henry Tilson strenuously attempted to refute the secret service allegation during the inquest, preferring his brother to be labelled 'temporarily insane', rather than a British spy. The *Star's* allegation cannot be proved, but neither can it be disproved. A witness with incriminating information may not have been called to testify, or authorities could have suppressed details about such a sensitive matter. One can only confirm that an English newspaper reported that George Tilson claimed to be a secret service agent, and that Henry Tilson partially rebutted those claims at the inquest. It is very relevant, however, that the spectre of espionage appeared in this incident.

SULLIVAN AND O'SULLIVAN

The third victim of the February killings was William Sullivan, an unemployed former Munster Fusilier. Cork city IRA intelligence officer Robert Aherne explained the Sullivan assassination in his testimony to the Irish Bureau of Military History in 1957.

> We received information that a civilian named William O'Sullivan was in contact with the enemy. This man was a local man living in 'D' Company, 2nd Battalion area. He was followed and watched for some time before it was finally established that he was an enemy agent. The facts were submitted to the brigade. O'Sullivan was taken into custody and executed by shooting at Tory Top Lane on 15 February 1921.[97]

One element of William Sullivan's killing bears closer scrutiny. IRA gunmen took Sullivan out of a pub and marched him to Tory Top Lane, an execution spot for other suspected civilian informers. (Timothy Quinlisk was shot there in February 1920, and James

Purcell was killed at the same location in May 1921.) Why didn't the Volunteers simply kill Sullivan where they found him, or somewhere along his way home, as they did with John O'Leary and William Mohally? Why take the risk of moving Sullivan under an armed escort? The most plausible answer is that the Volunteers wanted to question Sullivan before killing him. This would indicate that either the IRA did not have sufficient evidence again Sullivan (despite Aherne's claim) and wanted him to confess; or else the Brigade knew Sullivan was acting with others and wished him to implicate his accomplices. The latter case would point to IRA concern that Sullivan was part of a wider civilian informer conspiracy in Cork.

Less obscure is the case of Michael Finbar O'Sullivan (no relation to William Sullivan), whose body was pulled from the River Lee on 20 February. O'Sullivan was a tailor, and had been wounded on the Somme while serving with the Royal Medical Corps. A friend reported that O'Sullivan had recently re-enlisted in the British Army, signing on with the Royal Artillery.[98] In a city full of thousands of former British soldiers, such an action would not necessarily merit an IRA death sentence. However, IRA intelligence officer Robert Aherne claimed O'Sullvivan had 'joined the Black and Tans'.[99] That enlistment would likely spur an IRA response. O'Sullivan lived in Aherne's 'D Company' area, and according to Aherne, he was 'well acquainted with the IRA in the district'. There is some confusion over the date of O'Sullivan's execution. The city coroner testified that O'Sullivan had been missing for three weeks and he believed the corpse was in the water about that time. However, Robert Aherne claimed O'Sullivan was shot on 21 February (one day after his body was found). Aherne did say O'Sullivan was taken prisoner and removed to a location outside the city, until his execution 'on the instructions of the brigade'. It seems more likely that O'Sullivan was imprisoned for about three weeks before his killing, and the city coroner provided an incorrect date of death. Like William Sullivan, the IRA apparently wanted to question Michael O'Sullivan before shooting him.

O'LEARY AND MCDONNELL

The occupation of one of the February victims merits further consideration. John O'Leary, the second man shot in February, worked as a clerk in the Victoria Military Barracks. He was one of five Victoria

Barracks employees to be shot from February to April 1921. While there was an IRA boycott of the British Army in Cork, the Volunteers did not randomly kill workers at Victoria Barracks. If the IRA meant to make an example of O'Leary for working for the Crown forces, one would expect the Volunteers to explain O'Leary's infraction to the Cork public. However, the IRA accused O'Leary of spying, rather than collaborating. IRA leader Mick Murphy offered his own unsubstantiated explanation for O'Sullivan's killing. 'O'Sullivan was a civilian employee in the office of the British Military Intelligence Officer (Captain Kelly) ... He was known to be bringing information to the enemy.'[100] It will be noted that two IRA intelligence agents worked in Victoria Barracks and would have been in a position to identify potential informers on the civilian staff (see Chapter Seven for details).

The final February shooting is not mysterious. Daniel 'Monkey' McDonnell was well known in the city, memorable for his simian features. IRA leader Connie Neenan claimed McDonnell was a 'ne'er do well' whom the Volunteers had tarred and feathered for petty theft in 1919.[101] McDonnell lived in Robert Aherne's 'D Company' area. According to Aherne, McDonnell was 'well-known as an associate of enemy forces and the Brigade gave instructions that he should be executed'.[102] Aherne claimed IRA Volunteers fired half a dozen rounds into McDonnell at close range and left him for dead, but defective revolver ammunition saved 'The Monkey'.

Following his attempted assassination, McDonnell identified IRA Volunteers throughout the city. According to IRA veteran Seán Hendrick: 'he used to go around in a caged lorry and he pointed out people.'[103] Aherne remembered: 'He was frequently seen with military patrols at night, acting as a spotter in night raids on the houses of IRA men.'[104] To the young Olga Pyne Clarke, McDonnell was a kind of local ogre. 'He appeared to notice no one, and never a muscle moved in his inscrutable, wizened, chimpanzee-like face, but when he fired, either left or right, he never missed the mark. None of the city businessmen would ever look at him, because legend had it that if you did, he, being trigger happy, would have plugged you.[105] He was spiteful, recalled Connie Neenan. 'When he recovered he went around spotting everyone he knew whether they were in the IRA or not if he had a grudge against them.'[106] Brigade intelligence officer Seán Culhane claimed: 'My first arrest was due to The Monkey. I was with George Siske, whom The Monkey hated.'[107]

In May 1921, McDonnell's efforts proved fatal for captured IRA officer Charlie Daly (not to be confused with Volunteer Charlie Daly, who was killed in the Blackpool Railway Tunnel). British Army officials claimed Daly 'was shot attempting to escape.'[108] while the IRA reported that Daly was tortured before being unofficially executed in Victoria Barracks.[109] Before his death, Daly told his cellmate: 'He had given a wrong name and at the identification parade 'Monkey' McDonnell was present and he believed had identified him.'[110]

Another suspicion in McDonnell's case comes from the aftermath of his shooting. When the wounded 'Monkey' arrived at South Infirmary Hospital, police guarded him until his transfer to Victoria Barracks Military Hospital.[111] The Crown forces were clearly protecting McDonnell from an IRA attempt to finish him off, as had happened with William Mohally. (Detectives Maliff and Ryan, wounded in January, were removed to the military hospital the same day.) This official vigilance is suspicious. Throughout 1920–1, it was common for Cork citizens to be wounded by random British and IRA gunfire. Unlike other civilian casualties, the RIC placed McDonnell in protective custody. (This is the first case I have come across of a Cork civilian being so guarded, or treated at the Army hospital.) The police did so within hours of McDonnell's assault indicating a quick official conclusion that McDonnell's assailants were IRA gunmen. However, the police and military did not have time to investigate the crime and determine who was responsible. A plausible explanation for McDonnell's prompt protection is that police knew he was an informer wanted by the IRA. This would support IRA claims that McDonnell was a British informant.

'The Monkey' survived the conflict, though he fled Cork and was last reported serving a murder sentence in a British prison.[112] The only question about McDonnell is when he began to inform. It is possible McDonnell only started helping the Crown forces after his attempted assassination. However, local police reported that he had been 'friendly with police' at the time of his shooting.[113] When adding this information, along with the Crown forces' efforts to protect McDonnell after his wounding, and McDonnell's anti-Republican vigilance in the months following, it seems probable that 'The Monkey' was indeed a British informer.

SUMMARY

The IRA's nine February victims have been analysed. The two Unionist businessmen, Alfred Reilly and Charles Beale, appear to have been assassinated for suspected membership in a civilian spy ring. A third Unionist businessman, George Tilson, killed himself while fleeing Cork after receiving a threatening letter that linked him to the same supposed espionage group. Two victims, William Mohally and Michael Walsh, had been previously assaulted by the IRA, and were tracked by city Volunteers as suspected police informers before their deaths. Walsh had been sent to England by British military intelligence, which implicates him in civilian informing efforts. An IRA source reported that Volunteer surveillance of William Sullivan revealed his guilt. Michael O'Sullivan was likewise followed, and evidence shows he joined the British Army, and possibly the RIC, before his death. One victim, John O'Leary, worked in Victoria Barracks, and no other information is forthcoming about the reasons for his assassination. Circumstantial evidence links the intended victim Daniel McDonnell to Cork's Crown forces, whom he loyally served for the rest of the conflict.

There is no clear connection between the nine victims. While six of the men were former British soldiers and three were Protestant Unionists, their backgrounds do no appear to have been a criterion for the death sentences. So why were these specific men shot? Why were they shot in February? Why were they shot in such a short space of time?

There is an answer that aligns with events in Cork city during early 1921. In February the Cork No. 1 Brigade purged suspected informers in Cork city. The Crown forces had been receiving information from a population intimidated by British reprisals and the declaration of Martial Law. British forces made inroads against the IRA during January. Cork No. 1 Brigade weapons and safe houses had been uncovered in the city, probably through information given by local civilians. An IRA response, therefore, could be expected. The ferocity of this counterattack likely surprised the people of Cork. During this period, IRA Volunteers assassinated two prominent citizens, expelled other civic leaders, dragged two men from their sick beds and executed them, and for a two-week period killed someone about every other day. These were drastic and public actions, not previously entertained by the IRA in Cork city. The Volunteers of the Cork No. 1 Brigade had been excommunicated, the worst kind of condemnation to be suffered in a devout Catholic country like Ireland. Alienated, isolated, and under increasing pressure from the world's reigning superpower, the IRA must have felt compelled to take violent, decisive action against its perceived civilian enemies.

When the Cork No. 1 Brigade took the offensive in Cork city, it tended to attack in brief flurries. It followed this pattern in November during the assassination of suspected British Army intelligence operatives, and when it killed four Cork citizens suspected of espionage. The Brigade used the same method at least three more times between March and the July Truce.[114] The February killings conform with this model.

Evidence shows why the killings took place in February, and why in such a rapid succession. But an essential question remains. Why did the IRA target these people?

Strong evidence against the February victims is not forthcoming. Florence O'Donoghue, the key intelligence IRA officer in the city during this period, told IRA Chief of Staff Richard Mulcahy in 1921: 'the greatest care is taken in every instance to have the case fully proved and beyond all doubt.'[115] Unfortunately, the IRA kept no transcripts or records of their court-martials of suspected enemy spies. The British likewise left few details about the February casualties.

We cannot determine the strength of the IRA cases against all seven victims. The available evidence prevents us from concluding that each was guilty of providing information to the British in Cork. We can only attempt to detect trends in the local conflict that might illuminate the issue.

NOTES

1   Martial Law Declaration printed in the *Cork Examiner*, 11 December 1920; Also quoted in the *Irish Times*, 14 December 1920.

2   *Cork Examiner*, 13 December 1920; *Cork Constitution*, 13 December 1920; Department of Defence Archives, P918, A0413, NLI.

3   For details of the burnings, see the Confidential Report to the Irish Secretary, 'Statements on Incendiarism and Looting in Cork, with Report by Major-General Tudor, Police Advisor', CO 904/150; the Irish Labour Party and Trade Union Congress pamphlet *Who Burnt Cork City?* (Dublin: Irish Labour and Trade Union Congress, 1921); and the *Cork Constitution* and *Cork Examiner* for the week of 13–19 December 1920.

4   *Irish Times*, 14 December 1920.

5   Ibid. London's *Daily Chronicle* published and never repudiated an incorrect map of Cork that moved the City Hall across the River Lee, positioning it next

to the Patrick Street conflagrations. See *Who Burnt Cork City?* for details.

6   Greenwood in House of Commons Debates, 13 December 1920, reported in the *Irish Times*, 14 December 1920.

7   *Irish Times*, 14 December 1920.

8   *Cork Constitution*, 13 December 1920; *Cork Examiner*, 13 December 1920; Full extract in Ms. 31,148, NLI.

9   Brigade Chaplain D. O'Connor to Brigade Adjutant F. O'Donoghue, 15 December 1920, Seán Hegarty Papers, UI49, CAI.

10 Connie Neenan in the O'Malley Notebooks, UCD.

11 Ernie O'Malley *On Another Man's Wound* (Dublin: Anvil, 1979), p. 306.

12 Draft letter by O'Hegarty and O'Donoghue to Papal Nuncio P. Robinson, dated 1930, Ms. 31,268, NLI.

13 *Cork Constitution*, 5 January 1921.

14 *Cork Constitution*, 5 January 1921; *Cork Examiner*, 5 January 1921; RIC Inspector General's Monthly Report for January, CO 904/114; Florence O'Donoghue's article on the ambush, Ms. 31,301.

15 British strength in the city comes from Major Tudor's Report to the Irish Secretary, CO 904/150. IRA estimates of this number are much larger, likely because Cork's Victoria Barracks served as a staging area and replacement centre for military detachments across Munster. See also Ms. 31,213; General Seán Collins-Powell in P918, A0413, DDA, NLI; Charles Townsend *The British Campaign in Ireland* (London: Oxford University Press, 1975), pp. 53, 144, and 217–20.

16 *Cork Examiner*, 10 January 1921.

17 CI Report for Cork (City and East Riding), January 1921, CO 904/115. I believe Sheehan was the target rather than Constable Carroll. Two months earlier, the IRA had shadowed Carroll while planning the kidnapping of a suspected British Army intelligence officer (see Chapter Two). Volunteers held up Carroll and his companion Detective Thomas Ryan outside of Mass, and took Ryan away. They could have easily assassinated Carroll at that moment had they so desired.

18 *Cork Examiner*, 17 January 1921; *Cork Constitution*, 30 March 1921; Mick Murphy's Bureau of Military History statement.

19 Mick Murphy in the O'Malley Notebooks.

20 *Cork Weekly News*, 27 November 1920; *County Eagle and Munster Advertiser,* 22 January 1921.

21 CI Report for Cork (City and East Riding), February 1921, CO 904/115.

22 *Cork Constitution*, 10 February 1921; *Cork Examiner,* 10 February 1921.

23 Cork Chamber of Commerce and Shipping Annual Report 1920, Cork City Library.

24 *Cork Constitution*, 11 February 1921.

25 *Cork Constitution*, 14 February 1921; *Cork Examiner*, 14 February 1921.

26 *Cork Constitution*, 14 February 1921.

27 *Cork Constitution*, 15 February 1921; *Cork Examiner,* 15 February 1921; Report of Quarterly Sessions, 14 January 1922.

28 Cork Chamber of Commerce Report for 1920–1921; *Cork Examiner*, 9 August 1920.

29 *Cork Constitution*, 16 February 1921; *Cork Examiner*, 16 February 1921; Report of Quarterly Sessions, *Cork Constitution*, 4 June 1921.

30 *Cork Examiner*, 19 February 1921.

31 *Cork Constitution*, 19 February 1921; *Cork Examiner*, 19 February 1921.

32 *Cork Examiner*, 21 February 1921.

33 Report of the Mohally Inquest, *Cork Constitution*, 22 February 1921.

34 Robert Aherne Bureau of Military History Statement.
35 *Cork Constitution*, 22 February 1921, 23 February 1921; *Cork Examiner*, 22 February 1921, 23 February 1921.
36 Report of the Paddington Coroner's Jury, *Cork Constitution*, 25 February 1921. The *Cork Examiner* and the *Freeman's Journal* (23 February 1921) reported only the discovery of Tilson's body and a note reading 'Shadowed from Ireland'. Observers unaware of the Coroner's Jury findings could easily misinterpret Tilson's case as yet another assassination, rather than a suicide in unusual circumstances.
37 Report of the Cork Borough Sessions, *Cork Constitution*, 11 May 1921.
38 *Cork Constitution*, 23 February 1921; *Cork Examiner*, 23 February 1921.
39 *Cork Constitution*, 18 January 1921.
40 *Cork Weekly News*, 22 January 1921.
41 Interview reprinted in the *Cork Constitution*, 24 January 1921; A typed copy of the interview can be found in the Strickland Papers, IWM.
42 Anonymous letter to General Strickland, 24 January 1921, Strickland Papers, IWM.
43 CI Monthly Report for Cork, January 1921.
44 *Evening Standard* interview, reprinted in the *Cork Constitution*, 27 January 1921.
45 *History of the 6th Division in Ireland*, p. 97.
46 Mary Bowles' brothers were Volunteer officers and the family was staunchly Republican. See the *Cork Constitution*, 14 January 1921, 15 January 1921, and 26 January 1921; *Cork Examiner*, 14 January 1921, 15 January 1921; *Cork Weekly News*, 22 January 1921. One of the captured documents revealed the activities of IRA officer Con Conroy, then working undercover in British Army headquarters at Victoria Barracks. See Daniel Healy's BMH Statement for details.
47 *Cork Constitution*, 21 January 1921.
48 *Cork Constitution*, 21 January 1921. Writing in February 1921, Florrie O'Donoghue dismissed this report as '... purely invention. We have not lost a single article'. See *An tÓglach*, 15 March, 1921, Vol. III, No. 1, Cork Public Museum.
49 *Cork Constitution*, 25 January 1921.
50 *Cork Constitution*, 29 January 1921.
51 According to Florrie O'Donoghue, the IRA's First Southern Division held just 578 rifles and 1000 pistols in June 1921. The Division contained nine Brigades, including the Cork No. 1 Brigade. See O'Donoghue, *No Other Law*, p. 176.
52 The second Clogheen arms find, in particular seems suspicious. While various Cork Republicans spoke about the first Clogheen raid at the Bowles farm (four rifles lost), they did not mention a second raid, though it claimed a larger seizure (ten rifles lost). There were no independent newspaper reports to verify the British contention.
53 CI Monthly Report for Cork, January 1921.
54 *Cork Constitution*, 23 February 1921, 24 February 1921, 25 February 1921. One of Mary Bowles' brothers was among the captured. According to newspaper reports, most of the men were from outside the parish, indicating that the house was a meeting place for city Volunteers. Seán MacSwiney dramatically escaped from Spike Island Prison the following month, and succeeded Joe O'Connor as Brigade Quartermaster.
55 James Minighan in the O'Malley Notebooks.
56 Cork Chamber of Commerce and Shipping Annual Report for 1920–1921,

Cork City Library.

57   Ibid.

58   In late Februrary, O'Hegarty led the Brigade column to victory over a convoy of Auxiliary Cadets at Coolavokig, near Macroom. Numerous city officers and Volunteers participated in the Brigade's largest action of the conflict. See Pat Lynch in *Rebel Cork's Fighting Story* (Tralee: Anvil Books, 1961), pp. 139–45.

59   De Róiste Diary, 19 February 1921, CAI.

60   *Cork Constitution*, 25 February 1921.

61   Paddy O'Reilly in the O'Malley Notebooks.

62   CI Monthly Report for Cork (City and East Riding), March 1921, CO 904/114.

63   O'Callaghan, p. 63.

64   Cork Chamber of Commerce and Shipping Annual Report for 1920–1921.

65   Uinseann MacEoin *Survivors* (Dublin: Argenta Publications, 1980), p. 239.

66   IRA Record of Executions, MA.

67   *Cork Constitution*, 15 September 1920.

68   MacEoin, p. 239; Neenan in the O'Malley Notebooks, UCD.

69   Olga Pyne Clarke *She Came of Decent People* (London: Methuen Ltd, 1986), p. 53.

70   De Róiste Diary, 19 February 1921.

71   *Cork Constitution*, 10 February 1921.

72   *Cork Examiner*, 9 August 1920; *Cork Constitution*, 10 February 1921.

73   Mrs Reilly's testimony in the Cork Quarterly Sessions, *Cork Constitution*, 5 June 1921.

74   The following civic bodies passed resolutions condemning Reilly's assassination: the Cork Chamber of Commerce and Shipping, the Cork Savings Bank, the Cork Police Sessions Court, and the Cork Industrial Development Association. See the *Cork Constitution*, 15 February 1921, and 21 February 1921, for details.

75   For a list of JPs attending the Cork Summer Assizes in July 1920, see the *Cork Constitution*, 20 July 1920; Twenty-one JPs appeared at the opening of the Spring Assizes in March 1921. See the *Cork Constitution*, 12 March 1921.

76   Mick Murphy BMH Statement.

77   James Blemens Jr. attended Charles Beale's funeral in February (*Cork Examiner*, 16 February 1921), and was in Cork the following December 1921 (see the letter of James and Matilda Blemens to Minister of Defence Cathal Brugha, 21 December 1921, A/0535, MA).

78   Report of the Cork Quarterly Sessions, *Cork Constitution*, 4 June 1921.

79   Eamonn Enright in the O'Malley notebooks.

80   Report of the Cork Quarterly Sessions, *Cork Constitution*, 4 June 1921.

81   O'Donoghue Memoir, Chapter Four, Ms. 31,176, NLI.

82   *Cork Constitution*, 22 February 1921.

83   *Cork Examiner*, 11 September 1920.

84   *Cork Examiner*, 29 November 1920.

85   R. Langford Pension Statement, Langford Papers, Cork Archives Institute.

86   Greenwood written answer, House of Commons Debates, 21 March 1921, Vol. 139, c. 2246.

87   Eamonn Enright in the O'Malley Notebooks.

88   Greenwood written answer, HCD, 15 March 1921, Vol. 139, c. 1216.

89   *Cork County Eagle and Munster Advertiser*, 26 February 1921. I have found no mention of the infanticide in any other sources.

90   'Captured Documents', Ms. 31,223, NLI.

91   S. Lankford Pension Statements, Lankford Papers, UI69, CAI. Cork No. 1

Brigade Communications Officer Sheila Wallace appears to have been the highest-ranking woman in the IRA. See Florrie O'Donoghue's Brigade Staff list, Ms. 31,401, NLI.

92 Siobhan Lankford *The Hope and the Sadness* (Cork: Tower Books, 1980), p. 261.

93 Mick Murphy BMH statement.

94 Irish newspapers during this period operated under British censorship. The failure of local newspapers to mention possible connections between Cork's civilian victims and the Crown forces should be viewed in this context. It seems likely that the British repressed some of this information in local publications. Irish newspaper censorship is underscored in the Tilson case. While British newspapers freely discussed Tilson's possible ties to Crown force intelligence, such speculation was only mentioned indirectly in Irish papers. Ian Kenneally provides an excellent analysis of the *Cork Examiner's* publication under British censorship during 1920–1. See his 'Reports from a "Bleeding Ireland:" The Cork Examiner During the Irish War of Independence', *Journal of the Cork Historical and Archaeological Society*, Vol. 108, June 2003.

95 *London Star*, quoted in the *Cork Examiner*, 21 February 1921.

96 Report of the Paddington Coroner's Jury in the *Cork Constitution*, 25 February 1921.

97 Robert Aherne, BMH Statement. Sullivan was killed on 14 February.

98 *Cork Examiner*, 23 February 1921.

99 Robert Aherne BMH Statement.

100 Mick Murphy BMH Statement.

101 Connie Neenan in the O'Malley Notebooks.

102 Robert Aherne BMH Statement.

103 Seán Hendrick in the O'Malley Notebooks.

104 Robert Aherne BMH Statement.

105 Clarke, p. 46.

106 Connie Neenan in the O'Malley Notebooks.

107 Seán Culhane in the O'Malley Notebooks.

108 *Cork Constitution*, 1 July 1921.

109 Florrie O'Donoghue retained a medical examiner's autopsy of Daly's body. It reported that Daly suffered six bullet wounds, five bayonet wounds, a broken left eye socket, a crushed skull, fractured ribs and fingers, and a broken arm, tibia, and fibula. See Ms. 31,178, NLI.

110 Statement of Denis Murphy, Ms. 31,178, NLI.

111 *Cork Constitution*, 23 February 1921.

112 IRA veteran Dan Healy and another Cork Volunteer were dispatched to London to shoot McDonnell in 1921. Healy reported their inability to assassinate McDonnell because he was serving a seven-year jail term for murder. See Healy's BMH Statement.

113 CI Monthly Report for Cork (City and East Riding), February 1921, CO 904/114.

114 In January 1920, the Brigade planned to storm three RIC barracks on the same night (two attacks were made, and one was successful). In April 1920, IRA GHQ refused to sanction a simultaneous assault on all RIC foot patrols in the city. In April 1921, the Brigade shot four men in twelve days. At the end of May, city Volunteers kidnapped Ed Hawkins, Pat Hawkins, John Sherlock, and Francis McMahon on 20 May and killed Christy O'Sullivan on 26 May. On 18 June the IRA attacked three RIC posts in the city, all on the same day.

115 F. O'Donoghue Adjutant First Southern Division to R. Mulcahy, Chief of Staff GHQ, 4 May 1921, Mulcahy Papers, P7/A/16, UCD.

CHAPTER FOUR

Trends and Explanations

To understand the February slayings it is necessary to place them within the larger context of Cork's Anglo-Irish conflict. February saw more IRA assassinations of Cork civilians than any other period of the conflict. However, the Volunteers' shooting of suspected local informers did not end until the Truce of 11 July 1921.

ATTACKS ON SUSPECTED INFORMERS FROM MARCH THROUGH JULY 1921

During March, the Cork No. 1 Brigade killed one and wounded two local civilians accused of providing information to the British.[1] The three victims, Cornelius Sheehan (killed), John Good, and T.J. Poland, all worked in the city. John Good served as a clerk in Victoria Barracks before taking a position in the Cork Labour Exchange shortly before his assault.[2] Good, a Canadian Army war veteran, had been threatened by the IRA prior to his attack and ordered to leave the city within fourteen days.[3] T.J. Poland worked as a 'clerk in a city establishment'.[4] Unlike Good and Sheehan, T.J. Poland had no apparent connection with the Crown forces. He was a native of Bandon, and there is no record of his employer. Cornelius (Cors) Sheehan had been in the IRA's sights earlier that year. In January, Volunteers shot Sheehan in the shoulder while he walked with Constable Carroll, an officer connected with police intelligence in the city.[5] At that time Cork police claimed Sheehan 'was suspected of supplying information'.[6] Sheehan was a long-time attendant at the Cork Asylum, recently pensioned due to his January gunshot wound.[7] Like other IRA victims, Sheehan suffered from financial difficulties. In late 1920, the Cork City Corporation condemned Sheehan's house as unfit for human habitation. His landlord stated:

'the house was not fit for a dog, not to mind a human being, to live in at the present.'[8]

The RIC also blamed the IRA for two disputed city shootings during March. Michael J. Murray, a railway fireman and an ex-soldier, was shot dead near the city centre in the middle of the month.[9] Sir Hamar Greenwood told the House of Commons that a military sentry killed Murray while the latter attacked a female companion. 'The court of inquiry in lieu of an inquest returned a verdict of justifiable homicide.'[10] The RIC, however, reported that the IRA killed Murray. 'The object is believed to be that he was totally opposed to Sinn Féin and would not assist this body in the removal of goods from the station.'[11] The police account does not match the military inquest of the incident,[12] or any IRA records. The same month, the RIC County Inspector also claimed the IRA killed a jarvey driver 'who was in the habit of driving police'.[13] The driver, 20-year-old John Healy, was shot by men in civilian dress. Healy had dropped some passengers on Cork's Grand Parade, but they disputed the fare. During the exchange, one of the civilians produced a revolver and shot Healy.[14] Since Healy frequently drove police, it seems more likely that the killer was an officer in mufti, who tired of the dispute. It is possible an unidentified Volunteer was responsible for the killing, but such an episode cannot be found in IRA records. Personal shootings of this kind by the IRA were practically unheard of in Cork city in 1920–1, while they were relatively common among Cork's Crown forces. It seems likely that British gunmen were responsible for shooting both Murray and Healy, which underlines the relative unreliability of police reports in Cork during this period.

Attempted IRA assassinations of Cork civilians continued in April. On 1 April, three men fired on ex-soldier Thomas Goulding in Fitzgerald Park. They wounded Goulding in the neck, but he escaped by diving into the River Lee and swimming to the far bank. He recovered in the Military Hospital in Victoria Barracks under British protective custody, and IRA gunmen tried to kill him again in June.[15] On 4 April, ex-soldier James Flynn was shot while he returned to his home on Blarney Street. Although wounded twice, Flynn eluded his attackers. Like Goulding, he also recuperated in the Military Hospital.[16] The following week, on 12 April, the body of ex-soldier Denis Donovan was discovered seven miles outside the city. Donovan had been missing since 9 April, and a rosary was found in his hands.[17] Stephen O'Callaghan, still another ex-soldier, was shot to death shortly before curfew on 29 April. The former Munster Fusilier was an unemployed quay labourer, living off his military pension. On the evening of his death, O'Callaghan left a street card game and was shot in the company of a prostitute. His brother told an inquest: 'when he took a little bit of drink his head was not right.'[18]

May saw additional attacks in Cork. On 6 May, cattle trader and ex-soldier James Purcell disappeared in the city. His body was discovered the following day in Tory Top Lane, the sight of two previous IRA executions. The former Munster Fusilier was from Limerick and had been staying recently in Cork Quay boarding houses while looking for a job. Newspapers reported that 'he had been out of work some weeks', and Purcell was poorly dressed when found.[19]

Two weeks later, the IRA struck again. Edward Hawkins and John Sherlock were both ex-soldiers working at Victoria Barracks (Hawkins was a labourer, while Sherlock drove a lorry). While walking to the Barracks, Edward Hawkins was abducted with his father Daniel Hawkins and taken to a quarry on the edge of the city. There they saw John Sherlock, who had been picked up the same morning. The three men were forced to their knees, and then shot in the head. Miraculously, both Daniel Hawkins and John Sherlock survived, though the latter was critically wounded.[20] Faulty pistol ammunition, a constant IRA problem, probably saved their lives. The same morning, another former soldier named Francis McMahon was kidnapped while travelling to his office at the Cork War Pensions Office. McMahon was never seen again.[21] Two days later, on 26 May, the body of Christopher O'Sullivan was found near Dennehey's Cross, on the city outskirts. Six weeks earlier, O'Sullivan had lost his job as a motor mechanic in Victoria Barracks. A note found on his corpse read: 'Dear wife, I am going before my God.'[22]

The five shootings at the end of May were the closest repetition to the city's February killings. However, the May period claimed only five victims against February's eight and did not include any members of Cork's business establishment.

There were no reported civilian assaults in June until the last week of the month. On 25 June, railway worker and ex-soldier John Lynch disappeared from Cork. He was not seen again.[23] The next day, Thomas Goulding, who had been wounded in April, once again escaped IRA assassins. This time the gunmen failed to hit the nimble Goulding, and he found safety in a nearby RIC station.[24]

During the first twelve days of July, the IRA kidnapped and presumably killed three Cork civilians. W.J. Nolan, an ex-soldier and the son of a retired RIC constable, was abducted from his home on 7 July. According to police, Nolan had recently 'presented himself as a candidate', for the RIC.[25] That would explain his disappearance. The day after the July Truce, Major G.B. O'Connor, an esteemed member of Cork's Chamber of Commerce, was shot and killed outside his Douglas home. A prominent Protestant Unionist, O'Connor was well known in the city. He had also been a vocal Republican opponent and two months earlier had testified against IRA prisoners captured at Clonmult.[26] While O'Connor fits into the same demographic group as the Blemens, Reilly, and Beale, his role in the Clonmult affair makes him a possible candidate for an IRA revenge killing. His execution on the day following the July 11 Truce is also curious. No further evidence regarding his shooting is available.[27]

The third assassination in July was the interesting case of James Bagley. He disappeared from the city the same day as W.J. Nolan. Connie Neenan recalled: 'one of the group broke down in June 1921 when he was caught outside of Douglas. Bagley, one of Shields' crowd, said it was Shields who got him into this mess.'[28] Dan Shields was a former North Cork Volunteer who had given information that almost resulted in the capture of Cork No. 2 Brigade flying columns at Mourne Abbey and Nadd.[29] After becoming a British informer, Shields apparently recruited other spies for service in Cork, including a man named Saunders. Paid by British intelligence, Saunders moved about the city searching for wanted Volunteers. He was eventually arrested by the IRA and sentenced to death. Before his execution, Saunders identified Dan Shields as his controller in Cork city. Saunders' confession includes details about British intelligence operatives in the city during this period.[30]

The Cork No. 1 Brigade's campaign against suspected civilian informers peaked in February, fell and then levelled off during the final five months of the conflict. The total number of IRA attacks dropped significantly in March, but remained a disturbing feature of the fight in the city. The overall trend can be seen through a monthly listing of IRA shooting attacks on civilians.

The details of the incidents listed below have already been described. The cases listed are limited to those where the IRA's intention appears to have been to kill the victim.

Table One: IRA Assaults in Cork City Against Suspected Civilian Informers

1920	June	July	August	September	October	November	December
	–	–	–	1	–	1	3
1921	January	February	March	April	May	June	July
	1	8	3	4	6	2*	3

Source: RIC Monthly Reports, Newspaper Accounts, and IRA Records (MA A/0437, A/0535)

* Includes Thomas Goulding, who was previously shot in March 1921.

POLICE REPORTS ON THE SITUATION IN CORK

RIC monthly reports from Cork city do not explain the drop in local civilian shootings after February. One might anticipate the number of civilian assassinations to correspond with police depictions of the IRA campaign in the city. If the IRA faired poorly during one month, we could expect a matching spike in the shooting of Cork civilians. (According to this theory, the IRA would shoot civilians either to terrorize local residents from giving information, or to plug information leaks.) Conversely, IRA success in a period should translate into a subsequent drop in civilian shootings. However, neither of those trends appears in the RIC monthly reports. Local police reports indicate that after the February purge, the Cork city IRA acted against suspected civilian informers as they became apparent, on a case-by-case basis, rather than in response to local setbacks.

In March 1921, the RIC County Inspector wrote about Cork city: 'for the past two months the initiative has almost always been with police.' Despite this outlook, IRA assaults against suspected informers in the city dropped from eight in February to three in March. During April 1921, police reported: 'no improvement can be indicated in the state of the city and Riding.' However, the month's IRA attacks against civilians rose to four. The County Inspector was pessimistic about May, reporting: 'the state of the City and Riding has been bad.' However, May saw the second-highest number of IRA assaults against civilians of the entire war. In June the police were pleased to report: 'The State of the City and Riding has improved somewhat,' but IRA assaults on civilians dropped to two. While July was on pace to match February in assaults (three in the first twelve days of the month), the County Inspector reported: '... the City and Riding was in a very disturbed state to the 11th. In fact outrages and callous murders were carried out up the hour of the truce.'

Police described IRA setbacks in Cork city during March and June, yet IRA assassinations of civilians did not significantly increase in those months. Conversely, despite RIC reports of increased IRA activity in April, May, and July, those months each saw higher levels of attacks against accused informers. Based on the County Inspector's reports, no trend emerges to explain the February killings.

SUSTAINED IRA VIOLENCE IN CORK

A sharp increase or decrease in IRA activity in Cork could also explain surges in attacks against civilians. Some historians have suggested that the IRA deliberately targeted civilian enemies when it found British forces too difficult to attack. According to this theory, the Cork No. 1 Brigade would have assaulted ex-soldiers, political opponents, and Protestants as so-called 'soft targets'. Since the IRA was responsible for a vast majority of indictable crimes during this period, the County Inspector's monthly reports of these should provide a rough idea of IRA activity in the city. A clear drop of reported crimes along with a corresponding increase of civilian assaults would be consistent with the 'soft target' theory.

Table Two: RIC Report of Indictable Offences for Cork City & East Riding

1920	June	July	August	September	October	November	December
	60	37	60	81	65	80	88
1921	January	February	March	April	May	June	July
	60	62	54	49	103	80	78

Source: RIC County Inspector's Monthly Reports for Cork City and East Riding, June 1920–July 1921 (CO 904/113, 114, 115, PRO)
NOTE: Includes offences committed in East Cork

An examination of the County Inspector's reports (which include East Cork) does not support the 'soft target' theory. No trends emerge when comparing the area's crime figures against Table One's monthly account of IRA assaults on civilians in Cork city.

Table Two A: RIC Report of Indictable Offences for Cork City &
East Riding Against Civilians Assaulted by IRA

1920	June	July	August	September	October	November	December
Offences	60	37	60	81	65	80	88
Civilians Attacked	0	0	0	1	0	1	3
1921	January	February	March	April	May	June	July
Offences	60	62	54	49	103	80	78
Civilians Attacked	1	8	3	4	6	2	3

Source: RIC County Inspector's Monthly Reports for Cork City and East Riding, June 1920–July 1921
(CO 904/113, 114, 115, PRO)
NOTE: Includes offences committed in East Cork

While the above tables offer some evidence of IRA tendencies, they do not include all unreported crimes. Since large segments of Cork during this period boycotted local police, unreported offences likely would have added to the total. The RIC's crime reports are helpful, but alone they do not completely reflect local conditions during 1920–1.

Another measurement of IRA activity is the number of IRA attacks against Crown forces in the city. Unfortunately, it is extremely difficult to quantify Volunteer operations in Cork.

Although both police and local newspapers described major ambushes of British forces, minor actions and failed ambushes seemed to have gone largely unreported. For example, in July 1920, the RIC County Inspector reported seven IRA shooting attacks on city police (not including the assassination of Divisional Commissioner Smyth).[31] No details of these incidents were included in the inspector's report, and similar incidents went unreported during the rest of 1920. In January 1921, the County Inspector wrote: 'there have been many other cases in which the police have been fired at in the City during the month.'[32] Again the details are omitted. Newspaper articles frequently mention gunshots in the city during this period, and IRA sources claimed numerous armed attacks in 1920 and 1921. While it is clear that IRA sniping occurred in Cork in other months besides July 1920 and January 1921, the RIC did not report those attacks. Apparently, IRA actions were only remarkable when they resulted in British casualties. For example, on 24 March 1921, a large force of city Volunteers attempted to break IRA prisoners out of Cork Gaol. About 50 Volunteers took up positions around the gaol, detained 100 pedestrians, placed ladders against a prison wall, and exchanged gunfire with British sentries.[33] Yet, this spectacular escape attempt did not merit a mention in the County Inspector's March report. Such an oversight shows that RIC County Inspector reports, intended to provide just such information, are unreliable as a sole measure of local conditions.

British Army documentation from the period is not as thorough or comprehensive as police reports. Contemporary IRA documents are almost non-existent, and the testimony of IRA veterans differs in quality and quantity. However, a general idea of events in Cork city during 1920–1 can be ascertained with available materials.

Police and military casualties inflicted by the IRA in Cork offer some indication of the level of IRA violence during the Anglo-Irish War.

Table Three: Crown Force Casualties in Cork City, 1920–1

1920	June	July	August	September	October	November	December
Dead	–	1	–	–	3	4	1
Wounded	–	2	–	1	7	2	11
1921	January	February	March	April	May	June	July
Dead	2	6	–	1	5	2	4
Wounded	8	10	–	1	1	6	–

Source: Based on RIC Reports (CI Reports for July 1920–July 1921); Cork Newspaper Accounts; IRA Records (A/0437, A/0341, MA).
NOTE: Lists only those Crown casualties suffered in engagements with the IRA.
* Includes three British Army officers killed by City IRA forces at Waterfall, Co. Cork.

These statistics do not give irrefutable evidence of IRA activity in the city. For example, British casualties in February surpass any other month during the conflict. However, the February casualties came from a single IRA action, and the month as a whole was one of the war's quietest in terms of attacks on police and military. So the figures do not always directly correlate with what was occurring locally. These numbers, though, indicate that IRA operations remained relatively constant throughout 1921. In addition, Cork No. 1 Brigade activities do not correspond to any increase or decrease of attacks on Cork civilians suspected of informing.

Table Three A: Crown Force Casualties in Cork City, 1920–1
Against IRA Attacks on Alleged Civilian Informers

1920	June	July	August	September	October	November	December
Dead	–	1	–	–	3	4	1
Wounded	–	2	–	1	7	1	11
Civilian Assaults	–	–	–	1	–	2	3
1921	January	February	March	April	May	June	July
Dead	2	6	–	1	5	2	4
Wounded	8	10	–	1	1	6	–
Civilian Assaults	1	8	3	4	6	2	3

Source: Based on RIC Reports (CI Reports for July 1920–July 1921); Cork Newspaper Accounts; IRA Records (A/0437, A/0341, MA).

NOTE: Lists only those Crown casualties suffered in engagements with the IRA
* Includes three British Army officers killed by City IRA forces at Waterfall, Co. Cork.

Significant IRA activity in Cork city continued up to the July 11 Truce. There was a major Volunteer operation in March (the unsuccessful mass escape from Cork Gaol); two attacks on RIC patrols in April, and the assassination of a policeman;[34] in May an ambush of an RIC patrol in Blackpool (killing three policemen and wounding one), separate assassinations of an Auxiliary Cadet and a British soldier, and the failed ambush of the British intelligence chief Captain Kelly;[35] in June simultaneous attacks on three RIC barracks (one soldier killed, one wounded), the shooting of three soldiers outside their barracks the following week, and another RIC barrack attack three days later (one soldier killed, two wounded);[36] and in July the killing of four off-duty British soldiers the night before the Truce. The Cork County Inspector wrote of attacks continuing in the city up until the very hour of the ceasefire.[37]

It should also be noted there is little record of the IRA's numerous unsuccessful ambushes of Crown forces in the city.[38] While historian Michael Hopkinson suggests that such failures reflect poorly on IRA operations, I would argue the opposite.[39] Typically, armed Volunteers set up an attack position at a city thoroughfare, and waited for British forces.[40] If their target did not appear by a certain time, the Volunteers would withdraw. Even when an attempted ambush did not result in any fighting, such operations revealed three things: continued aggression by Volunteers in the city; the silence of local civilians during the ambushes, indicative of their tacit support of the IRA; and the lack of frequent Crown force patrols in many areas of Cork.

Does the sustained Cork IRA activity provide any explanations for the February killings? We have examined RIC report summaries, police lists of indictable offences, and British casualties in the city. These figures offer no clear connections or trends with IRA attacks on suspected informers. It would appear, therefore, that the February shooting spree stands largely alone in Cork's War of Independence experience.

TARGETING EX-SOLDIERS AS 'SOFT TARGETS'?

Two academic works are especially relevant to events in Cork city during 1920–1. Jane Leonard's article considers the large number of former soldiers assassinated by the IRA, while Peter Hart's more comprehensive county Cork study asserts that the February shootings were a 'tit-for-tat' response to British successes against the IRA. Neither of these works adequately explains events in Cork city during 1921. Each will be addressed below.

In her article 'Getting Them at Last: The IRA and Ex-servicemen' (in David Fitzpatrick's *Revolution? Ireland 1917–1923*),[41] Dr Jane Leonard focuses on the IRA's execution of military veterans during the War of Independence. Using the contemporary phrase 'soft-target', Leonard emphasizes the large number of former soldiers shot as suspected informers in Ireland during 1920–1. Her argument implies that the IRA executed Irish citizens because of their prior British military service. According to Leonard, as the guerrilla conflict progressed in 1920 and 1921, the IRA found it increasingly difficult to attack superiorly equipped and trained Crown forces. To preserve themselves, the Volunteers moved onto easier and unprotected symbols of British imperialism, such as ex-soldiers. Dr Leonard's theory is especially pertinent to Cork city. During the Anglo-Irish conflict, city IRA forces shot at least twenty-six former British servicemen as suspected spies. Nineteen of these men died.

Table Four: IRA Killings of Ex-Servicemen in Cork City

Name	Date of Death	Name	Date of Death
Quinlisk	20/2/20	Sheehan	23/3/21
S. O'Callaghan	15/9/20	Donovan	12/4/21
Downing	28/11/20	St. O'Callaghan	29/4/21
Horgan	12/12/20	Purcell	6/5/21
O'Leary	12/2/21	Hawkins	20/5/21
W. Sullivan	14/2/21	McMahon	20/5/21
Walsh	18/2/21	C. O'Sullivan	26/5/21
Mohally	20/2/21	Lynch	25/6/21
MF O'Sullivan	20/2/21	Nolan	11/7/21
		O'Connor	12/7/21

Source: Cork Constitution; Cork Examiner; O'Malley Notebooks, UCD; A/0535, MA.

When applying Leonard's thesis to Cork, it is necessary to review the individual cases of ex-servicemen victims in the city. A number of questions must be asked. Were the civilians shot solely because of their veteran status? What was the IRA's attitude towards ex-soldiers in the city? What else could explain the high ratio of veterans among civilian victims?

LOOKING BEYOND THE VETERAN STATUS

A closer examination of the ex-soldiers shot in Cork reveals three demographic commonalities besides their military service. Nineteen of the twenty-six ex-servicemen victims were either associates of the Crown forces, workers at Victoria Barracks, or unemployed at the time of their attacks. Their individual cases will be reviewed below.

Strong evidence shows that the first ex-soldier killed in Cork was indeed a British agent. Waterford native Timothy Quinlisk was an adventurer and former Royal Irish Regiment prisoner-of-war who served with the Casement Brigade in Germany (captured Irish soldiers enlisted by Sir Roger Casement to fight for Irish independence should the occasion arise).[42] Arriving in Dublin in late 1919, Quinlisk worked with Dublin Castle to arrange Michael Collins' capture. He managed to meet with Collins, but stirred misgivings among Dublin IRA officers. In early 1920, Quinlisk moved to Cork, after Collins' wary colleagues suggested that 'The Big Fellow' was hiding there. In Cork, Quinlisk quickly came under suspicion when he tried to infiltrate the city IRA by posing as a gun smuggler. Meanwhile, the IRA intelligence operation intercepted a coded telegram from Dublin Castle, telling Cork's police headquarters to expect a letter for a British agent operating in the city. The following morning Florence O'Donoghue held up the RIC messenger and found the letter, which incriminated Quinlisk as a British spy. City Volunteers then lured Quinlisk to Tory Top Lane by promising to show him a hidden weapons dump. There they shot him and pinned a warning on his corpse, in a manner that would soon become familiar to Cork's citizens.

While the city IRA proved no other local spy case as quickly as Quinlisk's, eight other ex-servicemen victims had connections to the police or military (Horgan, Downing, Walsh, Mohally, M.F. O'Sullivan, McDonnell, Sheehan, and Nolan). After George Horgan and Tom Downing disappeared in November, unidentified 'Black and Tans' threatened severe reprisals against the city, which indicates a relationship between the two men and local police. British military intelligence transported Michael Walsh to England before his execution in Cork. According to Sir Hamar Greenwood, William Mohally had 'friendly associations with the police and military',[43] while Cornelius Sheehan was shot while walking with RIC Detective Carroll. The final February victim Michael McDonnell was accused of providing information before he was shot, and definitely identified IRA Volunteers afterwards. Michael Finbarr O'Sullivan enlisted in the British Army (and possibly the RIC), and June victim W.J. Nolan had joined the RIC.

Employment at the British Army headquarters in Victoria Barracks was another common denominator among the IRA's ex-servicemen victims. Five ex-soldiers shot by the IRA worked at Victoria Barracks (John O'Leary, John Good, Edward Hawkins, John Sherlock, and Christy O'Sullivan). An obvious conclusion would be that they were shot for breaking a Republican prohibition on civilians working for the British Army. However, if these men were killed for such an offence, why did the IRA fail to broadcast the reason? The IRA issued no such warning at the time of the shootings, and Republican veterans never subsequently mentioned a campaign against civilian employees at Victoria Barracks. The failure to publicize such an explanation would defeat the entire rationale of an 'example' shooting. (As reported in the previous chapter, the IRA typically left a note on the bodies of civilians executed as spies, to warn others of the consequences of such activity.) During 1920 and 1921, hundreds of Cork civilians worked directly and indirectly for the British, including clerical and service employees at Victoria Barracks and the Haulbowline Naval Base, civil servants in government offices, domestic servants in the homes of military officers, and the staffs of dozens of local businesses supplying Crown forces with everything from lumber to drink. Using simple arithmetic, scores of such employees would have been former servicemen, yet they escaped harassment and assassination. What made these five Victoria Barracks employees so special in the eyes of the IRA? The most likely explanation is that the IRA believed the five men were providing information to British forces. The British Army reported that it received intelligence assistance from military contractors and civilians employed by the army or police during this period.[44] Two highly placed IRA agents operated in Victoria Barracks, and would have been in an excellent position to identify civilian employees acting in such a manner. (The work of these IRA agents will be studied in detail in Chapter Seven.)

Poverty was a second common denominator among a number of the IRA's ex-soldier victims. This was not uncommon among post-war veterans in Ireland. According to the British Government, over 21,000 ex-servicemen in Ireland were unemployed at the end of 1920.[45] The Munster Fusilier Ex-Comrades Association (serving Cork's home regiment, in which three of the victims served) complained: 'in the present state of affairs in Ireland, it was very difficult for an ex-serviceman to obtain employment of any kind.'[46]

Five IRA victims were jobless when they were assaulted. Michael Walsh was abducted from the Cork Workhouse. William Sullivan, Stephen O'Callaghan, and James Purcell were likewise unemployed. Cors Sheehan lived in an 'uninhabitable' home, 'not fit for dogs.'

IRA intelligence officer Florrie O'Donoghue reported that the Brigade shot a number of 'mercenary touts' in the city, as a 'stern warning to others'.[47] Since the British paid for information during this period, impoverished veterans had an incentive to gather intelligence on the IRA, though there is no evidence that any of the five listed victims received secret payments. It is possible that the IRA acted on an assumption that unemployed ex-servicemen were potential informers. However, there is little evidence that the IRA shot poor ex-soldiers as a class in the city. There were likely hundreds, possibly thousands, of impoverished ex-servicemen in Cork. If the IRA condemned the city's unemployed veteran population as possible informers, the number of executed would have far surpassed five.

Of the twenty-six ex-servicemen targeted by the IRA, only seven were unconnected with the Crown forces, working outside of Victoria Barracks, and gainfully employed. These three factors provide tenuous connections and motives for the executions. However, there is not enough evidence to prove a cause and effect in these cases.

THE IRA AND THE CORK BRANCH OF THE FEDERATION OF DEMOBILISED SOLDIERS AND SAILORS

The sheer number of former soldier victims would lead the casual observer to assume the city IRA deliberately shot ex-servicemen as a matter of policy. However, available evidence supports an opposite conclusion.

It must be remembered that Cork contained a very large veteran population. In 1915 alone, the RIC reported 2,256 men 'joining the colours' in Cork city and East Cork.[48] Of the approximately 38,000 males living in the city,[49] roughly 5500 were serving overseas with British military forces in December 1918.[50] The local veteran population rises significantly by adding the large number of discharged and retired ex-servicemen already living in Cork. Military veterans remained visible in Cork, and the President of the Irish Federation of Demobilised Soldiers and Sailors claimed a membership of 1000 in the Federation's Cork city branch.[51] With such a large ex-soldier population in Cork, it is doubtful to assume that the IRA shot ex-soldiers or sailors because of their veteran status.

If an IRA campaign against ex-soldiers in Cork city did exist, the local branch of the Federation of Demobilised Soldiers and Sailors would be a logical focal point for the Volunteers. However, this study reveals no clear antagonism between the Federation and the IRA in Cork.

An early and obvious occasion for conflict between the two organizations was the assassination of Cork Lord Mayor and Cork No. 1 Brigade Commander Tomás MacCurtain in March 1920. While early local rumours blamed ex-soldiers for the killing of MacCurtain, the IRA apparently did not believe this gossip.[52] The Volunteers did not attack ex-servicemen during this period, and allowed the Federation to march in MacCurtain's funeral cortege (the Brigade organised the procession).[53] The Cork Federation Branch condemned the shooting, and Mrs MacCurtain thanked them for the gesture in a letter published in the *Cork Constitution*.[54]

A second crisis appeared the following autumn, when MacCurtain's successor (as both Lord Mayor and Cork No. 1 Brigade commander) Terence MacSwiney went on hunger strike with IRA prisoners in Cork Gaol to protest against their detention without trial. Like the MacCurtain episode, the Cork Federation Branch received permission to march in MacSwiney's funeral procession. It also passed a resolution, which it sent to British Prime Minister David Lloyd-George and King George. The message read:

> That we, the survivors of the gallant Corkmen who cheerfully offered their lives on the altar of human liberty in the late war, strongly condemn the action of the Coalition Government in slowly sending to an early grave Cork's Lord Mayor. We feel, as men who desire to live in peace and accord with every section of our fellow countrymen, that the action of the present government in treating as common criminals the Lord Mayor and his fellow prisoners, whose only crime is love of country, shall have but one effect, that is to bring into contempt the present manner in which Ireland is governed.[55]

If there was an IRA campaign of intimidation against ex-soldiers in the city, one would expect veterans to disassociate themselves from a presumably suspect and dangerous body like the Cork Federation Branch. However, that does not appear to have occurred. In July 1920, 5000 ex-servicemen marched through the city in the funeral cortege of a fellow veteran killed by British troops.[56] On 11 March 1921, during the height of the Anglo-Irish conflict, over 250 Federation members gathered to elect city branch officers.[57] The following week, 1500 ex-soldiers rallied at the Cork Cathedral 'in memory of dead Great War comrades'.[58] The IRA did not interfere with any of these displays of ex-servicemen solidarity.

The dedication of the Cork branch's new Federation headquarters in September 1921 (two months after the July Truce) reinforces this point.[59] Showing that it was not a pariah in the city, the branch solicited and received enough funds 'to install themselves into that magnificent house, a club perhaps as good as any club in Ireland'. Demonstrating the dual nature of the organization, the Cork Federation Branch invited both General Strickland and Sinn Féin TD J.J. Walsh to attend the club dedication. Strickland did not attend, and Walsh was in Dublin for a Dáil meeting, but he did write: 'I wish to assure your men that no matter how radically I differed from them in the past, I owe them a duty as a Parliamentarian representative, and for this reason they can always rely on me to give careful and sympathetic consideration to any claims which they, as citizens, may deem it necessary to advance.'[60]

Perhaps the delicate status of the organization, and ex-servicemen in Cork city as a whole, is best captured in the remarks of the president of the Irish Federation of Demobilized Sailors and Soldiers, during the city club dedication. 'Their organization was non-political, non-sectarian, and strictly democratic, and he advised them not to discuss controversial topics in the club.'

EX-SERVICEMEN AND THE IRA

It would appear the Cork city IRA did not consider the ex-servicemen overtly hostile. While local Republicans opposed Irish involvement in the First World War and repeatedly broke up British Army recruiting meetings in the city, these activities were mainly confined to the tense Conscription Crisis in 1917 and 1918.[61] By 1920, Republican attention was focused on defeating the British civil and military administrations in the city, rather than punishing the thousands of Corkmen who enlisted in the British forces during the Great War. Cork city in this period was a small place, with neighbourhoods as intimate as country villages. Ex-servicemen were engrained in the city's social fabric. Such a large percentage of Cork's young male population served in the recent war that virtually every IRA activist in Cork would have been friendly with an older brother, neighbour, or co-worker who was a veteran.[62] There is little indication of open hostility in the city between Volunteers and ex-servicemen in 1920–1. There is certainly no evidence of an IRA murder campaign to persecute or purge ex-soldiers in Cork.

A number of ex-soldiers served in the Cork city IRA. Active city Volunteers such as James Coleman, Sean Healy, Con Conroy, Pat Margetts, and Eugene O'Connell were British military veterans. Seán Murray, the Brigade Training Officer and primary organizer of the Brigade Flying Column, was a former Irish Guard who saw action in Flanders. The popular Brigade chaplain Father Dominic O'Connor (brother of Brigade Quartermaster Joe O'Connor) served with the British Army in Salonika. Other veterans could be found throughout the Republican movement. The celebrated West Cork flying column commander Tom Barry fought in the Mesopotamia Campaign. Mid-Clare's flying column leader Ignatius O'Neal served in the Irish Guards. GHQ Director of Training Emmet Dalton won the Military Cross with the Dublin Fusiliers in France. Sinn Féin leaders Erskine Childers and Robert Barton were both decorated former officers. While the IRA was a tight organization that did not seek out new recruits after fighting started in 1920, it never prohibited ex-servicemen from joining its ranks.

Surprisingly, there is evidence of hostility in Cork city between ex-servicemen and the Crown forces. One of the largest outbreaks of violence during the Anglo-Irish War in Cork city was a bloody riot between ex-soldiers and British troops from Victoria Barracks. After a military patrol killed a local ex-soldier named James Burke (and was accused of using Burke's blood to write its regimental name on a nearby wall), hundreds of enraged former servicemen attacked and brawled with off-duty British soldiers throughout the city.[63] The disturbances continued for two days, and were finally broken up when British forces fired into a crowd of unarmed civilians, killing two and wounding twenty.[64] Days later, 5,000 ex-servicemen marched as a body in Burke's funeral (mentioned above). The city was put under military curfew, and according to the British Army, 'very bitter feelings existed between the Crown forces and the evil population of Cork for sometime afterwards'.[65] Antagonism appeared the following March, when police raided the Cork Federation branch office. They stole money, wrecked furniture, and beat ex-soldiers found inside.[66] At least seven Cork city ex-servicemen died at the hands of British forces in 1920–1.[67] However, this study has found no evidence of a British campaign to drive ex-soldiers out of Cork!

If the IRA intended to intimidate ex-servicemen in Cork city, one would expect assaults on high profile military veterans in town. However, such attacks did not occur. The area was home to scores of retired army and navy officers, including some of high rank. Former military officers administered military pensions in the city, and their schedules were frequently printed in local newspapers.[68] Active duty British Army officers lived openly in homes throughout Cork. If the IRA wanted to drive out these supposed political enemies, why would they focus almost exclusively on former enlisted men and ignore more inviting symbols of British imperialism?

The answer is that the Cork city IRA was not trying to purge former soldiers from a 'new' Ireland. Thousands of ex-servicemen lived in Cork during 1920–1. They could be found in all walks of life around town, and many were intimate with local IRA Volunteers. The IRA did not shoot local ex-servicemen because of their veteran status. They shot people they believed to be spies, and a disproportionate number of them were ex-soldiers. One question remains: why did so many ex-soldiers end up on IRA execution lists?

PETER HART'S 'THE IRA AND ITS ENEMIES'

The second academic explanation of Cork's February shootings comes from Peter Hart's finely researched *The Irish Republican Army and Its Enemies, Violence and Community in Cork, 1916–1923*. Although Hart focuses on all three Cork County IRA Brigades (Cork No. 1, Cork No. 2, and Cork No. 3), and extends his coverage through the Irish Civil War period (which this study does not), his work includes fascinating material about Cork city. However, Dr Hart also uses some of the city slayings to support his theory of 'tit-for-tat' cycles of violence, to explain IRA activity during the War of Independence.

First, one must address Hart's figures regarding IRA executions of Cork civilians. 'With almost every night producing another body,' Hart claims that, in the months following November 1920, '… the city IRA carried out 8 successful attacks on patrols and/or barracks – and 131 shootings of helpless victims.'[69] That latter number seems inflated. According to my research, city IRA forces attempted to kill thirty-three suspected informers in 1920–1.[70] This study's accounting of the city's fatal civilian attacks for the entire conflict comes to twenty-six,[71] still a sizable figure, but dramatically lower than Hart's. (My numbers are based on IRA records, police reports, British Army documents, and daily reviews of Cork's two major newspapers for the duration of the conflict.) While additional city victims likely 'disappeared' during the conflict (an August 1921 official list of missing persons adds three Cork names that do not appear on my list),[72] such isolated cases do not account for the significant discrepancy between Dr Hart's figures and mine.

Dr Hart's book also identifies a number of Cork city victims reviewed in this study, and subscribes questionable IRA motives for their assassinations. For example, he claims Alfred Reilly and Major O'Connor 'appear to have been shot because they refused to resign as justices of the peace'.[73] However, he offers no evidence to support his conclusion other than their Justice of the Peace titles, and does not venture to explain why these two men alone were targeted from the two-dozen active JPs in the city.[74] Hart likewise reports that 'three members of the *Cork Examiner* staff were gunned down after their paper had refused various IRA demands'.[75] This theory is fatally undermined by the fact that one of the victims, Stephen Dorman, was an active IRA Volunteer in the city's Second Battalion, was buried in the Republican plot at St Finbarr's Cemetery, and was listed in the Brigade casualty roll as 'bombed unarmed'.[76] (He and two co-workers were wounded by a hand grenade in a fashion almost identical to an RIC attack that killed three Volunteers in December.) Hart implies that John O'Leary, John Good, and Edward Hawkings were executed for working at Victoria Barracks, and Francis McMahon shot because of his employment at the War Pensions Office.[27] However, he cannot offer any evidence of the IRA's motivations other than the victims' occupation, and does not explain why these men were targeted instead of the scores of their co-workers. Tom Downing, kidnapped and killed in November, was allegedly shot as a 'political enemy' due to his prominence as a leader of the Cork Branch of ex-soldiers.[78] Again, Hart produces no evidence to support this claim, can point to no other members of the Cork Branch similarly targeted, and disregards the Black and Tans' threats of reprisals, intended to free him.

More surprisingly, Hart concludes that '... most of those shot (or denounced, expelled, or burned out of their homes) never informed.'[79] This is an extraordinary statement for the simple fact that there is no master record of Cork informers during 1920–1.

Crown forces did dispute IRA claims of success against civilian informants in Cork city. Referring to the February killings in Cork and elsewhere, the British Army later reported: 'In every case but one the person murdered had given no information.'[80] Describing the shooting of ex-servicemen as spies in Ireland, RIC Intelligence Branch Chief Sir Ormonde Winter claimed: 'Numbers of ex-soldiers and others have been murdered during the rebellion, not so much because they were ever discovered in active espionage – indeed, few of those who were assassinated had ever given information – but they had met their deaths partly because there was a possibility that they become informers and partly in order to keep alive the terrorism which it was considered desirable to impose.'[81] Monthly RIC reports typically recorded assaults on suspected civilian informers in Cork, but make no mention if the victim was indeed acting on behalf of the Crown forces. British reviews of specific Cork city cases are not available.

During the Anglo-Irish War, multiple British intelligence formations operated in the city. These were: the 'old' RIC (Irish constables with long service in the city); the 'new' RIC (Black and Tan British reinforcements to the RIC); the Auxiliary Cadets (an autonomous division of the RIC); the British Army; and presumably the shadowy British Secret Service agency MI5.[82] Official British histories and reports of the Anglo-Irish conflicts (both military and RIC) do not offer enough details to judge the individual victims in Cork city. Local unit documentation is incomplete, and in some cases missing. (For example, MI5 records are inaccessible.) No comprehensive debriefing projects were ever conducted with key British personnel from the area. Lost entirely are efforts of individual officers and soldiers operating on their own initiative. (For example, 'old' RIC officers routinely ran their own one-man intelligence networks, which were largely undocumented.)[83] No 'Truth Commission' ever met to record what occurred in the city in 1920 and 1921. For safety reasons the British (like the IRA) compartmentalized their information-gathering efforts, so that the right hand did not know what the left was doing. As a result, conclusions by one branch suffer due to ignorance about the activities of the other branches. Even then, British reports of the period are filled with inaccuracies and errors, often written to protect the authors from censure over their frequent indiscretions and failures in the city. (For example, RIC reports in late 1920 blame the 'Anti-Sinn Féin Society' for unofficial reprisals in the city, as shown in Chapter One.) Dependence on such limited sources is problematic. While Dr Hart's conclusions can be suspected, I do not believe they can be sufficiently documented.

Hart's explanation for the IRA attacks on Cork civilians is that as the Crown forces reorganized and counter-attacked in the city during late 1920, Volunteers became paranoid and attached sinister motives to local 'political enemies' and 'social deviants'.[84] Under pressure from the British and deluded by their own 'conspiracy theories', IRA Volunteers lashed out at their civilian enemies, allowing the real informers to go free. 'Driven by fear or a desire for revenge',[85] the IRA acted in 'tit-for-tat' violence cycles, as reprisals for defeats at the hands of British forces.

'TIT-FOR-TAT'?

Cork city offers an excellent laboratory for Hart's theory that the

IRA executed civilians as informal reprisals for IRA losses. City IRA forces suffered some of the worst Republican setbacks of the war. Cork No. 1 Brigade commanders Tomás MacCurtain and Terence MacSwiney both died at British hands in 1920. In 1921, seven Cork No. 1 Brigade Volunteers captured at Dripsey and Clonmult were executed at Victoria Barracks in the city.[86] In late March, Crown forces killed six Cork city Volunteers at their hiding place in Clogheen (commonly called 'Kerry Pike'). In each case, city Volunteers undertook violent responses to these defeats. Three of four episodes resulted in attacks on British forces rather than local civilians. The fourth case saw the Brigade execute one of its own members for betraying his fellow Volunteers.

ASSASSINATION OF TOMÁS MACCURTAIN

After RIC constables assassinated Tomás MacCurtain, the IRA attacked local policemen implicated in the killing. In May, two police officers 'complicit in the assassination of the Lord Mayor' were shot down while travelling on a Cork streetcar.[87] In July, an IRA party bombed and eventually burned down the King Street Police Barracks, where MacCurtain's killers were believed to have set out from.[88] Finally, after calling on Michael Collins' assistance, the Brigade leaders located District Officer Swanzy, whom they believed had organized the MacCurtain shooting. (He was named as a guilty party by a Cork Coroner's Jury.) On 22 August, two city Volunteers and two Belfast Brigade officers assassinated Swanzy as he emerged from Sunday services in Lisburn, Northern Ireland. The first shot was fired from MacCurtain's own gun, smuggled to Lisburn for the purpose. The Swanzy killing sparked a violent three-day Anti-Catholic riot in Lisburn, which saw scores of homes and businesses burned, and much of the Catholic population driven from the town.[89]

CORK HUNGER STRIKE

In the autumn of 1920, IRA prisoners in Cork Gaol went on hunger strike to protest against their detention without trial. Following his capture at Cork City Hall in August 1920, Cork No. 1 Brigade Commander Terence MacSwiney joined the strike, and was removed to Brixton Prison in London. During MacSwiney's long demise, his colleagues in Cork city plotted their revenge. First they tried to assassinate Sixth Division Commander General E.P. Strickland in Cork city. At the same time they dispatched a small assassination squad to London, to shoot senior members of the British Cabinet.

From the IRA's viewpoint, the attempted assassination of General Strickland was a missed opportunity that reinforced the Brigade's need for fulltime Volunteers. IRA intentions for the operation are not clear. Some Volunteers claim they wished to abduct the General and exchange him for MacSwiney, while others refer to the ambush as a failed assassination. The Volunteers' immediate firing on Strickland's car indicates that they probably intended to kill him. For about a week, Volunteers stood at the bottom of Patrick Hill in Cork, waiting to ambush the General as he drove from his home to Victoria Barracks. Inattentive due to their extended deployment, the Volunteers did not react quickly enough when Strickland's vehicle finally approached (he rode in a single automobile, containing some of his senior staff). Firing on the car, they managed to wound its driver, but had to dodge return fire from the passengers, including General Strickland. The general believed that had he been hit, his troops would have got completely out of hand in the city. His IRA counterparts asked their Dublin headquarters for funds to set up a fulltime staff capable of undertaking such long operations.[90]

Meanwhile, as Terence MacSwiney slipped closer to death in London, some of his subordinates were close by, plotting the Cork city IRA's response. With IRA GHQ approval, the Cork No. 1 Brigade had ordered three Volunteers (Patrick 'Pa' Murray, Jerry Dennehy and Jack Cody) to London with instructions to shoot a senior government minister in the event of MacSwiney's death. Pa Murray called on the assistance of local Volunteers from the IRA's London Battalion, and shadowed various politicians, including David Lloyd George and Lord Birkenhead. Murray was ultimately unable to plan an assassination that gave the assailants a reasonable chance to escape. (The officials did not keep regular hours or recognizable schedules to facilitate such a killing.) However, the Corkmen did find it quite easy to get close to Cabinet members, and on one occasion, Pa Murray exchanged pleasantries with former Prime Minister Balfour while they walked together to a building dedication at Oxford. The Cork Volunteers were eventually recalled to Ireland, probably because GHQ did not want to interfere with the great international sympathy generated by MacSwiney's death.[91]

EXECUTIONS OF IRA PRISONERS IN CORK

In late January 1921, British troops encircled an ambush position in Dripsey occupied by members of the Cork No. 1 Brigade's Sixth Battalion. The British raiding party succeeded in killing one Volunteer and capturing ten more. (The British were tipped off by the elderly loyalist, Mrs Lindsay. In a brutal response, Sixth Battalion officers executed Lindsay and her chauffeur.) Under new Martial Law restrictions, the Dripsey prisoners were convicted of levying war against the Crown, and sentenced to death. On 28 February 1921, a firing squad executed five of the Volunteers at Cork's Victoria Barracks. That evening, IRA gunmen attacked off-duty British soldiers throughout the city. They killed six unarmed soldiers and wounded ten more, including a number walking with local girls in the city's by-lanes.[92] The action was a vicious, but carefully planned retaliation for the execution of IRA prisoners. However, the Volunteers acted solely against British soldiers rather than Cork civilians.

The same month, Cork No. 1 Brigade's Fourth Battalion fell victim to the IRA's worst disaster of the entire Anglo-Irish War. On 20 February 1921, the Battalion's flying column was surrounded by British troops at Clonmult, near Middleton. At least five Volunteers were killed in the ensuing shootout, another seven died after the party surrendered, and nine were captured.[93] The Brigade took no retaliatory action following the Clonmult fight, though the Cork No. 2 Brigade shot an innocent traveller for allegedly informing on the column, after he was coerced into writing a dubious confession.[94] No reprisals against local Unionists or ex-servicemen occurred in the city. When the British executed two of the Clonmult prisoners in May, Munster IRA leaders planned coordinated reprisal attacks against British targets in the IRA's First Southern Division area. A number of ambushes occurred in county Cork, as well as Kerry and West Limerick (West Cork's Tom Barry used the occasion to machine-gun British soldiers playing football in Bandon).[95] City Volunteers attacked an RIC foot patrol in Blackpool, killing three constables. No IRA attacks on city civilians followed the executions (though it is possible Major G.B. O'Connor was later targeted in July 1921 for his testimony against the Clonmult prisoners).

'CROXY' CONNORS AND THE 'KERRY PIKE MURDERS'

In the early hours of 23 March, city IRA forces suffered their deadliest reverse of the war. Black and Tans surrounded a barn in Ballycannon, Clogheen, just outside Cork, and killed six Volunteers from the city's First Battalion found sleeping inside. The deaths were the worst losses inflicted on the city IRA, and were dubbed 'The Kerry Pike Murders' by Republicans. The six Volunteers were in hiding after their recent service with the Brigade flying column near Ballyvourney. Republicans hotly disputed British claims that the Volunteers were killed after a fight, and gathered testimony from local farmers that the men were beaten and then shot on the spot.[96] The funerals were the largest seen in Cork since the death of Terence MacSwiney.[97]

According to IRA and British military sources, a fellow member of the Brigade flying column betrayed the six city men. Patrick 'Croxy' Connors (also called Connor and O'Connor) was a decorated British Army veteran, whose moniker came from winning the French Croix de Guerre during the war. A former machine gunner, he was recruited to handle one of the flying column's Lewis guns.[98] He appears to have been one of the Brigade's few defectors of the conflict. The British military reported that Connors had previously been a police informer before joining the IRA.[99] Some members of the Brigade flying column believed Connors deliberately disabled his machinegun during the Coolavokig Ambush the previous month, compromising the IRA attack.[100] Others claimed that Connors returned to Cork after the ambush, and only turned informer after he was arrested while carrying a pistol and threatened with a death sentence.[101] All parties agreed that while in British custody at Victoria Barracks, Connors gave away the Clogheen hiding place and subsequently identified other captured IRA prisoners.[102]

Told of Connors' activities, the Cork No. 1 Brigade apparently attempted to poison him in Victoria Barracks. The plot failed when a group of hungry British soldiers consumed Connors' tainted meal, resulting in their severe food poisoning.[103] The British Army later helped Connors escape to London, but the Brigade tracked him there in July 1921 after intercepting correspondence to his family.[104] (This was an example of the IRA's control of the local post.) Cork assassins missed Connors in London, but late in August the Brigade was notified that a Corkwoman had spotted the fugitive in New York City. Florrie O'Donoghue recalled: 'At a time when every man and every shilling was needed, we went to the trouble and expense of sending three men after him to America.'[105] With the blessing of Michael Collins, the Cork No. 1 Brigade dispatched city commander Pa Murray and seasoned Volunteers Dan Healy and Martin Donovan to the United States in February 1922. The Brigade gunmen found Connors in Manhattan, and shot him outside Central Park on 13 April 1922. Despite being wounded three times in the body and once in the face, Connors miraculously survived the attack, though it is unclear if he ever recovered.[106]

The 'Kerry Pike Murders' episode illustrates the Cork city IRA's response to defeat. The loss of six veteran Volunteers was a significant blow to the IRA. However, the Brigade leadership showed cold discipline in its aftermath. No one from Clogheen was reported kidnapped or killed following the killings. The month of April was comparatively calm in terms of attacks on suspected civilian informers in the city. It would appear the Brigade identified Connors as the source of the British information and planned retribution solely against him. The Brigade's obsession with revenge is also underscored here. It took the extraordinary step of dispatching assassins to the United States, despite the costs and risks of the operation. However, after the Kerry Pike killings, it did not lash out in a 'panic', but moved in a relatively calm, if brutal fashion.

WHY SHOOT EX-SOLDIERS?

While the February killings were a part of a purge of suspected informers by the Cork city IRA, they were not as reactionary as Jane Leonard or Peter Hart conclude. The IRA did not target its ex-soldier victims because of their veteran status. IRA sources revealed no intention to terrorize political opponents or drive former servicemen out of Cork. Indeed the IRA believed it executed the correct persons. In some instances there is evidence supporting their assertions. However, the large number of ex-soldier victims in Cork must be addressed.

In Cork, the IRA suspected many more civilians of informing than they shot. For example, although a number of city women were accused of providing information to the British, none of them were killed.[107] While some Cork business leaders were likewise suspected of espionage, only a few of them were executed, while others were ordered out of the country. 'Croxy' Connors was the only Volunteer shot as an informer, though it seems probable that other IRA prisoners talked during their captivity. Pat Margetts, a British soldier stationed at Victoria Barracks who spied for the IRA, said of Brigade commander Seán O'Hegarty: 'It would have been better for him and his command if he had looked more closely at his own men for they needed looking after, and some of them were giving information as well as Connors.'[108] When considering the large number of Republicans in the city, it is likely that one or more of them informed. However, no Republican or member of a Volunteer family appears in the victims list. So how did the IRA choose who to shoot, who to exile, and who to leave alone? This study has only analysed thirty-three suspected informers in Cork city. We can assume many more Cork citizens informed on the IRA during the conflict. Ex-soldiers certainly make up a disproportionate number of the Volunteers' civilian victims in Cork. One must ask why the IRA seemed more willing to shoot ex-soldiers.

The social backgrounds of the ex-servicemen civilian victims in Cork provide the most likely explanation. Almost all were working class, with modest standings in the community. While the ex-soldiers victims may have been friendly with Republican activists, this study has shown no close connections or blood ties between them and any Cork Volunteers. A number of the suspected informers were impoverished war veterans, struggling to reintegrate themselves into their community. Faced with numerous cases of local complicity with the Crown forces, the city's IRA leadership probably found it easiest to assassinate isolated men of low social standing, rather than prominent pillars of the community, close associates, or members of Republican families. Although this theory is unproved, it does account for the high proportion of ex-servicemen shot in the city.

THE IRA AND PROTESTANT UNIONISTS IN CORK

The Cork city IRA also executed at least five local Protestant Unionists for espionage during the War of Independence period. (Some of the other local civilian victims may also have been Protestant, though their religion was not mentioned in newspaper, police, or IRA records, leaving the strong impression that religion was not considered relevant in their assassination.)[109] These five men (James Blemens, Fred Blemens, Alfred Reilly, Charles Beale, and Major G.B. O'Connor) were members of the city's 'business class', a different social strata than the other local victims, who came from the working or lower-middle classes. During this same period the IRA ordered additional Unionist businessmen out of the city under threat of death. However, this study shows no significant religious or political persecution of Protestant Unionists in Cork city.

Cork's Protestant community was vibrant in the 1920–1 period. Historian Ian d'Alton puts the city's Protestant population in the 1890s at 15% of the total.[110] By 1920, the city's Protestants likely numbered between 7,000 and 10,000.[111] Scores of Protestant Unionists could be found within the city's political and commercial elite, as well as in local civic bodies.[112] Cork's Unionist candidates garnered considerable support in the 1918 General Election, winning approximately 2,000 votes (about 8% of the electorate).[113]

Though the five Protestants killed in Cork were members of the city's Unionist establishment, four of the five would not be considered top leaders of that community. Alfred Reilly was one of many JPs to serve in the Cork's assizes in 1920, and managed, rather than owned the bakery where he worked. Charles Beale was a junior member of the Cork Chamber of Commerce, and a middle manager for Woodford Bourne Wine Merchants.[114] Neither James nor Frederick Blemens appear to have been active in Unionist politics. Even George Tilson (expelled from the city, but not assassinated) was overshadowed politically by his brother Henry, a Unionist activist and the city's former High Sheriff. With the exception of Major O'Connor (shot in July 1921), none of these men can be identified as important leaders of the city's Protestant Unionist community.

If the Protestant victims were executed as part of some kind of IRA 'pogrom' in Cork city, the Volunteers displayed a curious priority in their choice of victims. Certainly the IRA could have found far more prominent and active local Unionist opponents to assassinate. The 1918 Unionist MP candidates Williams and Farrington would have been a logical place to start, but both survived the conflict unharmed. The Executive Committee of Cork City and County Unionist Association would likewise have proved an inviting target. However, none of its nine local Executive Committee members were assassinated in the 1920–1 period.[115] The IRA could have sought out other former Unionist office holders or candidates in the city.[116] Yet these political opponents were not shot, burned out, or assassinated in 1920–1.

There were various centres of Protestant Unionist activity in the city, such as the offices of the Cork County and City Unionist

Association, the Cork Conservative Club, the Cork Cricket Club, the Cork Grammar School, the local Freemason Lodge, and the Cork YMCA. Despite heavy British reprisals in the city, the IRA did not bomb or burn any of these buildings, or target their organizations' leaders for assassination. While members of Cork's Freemason Lodge were suspected of assisting British intelligence gathering in the city,[117] none of its twenty officers were shot.[118] Neither did the Volunteers attack any of the city's Protestant churches or clergy.

Some attacks against Cork's Unionist establishment were made in 1920–1. The local Unionist newspaper, the *Cork Constitution*, a bitter and vocal opponent of the IRA, saw its presses wrecked and its publisher ordered out of the country in early 1920.[119] While harassed by the IRA, the *Constitution* continued to operate throughout the conflict, and its staff escaped serious harm. It should also be noted that the IRA likewise broke up the presses of the moderate Nationalist *Cork Examiner* in December 1920, after it endorsed Bishop Cohalan's Excommunication decree.[120] In April 1921, Volunteers burned down the Blackrock home of Unionist Robert Hill. However, this attack was apparently a response to Hill's reporting to the RIC of three Volunteers who had solicited him for IRA funds. The IRA did not shoot Hill as an informer, though it likely ordered him out of the country.[121] There were probably other assaults and harassments of Cork's Unionist population during the Anglo-Irish War, but they went largely unreported.

The most serious attack on Cork city's Protestants occurred in late May 1921. Following the IRA's ambush of a RIC patrol in Blackpool (killing three police), the British Army destroyed four local homes as an 'official reprisal'.[122] The following day city IRA forces burned down the residences of four local Unionists: Mr Eben Pike, JP; Sir Alfred Dobbin, JP; Mrs Jacob; and Mr W.H. Simpson. For good measure they also torched the Douglas Golf Pavilion, which IRA leader Mick Murphy called 'a den of imperialism'.[123] The IRA left a notice on Mr Pike's door reading: 'This is a reprisal for the Blackpool reprisal.'[124] These were premeditated and disciplined assaults. The Volunteer parties permitted and even assisted with the removal of furniture from the Jacob and Simpson homes, allowed Lady Dobbin to remove her painting collection, and gave the Douglas Golf Course caretaker an hour to clear his residence of valuables.[125]

The May arson attack was part of a wider IRA effort to stop British reprisals against Republican sympathizers throughout county

Cork. While brutal and sectarian in part, the IRA's counter-arson campaign proved effective, and the British called off 'official reprisals' in June.[126] The IRA's county Cork victims seem to have been chosen as much for their wealth and political prominence, as for their religion. (While the burned homes were typically mansions, their owners were almost entirely Protestant.) The Cork city IRA's contribution to the counter-reprisal campaign was limited to the May burnings. An important element of this arson is that the Cork No. 1 Brigade publicly took responsibility for the action. That acknowledgment indicates that the city Volunteers wanted to maximize the effect of their actions, undertaken with a specific result in mind (ending official British reprisals against local Republican sympathizers).

This last point should be noted when considering charges of a sectarian IRA campaign in Cork. Peter Hart places the execution of Cork Protestants within a wider IRA campaign of 'ethnic cleansing' in the area.[127] If the Volunteers intended to use assassination to prompt Protestants to leave Cork city, it would be logical for the IRA to target prominent Unionist leaders and then announce the reason for the attacks (as it did in the May counter-reprisals). Failure to do so would greatly diminish the impact of such an action. However, the city IRA did not execute prominent Protestants, or ever publicize a sectarian warning to vacate the city. Its five Protestant victims did not enjoy especially high profiles, and in the two cases where the IRA took responsibility, the victims were identified as spies rather than political or religious enemies. IRA veterans testified that they believed the victims were British agents, and there is no evidence to support a sectarian motivation for the executions, other than the dead men's religion. The circumstances of the killings of Cork's five Protestant civilian victims do not support allegations of an anti-Protestant conspiracy perpetrated by city Volunteers.

IRA attitudes towards Unionists in county Cork were hardly benevolent. Had the British employed scorched earth tactics against the Volunteers, local Unionists would have suffered heavily. The continued execution of IRA prisoners was already leading towards deadly Republican counter-reprisals against Munster Unionists. In May 1921, IRA First Southern Division commander Liam Lynch asked his GHQ for permission to take Unionist hostages to protect imprisoned Volunteers from execution. He wrote: 'In view of the fact that the enemy continues to shoot our prisoners, we suggest that for each prisoner shot in future we shoot one local loyalist.

Prominent Freemason officers to be the first to suffer.'[128] A month later he remarked: 'All lives must be considered sacred, and indeed we would all wish to be chivalrous, but when the enemy continues such an outrage, let it be barbarous war all around.'[129] Cork No. 2 Brigade leader Seán Moylan echoed Lynch's sentiments during the Dáil Treaty debates in early 1922. 'If there is a war of extermination waged on us ... I may not see it finished, but by God, no loyalist in North Cork will see its finish, and it is about time somebody told Lloyd George that.'[130] Fortunately for both sides, an apocalyptic 'war of extermination' was forestalled by the Truce of 11 July 1921. The First Southern Division project never received sanction from IRA GHQ, and no hostages appeared to have been executed.[131] In Cork city, the Volunteers apparently took no loyalist hostages during this period.[132]

The IRA's counter-reprisal policy should be placed within the context of Britain's colonial brutality during this period. When considering similar rebellions elsewhere in the British Empire, Liam Lynch and other IRA leaders had good reason to anticipate grievous British reprisals in Ireland. In 1919, British troops fired on a peaceful protest of Indian Nationalists in Armitsar, killing an estimated 400 civilians. In 1920–1, British forces committed substantial atrocities during the 'Arab Rebellion', including the use of poison gas against rebels and the indiscriminate bombing of Iraqi villages.[133] During the Anglo-Boer War, civilians were rounded up and interned in atrocious concentration camps, which resulted in the death of 27,000, mainly women and children.[134]

These tactics were not lost on IRA leaders. In response to IRA attacks in 1921, the Crown forces burned the homes of civilians, destroyed local industries, blockaded offending towns and villages, and carried civilian hostages in their lorries. Had the Irish rebellion continued another year, it is almost certain that the British Government would have waged the 'immediate and terrible war' threatened by David Lloyd George during the Anglo-Irish Treaty negotiations. Severe reprisals against Irish civilians would be expected in such a campaign. In 1919–20, there were few reports of IRA attacks on Ireland's Protestant population. However, during the spring of 1921, in the wake of sustained British reprisals and collective punishments, and anticipating much worse, the IRA planned equally brutal counter-reprisals against Irish Unionists. While regrettable, that decision is hardly surprising.

Though the IRA in Munster prepared ruthless contingency plans against local Unionists, these operations were not undertaken in Cork city. When considering Cork in 1920–1, it is important to recognize what did not happen. Leading Unionists were not harmed. Outside the May counter-reprisal, the IRA did not disturb Protestant property. Local Unionist institutions remained intact.

The IRA's execution of the five accused Protestant civilian informers does not point to a wider campaign of 'ethnic cleansing' in Cork city. Amid a very large and active Protestant Unionist community in the city, only five of its members were targeted. Symbols of Protestant and Unionist authority survived the conflict unharmed. Testimony from a number of IRA veterans provides no evidence that the five city victims were shot because they were Protestants or Unionists. Like the ex-soldier victims, they were executed because the IRA believed they were informers. Whether the Volunteers' suspicion was accurate is an entirely different question.

SUMMARY

The shooting of informers in Cork peaked in February, but continued throughout the rest of 1921. IRA actions against city residents do not follow any easy trends. The IRA campaign continued at a steady pace throughout 1921, offering no correlation between levels of guerrilla violence and attacks on civilians. Ex-soldiers composed a high percentage of civilian victims in the city, but were not targeted because of their veteran status. The large ex-serviceman population in the city and the lack of IRA action against local veteran groups indicates little violent animosity between the IRA and ex-servicemen in Cork. Theories that the IRA targeted ex-soldiers as 'soft targets', or as part of 'tit-for-tat' reprisals to Republican setbacks, are not applicable to Cork city. Evidence does not bear out similar accusations regarding the city's Protestant Unionist victims.

While it is easy to offer theories about civilian informers in Cork, it is very difficult to provide definite proof in many cases. Reconstructing IRA motives, intentions, and effectiveness from incomplete recollections, newspaper reports, and official records can lead to spurious conclusions. It is impossible to provide full and complete reviews of every single case in Cork. The nature of this subject prevented the compilation of written records, and the shootings themselves were irretrievably blurred by reticence, self-service, and the faulty memories of both the Irish and British parties. It is irresponsible to judge many of these cases. However, it is equally irresponsible to discount IRA claims of guilt without exploring other events in Cork in 1920 and 1921, and reviewing British and IRA intelligence-gathering capabilities.

NOTES

1   'IRA Activities Cork City', chronology compiled by Florence O'Donoghue, Ms. 31,401, NLI.
2   Report of Cork Borough Sessions, *Cork Constitution*, 11 May 1921. See also the *Cork Constitution*, 11 March 1921.
3   *Cork Constitution*, 25 March 1921.
4   *Cork Examiner*, 25 March 1921.
5   Daniel Healy BMH Statement; *Cork Examiner*, 10 January 1921.
6   CI Report for Cork City and East Riding, January 1921, CO 904/114.
7   Report of Cork Borough Sessions, *Cork Constitution*, 11 May 1921; *Cork Constitution*, 22 March 1921; *Cork Examiner*, 10 January 1921, 22 March 1921.
8   Report of Cork Quarterly Sessions, *Cork Constitution*, 1 June 1921. The Sheehans' landlord sued the couple for back rent, after a drunk Mrs Sheehan attacked him with a hurley.
9   *Cork Examiner*, 15 March 1921.
10   *Cork Examiner*, 19 March 1921.
11   CI Report for Cork City and East Riding, March 1921, CO 904/114.
12   *Cork Examiner*, 16 April 1921.
13   CI Report for March 1921, CO 904/114
14   *Cork Weekly News*, 29 March 1921.
15   *Cork Examiner*, 2 April 1921; Report of Cork Borough Sessions, *Cork Constitution*, 16 June 1921; CI Report for Cork City and East Riding, June 1921, CO 904/115.
16   *Cork Examiner*, 5 April 1921; Report of Cork Borough Sessions, *Cork Constitution*, 16 June 1921.
17   *Cork Examiner*, 13 April 1921, 14 April 1921; *Cork Constitution*, 13 April 1921.
18   *Cork Constitution*, 30 April 1921; *Cork Examiner*, 30 April 1921; Report of Military Inquiry, *Cork Examiner*, 3 May 1921.
19   *Cork Constitution*, 9 May 1921, 11 May 1921; *Cork Examiner*, 9 May 1921, 11 May 1921.
20   *Cork Constitution*, 21 May 1921.
21   Dublin Castle List of Missing Persons, *Irish Times*, 22 August 1921.
22   *Cork Constitution*, 28 May 1921; Report of Cork Quarterly Sessions, *Cork Constitution*, 15 October 1921.
23   CI Report for Cork, June 1921, CO 904/114.
24   Ibid.
25   CI Report for Cork City and East Riding, July 1921, CO 904/115.
26   *Cork Constitution*, 21 April 1921.
27   O'Connor's death is a mystery. As stated above, he could have been assassinated because of his testimony against the Clonmult prisoners. He may also have been kidnapped as a hostage for IRA prisoners facing execution, and then executed after the Truce when he was no longer needed by the Volunteers. It

is possible he was shot for membership in the 'Anti-Sinn Féin Society'. However, there is no clear record of what happened to O'Connor and why.

28   Connie Neenan in the O'Malley Notebooks.

29   Michael Hopkinson *The Irish War of Independence* (Dublin: Gill and MacMillan, 2002), p. 111; Seán Moylan *Seán Moylan in his Own Words* (Millstreet: Aubane Historical Society, 2004), pp. 111–12; and Meda Ryan *The Real Chief, Liam Lynch*, (Cork: Mercier Press, 2005), pp. 73–4.

30   'Statement by the Spy Saunders', included in IO First Southern Division F. O'Donoghue's Report to Chief of Staff R. Mulcahy, 24 June 1921, Mulcahy Papers, P17A/20, UCD. Saunders' account is fascinating, and seems to indicate MI5 'secret service' activity in the city.

31   CI Report for Cork City and East Riding, July 1920, CO 904/113.

32   CI Report for Cork, January 1921, CO 904/114.

33   *Cork Examiner*, 25 March 1921; James Minighan and Mick Murphy in the O'Malley Notebooks, UCD.

34   CI Report for Cork, April 1921, CO 904/115; *Cork Examiner,* 14 April 1921; 18 April 1921; *Cork Constitution,* 13 April 1921, 23 April 1921, 7 July 1921; Abbott, p. 222.

35   CI Report for Cork City and East Riding, May 1921, CO 904/115; *Cork Examiner,* 9 May 1921; *Cork Constitution,* 16 May 1921, 23 May 1921.

36   CI Report, June 1921, CO 904/115; CI Report, July 1921, CO 904/115.

37   CI Report, July 1921, CO 904/115.

38   For examples, see Pa Murray in the O'Malley Notebooks; Pa Murray's BMH Statement; Robert Aherne's BMH Statement; and Dan Healy's BMH Statement.

39   Hopkinson, *The Irish War of Independence*, p. 108. In June 1921, the British sharply curtailed their patrols in Cork city, probably to protect their forces from ambush. I suspect the same happened elsewhere in Ireland. For example, during the IRA ambush of Auxiliary Cadets at Coolavokig, the Cork No. 1 Brigade flying column waited for eight days before the police convoy appeared. This ambush occurred on the major road connecting Ballyvourney with Macroom, meaning no British forces travelled to that village for over a week.

40   British forces do not appear to have detected any pre-prepared ambushes in Cork city. Such a discovery would be apparent by a British attempt to round up the guerrillas, as occurred in similar circumstances at the Cork Viaduct, Dripsey, and Mourne Abbey.

41   David Fitzpatrick (ed.) *Revolution in Ireland? Ireland 1917–1923* (Dublin: Trinity History Workshop, Trinity College Dublin, 1990).

42   P. Beaslai *Michael Collins and the Making of a New Ireland, Vol. I* (Dublin: Phoenix Publishing Company, 1926) [This book includes a captured letter from Quinlisk to Dublin Castle]; *Cork Examiner*, 20 February 1920; Mick Murphy's Bureau of Military History Statement; David Nelligan *A Spy in the Castle* (Dublin: McGibbon and Kee, 1968), p. 60; Statement of Company Captain J. O'Dwyer, A/0535 XV; MA; O'Donoghue, *Tomás MacCurtain*, p. 164; O'Donoghue in the O'Malley Notebooks, UCD; O'Donoghue Military Lecture, p. 23, Ms. 31,443, NLI; and O'Donoghue, *Florence and Josephine O'Donoghue's War of Independence*, pp. 67–9.

43   Sir Hamar Greenwood written answer, HCD, 21 March 1921, Vol. 139, c. 2246.

44   Hart, *British Intelligence in Ireland,* p. 47.

45   Those figures were current in 19 November 1920. Dr MacNamara written answer, HCD, 1 December 1920, Vol. 135, c. 1261.

46   Report of Association Dinner in London, *Cork Examiner*, 20 June 1921.

47 O'Donoghue, *Florence and Josephine O'Donoghue's War of Independence*, p. 84.

48 Brendan MacGiolla Choiller *Intelligence Notes, 1913–1916* (Dublin: State Paper Office, 1966), p. 147.

49 Based on the 1911 and 1926 Census for the City of Cork, from the 1926 Census of Population, Cork City Library.

50 During the 1918 General Election, a total of 5,665 soldiers and sailors serving abroad were eligible to cast absentee ballots in the City constituency, according to the *Cork Constitution*, 30 December 1918.

51 Remarks of the General Secretary of the Federation in Ireland, *Cork Constitution*, 12 September 1921.

52 De Róiste Diary, 27 March 1920.

53 *Cork Examiner*, 23 March 1920.

54 *Cork Examiner*, 23 March 1920; *Cork Constitution*, 16 April 1920.

55 *Cork Examiner*, 30 August 1920.

56 *Cork Weekly News*, 24 July 1920.

57 *Cork Constitution*, 13 March 1921.

58 *Cork Examiner*, 18 March 1921.

59 *Cork Constitution*, 12 September 1921.

60 Ibid.

61 There was tension between the Volunteers and ex-servicemen during the 1918 General Election, as the latter largely supported Nationalist candidates. For example, Republicans attacked the Discharged Soldiers and Sailors marching band during a December election rally. See the *Cork Weekly News*, 14 December 1918.

62 For example, Brigade leader Florrie O'Donoghue recalled that early in the war most of his intimate friends joined the British Army, while Brigade Transportation Officer Jim Grey (one of the city's most active Volunteers) was the son of a former British soldier. See O'Donoghue *Florence and Josephine O'Donoghue's War of Independence*, p. 16.

63 De Róiste Diary, 19 July 1920; *Cork Weekly News*, 24 July 1920; A photograph of the inscription appears in Goddard Lieberson *The Irish Uprising, 1916–1922* (New York: CBS Records, 1968), p. 133.

64 *Irish Times*, 19 July 1920, 20 July 1920.

65 *History of the 6th Division in Ireland*, p. 45.

66 Mr Hogge to Sir Hamar Greenwood, HCD, 17/3/21, Vol. 139, c. 1678. The incident took place on 26 February 1921, according to Hogge. No local newspapers reported the incident, which is not surprising since Cork's newspapers at this time were published under strict military censorship.

67 As mentioned above, James Burke was killed in July 1920 (*Cork Weekly News*, 24 July 1920); ex-soldier William McGrath was shot dead during the ensuing riot over Burke's death (*Cork Weekly News*, 31 July 1920); John Fleming, a Royal Navy veteran, was fatally struck by random police gunfire the following month (*Cork Weekly News*, 1 August 1920); Eugene O'Connell, an IRA Volunteer and ex-soldier, was killed in his bed as a reprisal for the IRA shooting of RIC Constable O'Donoghue (*Cork Examiner*, 22 November 1920); ex-soldier Michael Murray was shot by a military curfew patrol in March 1921 (*Cork Constitution*, 6 March 1921); ex-soldier James Mullane likewise died at the hands of a curfew patrol the same month (*Cork Examiner*, 21 March 1921); and ex-soldier Patrick Keating was shot by yet another military patrol in Shandon Street (*Cork Examiner*, 23 May 1921).

68 For an example, see Lt Col Holmes-Wilson in the *Cork Constitution*, 10 June 1921.

69 Hart, *The I.R.A. and Its Enemies,* p. 99.
70 In addition to the twenty-six fatalities listed below, the IRA tried to kill the following civilians: Daniel McDonnell (22 February 1921); John Good (10 March 1921); P.J. Poland (24 March 1921); Thomas Goulding (1 April 1921); James Flynn (4 April 1921); John Sherlock (20 May 1921); and Daniel Hawkins (20 May 1921).
71 I count twenty-six fatalities in 1920–1. The victims are as follows: Timothy Quinlisk (20 February 1920); Seán O'Callaghan (15 September 1920); Tom Downing (28 November 1920); James Blemens (2 December 1920); Frederick Blemens (2 December 1920); George Horgan (12 December 1920); Alfred Reilly (9 February 1921); John O'Leary (12 February 1921); William Sullivan (14 February 1921); Charles Beale (15 February 1921); Michael Walsh (18 February 1921); William Mohally (20 February 1921); Michael Finbarr O'Sullivan (20 February 1921); Cornelius Sheehan (23 March 1921); Denis Donovan (12 April 1921); Stephen O'Callaghan (29 April 1921); James Purcell (6 May 1921); Edward Hawkins (20 May 1921); Francis McMahon (20 May 1921); Christopher O'Sullivan (26 May 1921); John Lynch (25 June 1921); James Bagley (11 July 1921); W.J. Nolan (11 July 1921); and Major G.B. O'Connor (12 July 1921). The twenty-six includes two undated killings reported by the IRA: 'the lad Parsons', and 'the spy Saunders'.
72 'List of the Missing', *Irish Times,* 22 August 1921. The three names are John Coughlin (14 August 1920); Patrick Ray (22 January 1921); and E. Swanton (5 June 1921). 'The lad Parsons' and the captured spy 'Saunders' are omitted in the *Irish Times* list, but I include them in my group of twenty-six victims. For details on Saunders, see the Mulcahy Papers, P17A/20, UCD.
73 Hart, *The IRA and Its Enemies,* p. 299.
74 Eleven local JPs attended the Cork County Grand Jury Summer Assizes session in July 1920, though citizens summoned for regular jury service almost entirely boycotted the proceedings. See the *Cork Constitution,* 20 July 1920. As noted previously, twenty-four JPs appeared at the Assizes in March 1921 (*Cork Constitution,* 9 March 1921). Similarly, the IRA did not assassinate prominent Unionists in the city. For example, a meeting report from the October 1919 Executive Committee of the County and City of Cork Unionist Association lists nine attendees, including two JPs and two members with military titles. None of them were targeted in the city. See the *Cork Constitution,* 13 October 1919.
75 Hart, *The IRA and Its Enemies,* p. 299.
76 Cork No. 1 Brigade Casualty Roll, Seán Hegarty Papers, Cork Archives Institute. Dorman's death occurred the night after two British assassination attempts on city Republicans. These were apparent reprisals for an IRA attack on an RIC patrol in Blackpool, mentioned on p. 121. See Chapter Five for details.
77 Hart, *The IRA and Its Enemies,* p. 298.
78 Ibid., p. 299.
79 Ibid., p. 303.
80 Hart, *British Intelligence in Ireland,* p. 28.
81 Ibid., p. 73.
82 See Lauran Paine *Britain's Intelligence Service* (London: Robert Hale, 1979), p. 99.
83 A British Army review of Irish intelligence operations said of the RIC: 'They all thought they were intelligence officers.' See Hart, *British Intelligence in Ireland,* p. 41.
84 Hart, *The IRA and Its Enemies,* pp. 299 and 311.

85   Ibid, p. 314.
86   Victoria Barracks saw more executions than anywhere else in Ireland during 1920–1. The Cork No. 1 Brigade accounted for seven of the twenty-five IRA prisoners executed, and with the exception of the Dublin Brigade, lost more men to executions than any other IRA unit.
87   R. Langford Pension Statement, CAI; Dan Healy's BMH Statement; Pa Murray's BMH Statement; and RIC County Inspector's Report for May 1920, CO 904/112.
88   *Cork Constitution*, 1 July 1920, 10 July 1920, 11 July 1920, 12 July 1920; Mick Murphy BMH Statement.
89   See the *Cork Examiner, Cork Constitution*, and the *Irish Times* for the week of 22 August; Seán Culhane in the O'Malley Notebooks; Sean Culhane Bureau of Military History Statement; MacSwiney to Arnot, 24 April 1920, Ms. 31,163; Florence O'Donoghue in the O'Malley Notebooks, UCD; O'Donoghue's research into the assassination containing correspondence and his account, Ms. 31,313; RIC County Inspector's Report for Down, August 1920, CO 904/112.
90   *Cork Examiner*, 25 September 1920; the *History of the 6th Division in Ireland*, Appendix II, IWM; General Strickland's diary entry for 24 September 1920; Mick Murphy's BMH Statement; captured IRA correspondence concerning the operation, printed in the British Army pamphlet, *The Irish Republican Army*, p. 363, issued by the Irish Command General Headquarters Staff, Strickland Papers.
91   Florrie O'Donoghue exchanged a series of letters with Cork IRA leaders Pa Murray, Moss Twomey, and Dan 'Sandow' Donovan about the visit in 1959. That correspondence can be found in Ms. 31,296, NLI. See also Pa Murray and Stan Barry in the O'Malley Notebooks, UCD; and Pa Murray's BMH statement.
92   *Cork Constitution*, 1 March 1921; *Cork Examiner,* 1 March 1921; and *Times of London*, 1 March 1921.
93   The British denied that they shot the Clonmult Volunteers after their surrender, though court-martial testimony described a number of the dead as having their hands tied. See the *Cork Constitution*, 9 March 1921.
94   This is the clearest example of a case of mistaken identity with a suspected civilian informer. The depressing document can be found in Florrie O'Donoghue's papers, Ms. 31, 249, NLI.
95   In addition to Barry's attack, there were actions at Inishannon, East Ferry, Middleton, Rossmacowan, and Dunmanway, resulting in the deaths of four constables and six soldiers. The West Limerick Brigade killed a policeman in Drumcollogher, and Kerry Volunteers assassinated a head constable in Tralee, and failed to inflict casualties during attacks in Cahirciveen, Rathmore, and Kenmare. See Abbott, pp. 237–9; Tom Barry *Guerrilla Days in Ireland* (Boulder, CO: Roberts Rinehart Publishers, 1995), pp. 166–73; and Dwyer, pp. 314–15.
96   Daniel Healy's BMH Statement includes a number of witness affidavits.
97   *Cork Constitution*, 24 March 1921, 27 March 1921; *Cork Examiner*, 24 March 1921, 26 March 1921, 28 March 1921; Stan Barry in the O'Malley Notebooks, UCD. (Barry visited the Kerry Pike safe-house shortly before the raid.)
98   See Stan Barry, Mick Leahy, and Pat Margetts in the O'Malley Notebooks. Margetts' testimony is especially damaging, since he worked in Victoria Barracks, and apparently had first-hand knowledge of Connors' informing.
99   The British Army's *Sixth Division in Ireland*, p. 55. Also, a captured letter

from the British Army's 6th Division intelligence officer Captain Kelly to H.H. Davis of the Eighteenth Brigade, refers to Kelly's employment of Connors at £2.10 per week. See Ms. 31,228, NLI. Michael Collins made an apparent reference to this letter in an exchange with Florrie O'Donoghue dated 5 April 1921, Ms. 31,192, NLI.

100 Dan Corkery and Mick Sullivan in the O'Malley Notebooks, UCD.

101 Daniel Healy BMH Statement; Mick Leahy and Florrie O'Donoghue in the O'Malley Notebooks, UCD. O'Donoghue repeated this version in his memoir, *Florence and Josephine O'Donoghue's War of Independence*, p. 83.

102 Dan Corkery, Mick Leahy, Florrie O'Donoghue, Stan Barry, Raymond Kennedy, and Pat Margetts in the O'Malley Notebooks; Daniel Healy BMH Statement; *Sixth Division in Ireland*, p. 55.

103 Stan Barry and Raymond Kennedy in the O'Malley Notebooks.

104 Daniel Healy BMH Statement. Healy and fellow city Volunteer Liam O'Callaghan staked out a London post office for ten days, expecting Connors to pick up a letter, but he never showed.

105 O'Donoghue, *Florence and Josephine O'Donoghue's War of Independence*, p. 83.

106 Dan Healy described the shooting in detail, and claims Connors died, though the *New York Times* reported that he initially survived. Pa Murray apparently told IRA colleague Todd Andrews that Connors lived. See C.S. Andrews *Dublin Made Me* (Dublin: Mercier Press, 1969), p. 257. For further details see Healy's BMH Statement; correspondence between Florrie O'Donoghue, Dan Donovan, Moss Twomey, and Pa Murray, Ms. 31,296; and the *New York Times* 14 April 1922, 15 April 1922, and 17 April 1922. Cork No. 1 Brigade veterans told Father Patrick Twohig that Connors died from his wounds a year later, which would explain the conflicting accounts of his fate. Twohig was also informed that Connors refused to identify his assailants to police, though he knew them by name. (Author's interview with Fr. Twohig, 24 September 2005). If Connors did collapse under British interrogation, his weakness is understandable in light of his nightmarish experiences in Flanders, as well his time as an IRA guerrilla. He remains a tragic and haunting figure.

107 According to Captain Kelly, Mrs. Marshal, 'a lady of easy virtue', was sentenced to death by the IRA for informing, but the penalty was not carried out. See his letters of 22 and 27 February 1921, Ms. 31,223, NLI. Michael Collins wrote to Florrie O'Donoghue about a Miss Staunton, a solicitor's daughter in Cork, who was passing information to British authorities in Dublin. See Collins to O'Donoghue, 21 August 1920, Ms. 31,175, NLI. Police reported that Mrs Fletcher was ordered out of the city in March 1921 for being 'on friendly terms with police and military'. See the CI Report, March 1921, CO 904/115. The 'British spy Saunders' told the IRA that Mrs. O'Brien of Cork city helped him track local Volunteers. See the Mulcahy Papers, P17A/20, UCD.

108 Pat Margetts in the O'Malley Notebooks.

109 I have not found record of the faith of the other local civilian victims in Cork, so I will not speculate as to their religion. In the case of the Blemens, Alfred Reilly, and Charles Beale, police reports make special mention of their religion, as opposed to the other cases.

110 Ian d'Alton, 'Keeping Faith: An Evocation of the Cork Protestant Character 1820–1920', in *Cork History and Society* (Dublin: Geography Publication, 1993), p. 778.

111 The city's overall population numbered 76,000 in 1920.

112 In 1899, Protestants accounted for 36% of the Cork Corporation (twenty of

fifty-six members). See John O'Brien, 'Population, Politics and Society in Cork, 1780–1900', *Cork History and Society*, p. 710. In 1896, Protestant Unionist Sir John Scott was elected Lord Mayor of Cork (see d'Alton, p. 778). In the late nineteenth century, the staunchly pro-Empire Primrose League boasted a strong organization in county Cork, with 4000 members split into four branches, including one in the city (D'Alton, p. 770). Ian d'Alton also claims that by 1911, Cork Unionists were 'well represented in local government'. (See d'Alton, p. 779.)

113 Returns from the 1918 General Election, *Cork Constitution,* 16 December 1918. The two Unionist candidates, Williams and Farrington, won 2,519 and 2,254 votes respectively.

114 Though a member of its Executive Committee, Beale was not an officer of the organization. See the *Cork Chamber of Commerce and Shipping Annual Report for 1920,* Cork City Library. Of the twenty-seven officers or Executive Committee members of the Chamber, Reilly and Beale were the only ones to face IRA assassins.

115 Report of the Executive Committee meeting, *Cork Constitution,* 13 October 1919.

116 In the 1910 Municipal Elections, sixteen Protestants stood for office, though not all were Unionists. (D'Alton, p. 791.)

117 Florence O'Donoghue in the O'Malley Notebooks.

118 List of Cork city lodge officers, Ms. 31,200, NLI. The information lies in Florrie O'Donoghue's papers, indicating his investigation of the lodge for possible informers.

119 Hart, *The IRA and Its Enemies,* p. 103; See the IRA's anonymous letter to publisher H.L. Tivey, L1960, 344, Seán Hegarty Papers, Cork Public Museum. According to Cork police, in April 1920 Tivey received another threat for an editorial calling Alan Bell's IRA killers 'human brutes'. (Bell was a suspected British intelligence operative assassinated by Michael Collins' 'Squad' in Dublin.) See Outrages Against Police, 14 April 1920, CO 904/148, PRO.

120 Kenneally, p. 99; *Cork Examiner,* 28 December 1920.

121 The only person in Hill's home during its burning was an auctioneer, indicating that Hill had wisely decided to sell the house and leave Cork. See the *Cork Constitution,* 4 April 1921, 6 April 1921; *Cork Examiner,* 5 April 1921; and the *Skibbereen Star,* 9 April 1921.

122 *Cork Constitution,* 25 May 1921.

123 Mick Murphy BMH Statement.

124 *Cork Constitution,* 27 May 1921.

125 *Skibbereen Star,* 28 May 1921.

126 Hopkinson, *The Irish War of Independence,* p. 93.

127 Hart 'The Protestant Experience of Revolution in Southern Ireland', in *Unionism in Modern Ireland* (Dublin: Gill and MacMillan, 1996), p. 92. In his study of Cork, Hart concluded: '... The war on informers must be seen as part of the tit-for-tat dynamics of violence, driven by fear and the desire for revenge. It was not, however, merely (or even mainly) a matter of espionage, of spies and spy-hunters. It was a civil war within and between communities, with the battle lines drawn by a whole range of social bonds and boundaries. As used by the men of the Cork IRA, the term informer meant simply 'enemy' and enemies were defined by their religion, class, connection.' (Hart, *The IRA and Its Enemies,* p. 314).

128 Liam Lynch, O/C First Southern Division, to IRA GHQ Chief of Staff Richard Mulcahy, 4 May 1921, Mulcahy Papers, P/7/A/16, UCD.

129 Lynch to Mulcahy, 10 June 1921.

130 Dáil Éireann Treaty Debates, Volume 3 – 22 December, 1921.
131 In July Lynch told Mulchay that no action would be taken against hostages without GHQ authorization. He apparently wanted to wait for approval before issuing a public warning to kill hostages if any additional IRA prisoners were executed. Again, this shows the Volunteers' reluctance to commit a counter-reprisal without first announcing it. See Lynch's letter to Mulcahy dated 5 July 1921, Mulcahy Papers.
132 Again, the mysterious case of Major G.B. O'Connor is a possible exception. While there is no evidence O'Connor was an IRA hostage, it is plausible that he was abducted for that reason, and then shot after the Truce to protect his Republican captors from identification. However, this theory is speculative, and the discovery of his body near his Douglas home indicates he was shot on the spot. The Cork No. 1 Brigade's most notable hostage episode took place in February 1921. The Brigade's Sixth Battalion arrested the elderly Cork Unionist Mrs Mary Lindsay, after she had told the British Army about an IRA ambush in Dripsey, resulting in the death and capture of a number of Volunteers. Facing the execution of five Volunteers, the Sixth Battalion threatened to shoot Mrs. Lindsay and her chauffer James Clarke unless the IRA prisoners were reprieved. The executions went forward, and the IRA killed Lindsay and Clarke as a reprisal. It remains unclear whether the Cork No. 1 Brigade leadership sanctioned the Sixth Battalion's action. For details, see Seán O'Callaghan's *Execution*.
133 David Omissi, 'Baghdad and British Bombers' (*The Guardian*, 19 January 1990).
134 The impact of the Anglo-Boer conflict should not be underestimated. Irish regiments (including Cork's Munster Fusiliers) fought with the British Army in South Africa, and the war was followed closely in Ireland. During the Boer's guerrilla campaign, British forces burned farms, destroyed livestock, and forced civilian sympathizers into concentration camps. Republicans studied the conflict and likely anticipated similar tactics in the future. (For example, see Florrie O'Donoghue's letter dated 5 May 1921, Ms. 31,176; or the report of Boer guerrilla Christian De Wet's portrait hanging in the city's main Sinn Féin Hall, *Cork Examiner*, 11 March 1920.)

CHAPTER FIVE

'The Murder Gang'

An important element of the Anglo-Irish conflict in Cork concerns disguised Crown forces, known to city Republicans as 'The Murder Gang'. The appearance of this group (or more accurately groups) towards the end of 1920 corresponded roughly with the emergence of Anti-Sinn Féin Society reprisal threats in the city, and an upsurge of IRA attacks against suspected informers.

The term 'Murder Gang', commonly used by British authorities in 1920 and 1921 to describe the IRA, was also employed by Cork Republicans to identify parties of Crown forces who attacked local Volunteers and Sinn Féin leaders after curfew. In January 1921, Lord Mayor Donal 'Óg' O'Callaghan provided a telling description of the 'murder gang' to the American Commission on Conditions in Ireland.

> Q. What do you call the Murder Gang?
> A. It is where a raid takes place to murder a man, to shoot him in his bed, as it often happens. We call that the murder gang, as opposed to a raid to arrest him and search his house.[1]

These nocturnal raiders typically disguised themselves, did not take prisoners, and often left wrecked and burned property in their wake. The purpose of their attacks was assassination rather than arrest. The parties were almost certainly Crown forces, composed of British Army and RIC personnel, probably led by military and police intelligence specialists. Bishop Cohalan placed them within a larger British policy of reprisals in Cork.

> Instead of defending the lives and property of the innocent, the Government, by a carefully laid plan, for which not even a cloak of legality has been provided, has conducted through its servants a reprisal campaign of murder of the innocent and of the destruction of their property, with the view of securing the submission of the

Republican Army by terrorism exercised over the innocent and unof-
fending.[2]

It is unclear if the British Government authorized these activities.
However, since no one was ever arrested for the attacks, and as most
took place during curfew hours when the city was under British
Army control,[3] it seems likely that military authorities in Cork tacitly
approved them.

DISGUISED ATTACKS ON CORK REPUBLICANS IN 1920

The first night time assassination of a Cork Republican took place
in March 1920. The killing of Lord Mayor Tomás MacCurtain on
19 March and the attempted assassinations of Sinn Féin Aldermen
Stockley and Sullivan during the preceding week, were unofficial
RIC reprisals for two attacks on policemen in Cork city.[4] The assailants appear to have been members of the 'old' RIC, Irish constables
with numerous years of service in the police.

Following an IRA assassination campaign against 'active' constables in Cork, the RIC became much less assertive in the city.
Throughout 1920, a number of prominent police were shot, and
others were transferred out of the city for their own protection.[5] The
loss of these aggressive constables, combined with the international
furore over MacCurtain's killing, likely helped curtail violent
reprisals against Cork Republicans until late 1920. However, the
danger remained apparent to the city IRA. After MacCurtain's assassination, Volunteer Seán Daly was posted as a bodyguard to
Alderman Stockley,[6] and the IRA maintained a 24-hour armed guard
over Lord Mayor Terence MacSwiney until his arrest in August
1920.[7]

Violent late-night raids on Republicans became common in Cork
city in the late autumn of 1920. These attacks coincided with inte-
gration of 'Black and Tan' British constables into the Cork city RIC,
and the arrival of a newly raised company of Auxiliary Cadets. The
Cadets, composed of former British military officers, seem to have
instigated the reprisal campaign in the city. Lord Mayor Donal
O'Callaghan (Terence MacSwiney's successor) claimed that in
November alone there were ten failed assassination attempts against
city Republicans.[8] These assaults were often deliberate responses to
local IRA attacks against British forces.

The nocturnal attacks kicked off in earnest on 17 November when IRA Volunteers shot down the popular RIC Sergeant James O'Donoghue as he walked to his city station.[9] After midnight, a group of men in police uniforms invaded four Cork homes.[10] At 28 Broad Street, Eugene O'Connell, a Volunteer in the Cork No. 1 Brigade's First Battalion (and ex-British soldier), was shot and killed. Nearby, at 2 Broad Lane, disguised assailants shot to death Fianna Boy Scout Patrick Hanley, and wounded two other young men in the home. Moments later, a man wearing a police uniform and goggles entered 17 Broad Lane, marched into the room of another Fianna Scout and shot him in the face. Later, an assailant wearing a policeman's cap killed Sinn Féin activist James Coleman in his North Mall home. In all, three people were killed and three seriously wounded during the night. The three fatal victims were all Republican activists.

Three nights later, a similar group hunted for veteran city IRA officer Bob Langford. He later recalled: 'On the night of the capture of Constable Ryan [20 November 1920, See Chapter Three], my home at Ashburton was raided for me by what was known as the "murder gang" some of whom wore a mask. The raid took place about midnight.'[11] Langford escaped his assailants, and like many prominent Republicans, went 'on the run' for the remainder of the conflict.

On the evening of November 23, three nights after the attack on Bob Langford, some Volunteers were walking home together shortly before curfew. A passing police constable tossed a grenade into the group, killing Volunteers Trahy, O'Donoghue, and Mehigan. All three were seasoned IRA veterans.[12]

Four nights later, on 27 November, armed and disguised men with 'foreign accents' burst into the home of Sinn Féin Alderman Coughlan.[13] His wife testified that they were: 'looking for my husband to shoot him',[14] and the leader wore a military cap and 'a black mask over his complete face, having two slits to see through'.[15] The same group returned to Coughlan's house on the evening of 11 December, hours after city IRA forces ambushed Auxiliary Cadets at Dillon's Cross, sparking reprisal burnings in Cork city centre. Again, the disguised party did not find Alderman Coughlan, but they appear to have located two sleeping Cork IRA Volunteers across town. While fires consumed Cork's Patrick Street, unknown assailants executed Con and Jeremiah Delaney, members of the city's First Battalion, in front of their father. Mr Delaney later testified:

The men who went upstairs entered my sons' bedrooms, and said, in a harsh voice: 'Get out of that.' I was in the room with them. They asked them if their name was Delaney. My sons answered, 'Yes.' At that moment I heard distinctly two or more shots, and my boys fell immediately ... As far as I could see, they wore long overcoats and spoke with a strong English accent.[16]

Later that month, Cork No. 1 Brigade Headquarters ordered its members to be vigilant of possible reprisal attacks. 'A Crossley tender conveying a murder gang passes your road. Later on you hear of some Irish citizen being brutally murdered. If you have taken the number of that tender you may be able to deal with it the next time you see it.'[17]

The case of shopkeeper and Sinn Féin city councillor Eamon Coughlan was typical of these assaults.[18] According to Mrs Coughlan, some men called on her husband and ordered him to change the shop name on the storefront from Irish to English. They threatened to burn the premises within twenty-four hours if he did not remove the Irish sign. When Mrs Coughlan reported the matter to the RIC, she claimed the sergeant told her, 'Nobody has control over the Black and Tans; That they were out on their own ... Irish to these fellows is like a red flag to a bull. They're mad ... If these fellows (meaning the Black and Tans) find out that you have reported them, they will be worse than ever on you.' A couple of nights later, men in mufti speaking 'in a pronounced English accent', set fire to Coughlan's shop.

ATTACKS IN EARLY 1921

A brutal and documented raid took place on Griffin Street, Cork. On 8 February 1921, two men wearing police uniforms and white linen masks invaded the home of Denis and Norah Healy. Apparently the visitors had gone to the wrong address. Regardless, one of the intruders prepared to shoot Mr Healy. According to Denis Healy: 'his accent (as was his comrade's) was English.' Norah Healy convinced the assailant that he was in the wrong house, and with greater difficulty persuaded him from shooting her husband. Her success came at a price. She reported that the attacker: '... caught hold of me, and pushed me into the back-kitchen and closed the door ... In spite of my every resistance he then succeeded in criminally assaulting and raping me.'[19]

Siobhan Lankford wrote of the attempted assassination two

nights later of her husband Seamus, then a Sinn Féin activist and
Vice-Guardian of the Cork Poor House. The attack occurred at a
time when 'the cloak and dagger men of the British Army and the
Black and Tans were at their busiest.'[20]

> After midnight, Seamus was in one of the wards facing the road. He
> was speaking to the nurse in charge. Suddenly she said 'look out', and
> there, coming over the wall, was a 'murder-gang'. They carried small
> arms and a machine gun. Covering this group of four or five was a
> force of eighteen police, heavily armed and with blackened faces, who
> stealthily climbed over the lane wall. A figure in skirts nimbly jumped
> over with them. This was a prostitute who had been in and out of the
> workhouse, and who had gone to British Intelligence and offered to
> identify Lankford for a certain amount of money ... It was the night
> of 10 February 1921, the eve of the Our Lady of Lourdes to whom
> Seamus had a long devotion.[21]

Brigade officer Seán MacSwiney (brother of Terence), captured in
the Rahinisky House raid, referred to these assaults during his court-
martial in February 1921, the same month of the Seamus Lankford
and Norah Healy attacks:

> Court: Why do you carry weapons?
> Witness [MacSwiney]: For self-defence, because before and after
> Christmas, I had definite information that what we know as the
> murder gang of the Black and Tans were after me.
> President: You stated you were in danger of your life from a murder
> gang of Black and Tans. The Court does not understand that. Is there
> a special section of Black and Tans?
> Witness: Well, so far as I know there has been a special section going
> around looting and shooting.
> President: A special section?
> Witness: Well, I would not say a special section. Whether or not they
> have specially selected for that kind of work I don't know. What I say
> is that there were Black and Tans going around for some time past.
> They had a pretty fair hand in the city to do what they liked after
> curfew, and they went around looting and shooting, and I have defi-
> nite information that they called to certain houses for me.[22]

In the wake of these assaults, known Volunteers and prominent
Sinn Féin activists went 'on the run' throughout the city. For many,
this meant sleeping outside their homes, while others became fulltime fugitives.

The assaults dwindled after February, but continued throughout the rest of the conflict. On the evening of 1 March, three disguised men called to the goods office at the Cork train station. There they found Second Battalion Volunteer Charlie J. Daly, a clerk in the office. The men dragged Daly into the Blackpool Railway Tunnel, beat him for some time, and finally shot him to death.[23] In the coming weeks, a party of masked gunmen also visited and terrorized the family of another Charlie Daly, who was Adjutant of the Brigade's Second Battalion.[24] (It seems possible that Charlie J. Daly was confused with the latter Charlie Daly.)

Even when the raiders missed their intended targets, the results could still be a nightmare for any male found in the house. The *Cork Constitution* reported this encounter on 10 March 1921:

> Shortly after 4 o'clock yesterday morning, a party of four armed men with blackened faces knocked at the house of Mr McIlwraith, South Douglas Road, and after sometime were admitted. Here they inquired for a certain young man and upon being told he did not live there, they went next door to Mr Hickey's on a similar mission. The loud knocking at Mr McIlwraith's house alarmed the residents of the terrace, and it is stated that two young men made good their escape in their shirts and pants by a back door, and found refuge in another street. When the armed men could not find the man they were looking for, it is stated they burned some beds. Then they returned to Mr McIlwraith's where a pitiful scene was witnessed. It is stated that the raiders ordered him out on to the public road, but some girls in the house protested and appealed to them not to shoot so old a man, who was guilty of no offence whatever. The request would not be listened to at first, but eventually the entreaties of the girls saved Mr McIlwraith's life. After the raiders had taken their departure, the Fire Brigade was summoned to the scene and on arriving there found some furniture and bedding ablaze, which they promptly extinguished. The incident caused profound alarm in the locality, and the residents spent the remainder of the night in a state of abject terror.[25]

A more startling event followed the IRA's 14 May bomb attack on a police patrol in Blackpool. The ambush was part of the First Southern Division's 'shoot-up' (mentioned in the previous chapter), a reprisal for the execution of IRA prisoners in Victoria Barracks. After three constables were killed and a fourth wounded, armed British parties sought vengeance around the city.[26] At 2 am, a group of disguised men called at Miss Crowley's home in the city. They walked into the house and asked a man: 'Are you Patrick Sheehan?' When he replied in the affirmative, they shot and killed him.[27] An hour later, a number of police invaded the residence of Sinn Féin TD Liam de Róiste. Fearing assassination for some time, de Róiste had taken the precaution of sleeping at a neighbour's house up the street. He wrote of hearing the intruders. 'A voice, English accent, enquired somewhere nearby, "Is this where Mr Roche lives?"'[28] The attackers entered the de Róiste home, including one who climbed through the bedroom window, apparently drunk, and ended up brawling with Mrs de Róiste and her elderly mother. When the de Róiste's lodger, a Catholic priest named Father James O'Callaghan, called on the intruders to leave, they fired on the curate and killed him.[29]

The following night, five members of the *Cork Examiner* staff were walking home during curfew. An unknown assailant flung a grenade at them, killing Second Battalion Volunteer Stephen Dorman, and wounding three of his colleagues. It appears that Dorman was the target of this attack, and he died in an almost identical fashion to the three Volunteers bombed in late November 1920.[30]

WHO WERE THEY?

It is likely that the covert squads were mixed groups of Black and Tans, Auxiliary Cadets, and British soldiers. Coordination with the British Army was necessary to prevent military curfew patrols from firing on the 'murder gangs'. Armed bodies of civilians could not have moved unmolested through the city otherwise. British soldiers were also reported as participating in some of the unofficial reprisals in late 1920. The killing of Charlie Daly in the Blackpool Tunnel casts suspicion on military intelligence officers, as Daly was questioned (and tortured) for some time before his death. Undoubtedly 'Black and Tans' were also involved in these operations.[31] We know that the military and RIC coordinated their intelligence efforts.[32] The RIC Divisional Commissioner's staff included a military intelligence officer to act as a 'connecting link between the military and police Intelligence organizations'.[33] In Cork, this officer was the infamous Lt Keogh, previously implicated in the torture of Cork No. 3 Brigade commander Tom Hales.[34] The Cork No. 1 Brigade casualty roll blames Auxiliary Cadets for the death of the Delaney brothers, indicating their involvement in some of the attacks.[35] Though Auxiliary Cadet Company K was transferred out of Cork after it torched the city centre in December, Cadets still frequently patrolled Cork.[36] The participation of Auxiliary Cadets is especially relevant, since they appeared to have been the prime culprits of the 'Anti-Sinn Féin Society' arson campaign in late 1920.

THE 'MURDER GANG' AND IRA CASUALTIES

The Murder Gang made a considerable impact on city IRA forces. The Cork No. 1 Brigade casualty roll for the city's First and Second Battalions illustrates the deadly results of these attacks.

Table Five: Chronological List of City IRA Fatalities

Name	Enrolled IRA	Age	Circumstance	Date
JP O'Brien	1918	17	Shot helping woman	18/7/20
C Lucey	1916	23	Shot Ballingeary evading arrest	10/11/20
P Hanely*	1918	18	Shot at home	17/11/20
E O'Connell	1918	20	Same	Same
P O'Donoghue	1914	32	Bombed Unarmed	23/11/20
J Mehigan	1914	28	Same	Same
P Trahy	1917	26	Same	Same
C Delaney	1914	28	Shot in bed by Auxiliaries	11/12/20
J Delaney	1918	33	Same	11/12/20
CJ Daly	1917	23	Shot at work GS&WR	1/3/21
T Dennehy	1916	23	Killed Sleeping at Ballycannon	24/3/21
J Mullaine	1915	23	Same	Same
W Deasy	1915	21	Same	Same
D Murphy	1916	24	Same	Same
D Crowley	1916	22	Same	Same
M O'Sullivan	1917	20	Same	Same
T O'Sullivan	1914	29	Shot unarmed	19/4/21
S Dorman	1918	22	Bombed Unarmed	23/5/21
C Daly	1917	30	Murdered in Barracks	28/6/21
D Springs	1920	20	Taken from home and shot	9/7/21

Source: Cork No. 1 Brigade Casualty Roll, CPM.
NOTE: Does not include Tomas MacCurtain, or those who died in accidents or on hunger strike.
* Member of Fianna Eireann
Italics denotes evidence of disguised Crown forces in the attack.

The Brigade casualty list is remarkable because it shows that no member of the city IRA died in combat with British forces. At the time of their deaths, all the Volunteers were unarmed and were killed either in their homes, on city streets, or while in British custody. Newspaper reports support the IRA version of events listed in the 'Circumstance' column.[37] Six of the attacks accounting for ten dead Volunteers, occurred during the city's curfew hours, and were officially committed by 'persons unknown'. Strong evidence implicates Crown forces in each of the attacks, which is consistent with Republican descriptions of British 'murder gangs' operating in the city.

The highest concentration of IRA deaths occurred during the four weeks between mid-November and mid-December. In three separate incidents, disguised Crown forces killed seven Volunteers (see the names listed in italics). In the remaining seven months of the conflict, just three IRA members died in similar circumstances (eight more Volunteers died evading arrest or while in police or military custody). The decline in 'murder gang' fatalities may be relevant.

In a lecture to Irish Army officers twenty years later, Brigade leader Florrie O'Donoghue remarked:

> There was a semi-secret organization within the RIC, led by foreign elements now gaining influence in that body, which carried out a number of murders, including that of Tomás MacCurtain, then Brigade O/C and Lord Mayor of Cork.[38] Not much was known of the intelligence activities of this body, but there was evidence that their actions were based on detailed information which they had, in part at least, acquired through their own efforts.[39]

O'Donoghue's statement is important. Since witnesses usually describe 'murder gang' assailants as speaking with English or 'foreign' accents, it is probable that the perpetrators were not Irish, meaning they likely came from the Auxiliary Cadets, the Black and Tans (distinct from the 'old' RIC), and/or the British Army. As newcomers to Cork, how did the gunmen identify their targets? It seems likely that the murder gang (or more accurately, murder gangs) acted on information received locally. The dead Volunteers' enrolment date (listed in Table Five) supports this contention. The slain were all IRA veterans, each having served an average of about three and a half years in the Volunteers. The victims' long connections to the IRA would make them known locally as Republican activists. Constables of the 'old RIC' could have identified these targets. It is also possible the details came from civilian informers.

The highest concentration of 'murder gang' killings of Cork Volunteers occurred in late 1920, the same time as an unofficial arson campaign and the 'Anti-Sinn Féin Society' warnings rocked the city. During the next three months, the IRA executed Cork civilians accused of belonging to an 'Anti-Sinn Féin Society'. After the February killings, the 'murder gang' was less successful in its attacks on IRA Volunteers. Though unproved, it is possible the IRA stopped the sources of information used by British gunmen to target city Volunteers.

SUMMARY

Unofficial police attacks on Cork Republicans began in early 1920, but halted after the assassination of Tomás MacCurtain. The situation changed in late 1920 as British police reinforcements appeared in the city. In October and November, Anti-Sinn Féin Society warnings threatened drastic reprisals against Republicans and their sympathizers in Cork city. Shortly afterwards, Cork experienced arson attacks attributed to the Anti-Sinn Féin Society. At roughly the same time, the 'murder gang' began an assassination campaign against local Republicans. These assaults were deliberate killings made by disguised members of the Crown forces. Their success against IRA Volunteers peaked in late 1920, declining in 1921, though attacks on Republican activists continued for the remainder of the conflict. In late 1920, Cork citizens accused of belonging to an Anti-Sinn Féin Society disappeared in Cork. Two months later, the IRA killed more civilians they suspected of membership of the same group. These events may be connected.

NOTES

1 Donal O'Callaghan's testimony to the American Commission on Conditions in Ireland, 13 January, 1921. See American Commission on Conditions in Ireland *Evidence on Conditions in Ireland* (Washington DC, 1921), p. 740.
2 Bishop Cohalan Excommunication Pastoral, Ms. 31,148, NLI.
3 IRA operations in the city were almost always conducted in the daytime. During the evening, anyone seen moving about was subject to immediate arrest. This cleared the streets of civilian traffic, depriving the Volunteers of their greatest asset: the ability to melt into the civilian population before and after an attack. In Cork city at least, the night belonged to the Crown forces.
4 *Cork Examiner*, 19 March 1920; De Róiste Diary, 18 March 1920. The Sullivan and Stockley attacks followed the shooting of District Inspector MacDonagh by IRA officers. MacCurtain was shot two hours after the IRA assassinated Constable Murtagh in Cork.

5 Local Volunteers killed Detective Murtagh, Constable Cheve, Sergeant Garvey, and Constable Harrington. IRA veterans accused each of aggressively pursuing local Republicans. The July 1920 assassination of Divisional Commissioner Smyth (commander of the RIC in Munster) fits into this pattern. Smyth had recently suggested that his officers shoot Volunteers out-of-hand, rather than take prisoners. A few days after his remarks were reported in the Cork newspapers, city Volunteers killed him in the Cork Conservative Club. During this period other active constables transferred out of Cork. These included District Inspector Swanzy (who was shot by Cork Volunteers in Lisburn, in August 1920), Head Constable Cahill, Head Constable Clarke, Detective Maliff, and Sergeant Ferris, who subsequently survived an assassination attempt in Belfast, despite being shot four times.

6 Sean Daly in the O'Malley Notebooks.

7 Pa Murray initially guarded MacSwiney, but was succeeded by the formidable Christy MacSweeney. Florrie O'Donoghue shared lodgings with Terry MacSwiney in an IRA safe-house, so he took the night shift. See Pa Murray's BMH Statement; and O'Donoghue, *Florence and Josephine O'Donoghue's War of Independence*, p. 94.

8 'Report of Cork Municipality' read by Lord Mayor O'Callaghan to the American Commission on Conditions in Ireland. See the *American Commission on Conditions in Ireland Interim Report* (London: Hardin & Moore Ltd, 1921), p. 63.

9 CI Report for Cork (City and East Riding) November 1920, CO 904/113.

10 *Cork Examiner*, 18 November 1920, 19 November 1920; *Irish Bulletin*, 19 November 1920, Vol. 3, No. 56; Cork No. 1 Brigade Casualty Roll, CPM; and Bishop Cohalan's Excommunication Pastoral.

11 Langford Pension Statement, CAI. See also Hart, *The IRA and Its Enemies*, pp. 1–6.

12 *Cork Examiner*, 24 November 1920; Cork No. 1 Brigade Casualty Roll, CPM.

13 *Cork Examiner*, 29 November 1920.

14 Statement of Mrs Eamon (Ellen) Coughlan, *Who Burnt Cork City?*, pp. 23–4.

15 Statement of Mrs Eamon (Ellen) Coughlan presented to the American Commission on Conditions in Ireland. See *Evidence on Conditions in Ireland*, p. 741.

16 Statement of Daniel Dalaney, *Who Burnt Cork City?*, p. 65.

17 Cork No. 1 Brigade Order, 22 December 1920, Ms. 31,202, NLI.

18 Affidavit of Mrs Ellen Coughlan, dated 25 January 1921, corroborated by affidavits from other witnesses. See the Alfred O'Rahilly Papers, U118, University College Cork.

19 Affidavit of Norah and Denis Healy, 7 April 1921, Op Cit. Sinn Féin propagandists collected the testimony, but did not publicise Mrs Healy's rape. Seamus Fitzgerald's BMH Statement indicates she was pregnant when assaulted.

20 Lankford, p. 269.

21 Lankford, p. 260.

22 Report of MacSwiney's Court-martial, *Cork Constitution*, 25 February 1921.

23 *Cork Examiner*, 2 March 1921, 3 March 1921; Brigade Casualty Rolls, CPM.

24 Adjutant Charlie Daly's sister Catherine testified that this group frequently threatened to kill her brother. 'They came several nights but did not come into the house.' The visitors instead stood outside whistling and throwing gravel at the windows from midnight until 5 am. Charlie Daly was subsequently captured at Waterfall on 28 June, and apparently beaten to death in Victoria Barracks. Details of the case, including Catherine Daly's affidavit can be found in Ms. 31,178, NLI.

25 *Cork Constitution*, 10 March 1921.

26 *Cork Examiner*, 16 May 1921; Pa Murray in the O'Malley Notebooks, UCD; and Pa Murray BMH Statement.
27 *Cork Constitution*, 16 May 1921.
28 De Róiste Diary, 15 May 1921.
29 *Cork Examiner*, 16 May 1921, 17 May 1921; and the De Róiste Diary, 15 May 1921. De Róiste's diary entry for 15 May captures the terror of such a visit. His family's experiences illustrate the precarious position of prominent Sinn Féin politicians, many of whom disagreed with the IRA's violent tactics, yet found themselves held accountable by Crown forces.
30 *Cork Examiner*, 23 May 1921, 24 May 1921. As stated in Chapter Four, Peter Hart blamed the IRA for this attack, though it seems highly unlikely city Volunteers would have killed one of their own. Dorman is listed in the Brigade Casualty Roll and is buried in the Republican plot at St Finbarr's Cemetery in Cork. The Brigade Casualty roll 'circumstance' description indicates British involvement, and it was almost identical to the November killing of Volunteers Trahy, O'Donoghue, and Mehigan. The timing of the attack likewise implicates the Crown forces, as it occurred a day after the Blackpool bombing, which produced two unofficial reprisals against Cork Republicans.
31 Many of the assailants wore police uniforms. See the attacks of 17 November 1920, 8 February 1921, and 10 February 1921 for examples.
32 Pat Margetts in the O'Malley Notebooks.
33 OC 6th Division to GHQ Ireland, 17 May 1920, Strickland Papers, IWM.
34 IRA Intelligence Report, Ms. 31,227, NLI; R. Langford Pension Statement, CAI; Tom Hales Torture Statement, Hales Papers, CAI; Michael Collins to Florrie O'Donoghue, 19 December 1920, Ms. 31,192, NLI. During the Truce period, members of the Cork No. 1 Brigade secretly killed Keogh and two other military intelligence officers (and their driver) after they stopped for a drink in Macroom. Apparently they were caught armed and with map-making equipment, so the Volunteers shot them as spies. For details, see Patrick Twohig, *Green Tears for Hecuba* (Cork: Tower Books, 1994), pp. 337–43.
35 See Table Five.
36 General Tudor's Report of the Cork Fire, CO/904/150; Captain Sean Collin-Powell, A/0431, DDA.
37 The first description in the 'Circumstances' column refers to JP O'Brien's death during the ex-soldier riots of July 1920, described in the previous chapter. Under British fire, a crowd of protestors stampeded, injuring a woman. O'Brien was shot while he tried to drag her to safety.
38 The constables implicated in MacCurtain's killing were Irish, though it is possible some newly-arrived 'Black and Tans' participated in the assassination.
39 'Military Intelligence Lecture', Ms. 31,443, NLI.

CHAPTER SIX

British Intelligence in Cork

W hen analysing the execution of suspected civilian spies in Cork, British intelligence efforts in the city must also be ascertained. One must review the Crown forces' intelligence operation, judge its effectiveness, and determine if the British recruited a civilian intelligence auxiliary in Cork.

COLLAPSE OF THE RIC

Since the nineteenth century, the British Administration in Ireland had relied on the Royal Irish Constabulary for information about its political opponents. However, in 1920 the RIC collapsed as an intelligence force. Sir Ormonde de l'Epree Winter, Chief of RIC Intelligence, described the situation.

> A large number of men with local knowledge had either left the Force, or been transferred for reasons of safety, and those who remained, being unable to move about, had no means of obtaining information. Persons seen holding converse with a policeman were, at best, subjected to a severe boycott. The state of affairs had been arrived at when the tittle tattle, open to the ordinary village policeman in England, was no longer available to his Irish confrere.[1]

The British tried to reorganize RIC intelligence operations under the leadership of Sir Ormonde 'O' Winter, a flamboyant and occasionally absurd character described by senior Dublin Castle civil servant Mark Sturgis as 'the typical Colonel of light comedy'.[2] Winter staffed his office with amateurs considered by Sturgis to be a 'surprising set of ruffians', who also proved disloyal to their chief.[3] Though 'O' worked hard,[4] Sturgis reported displeasure over Winter's poor performance among Ireland's top civil and military leaders.

Sturgis wrote: 'Poor "O" has been struggling against a rising tide of overwork and insufficient (or inefficient, perhaps both) staff.'[5] General Macready, head of the Irish military command, believed: '"O" is not the man for the job,' while the Irish Joint Undersecretary Sir John Anderson wrote: 'his show is thoroughly bad and I don't see it getting any better.'[6] Winter failed to reshape and recharge RIC intelligence-gathering efforts, and the police force continued to lose its intelligence war with the IRA.

A 1922 British Army intelligence report claimed that by early 1920, police information gathering was 'paralysed',[7] and the RIC leadership: 'failed to realise their own system had broken down.'[8] During a British Army intelligence conference in late 1921, Colonel French (Hampshire Regiment) reported: 'Sinn Fein became gradually more military and as guerrilla war developed the RIC became less able to compete with it both by organization and owing to casualties.'[9] Writing in May 1921, General Strickland complained to his superiors: 'At present there is an enormous waste of valuable information which cannot be rectified until the RIC possesses an Intelligence Organisation in some form.'[10] Cork Republicans agreed. In mid-1920, Liam de Róiste believed: 'The English spy department, in so far as it concerns Volunteer movements or definite action, has broken down completely.'[11] Florrie O'Donoghue later remarked: 'In Cork they had lost the RIC as an intelligence service.'[12] In Cork city, police had suffered through a local boycott, and Cork citizens refused to serve on juries or otherwise participate in the British judicial system.[13] The alienation of local constables pushed Cork's RIC to a tipping point in early 1920.

TARGETED ATTACKS ON THE RIC IN CORK CITY

The Cork city Volunteers seem to have ultimately disabled the local RIC through a targeted assassination campaign. The IRA began to shoot specific 'dangerous' police officers in early 1920. In March 1920, the Brigade attempted to assassinate two city constables who 'made themselves particularly obnoxious by their aggressiveness towards us'.[14] IRA gunmen killed 'Detective' Constable Murtagh and fired shots at Sergeant Ferris (wounding his companion District Inspector MacDonagh), resulting in Ferris' transfer from the city.[15] Constable Harrington and Sergeant Garvey were killed in May 1920 for their alleged role in the assassination of Tomás MacCurtain. Both were considered aggressive officers, and had roughed up Cork Republicans during a brutal raid on a Sinn Fein Club in 1917.[16] Pa Murray, leader of the IRA squad that assassinated the two men, reported that he did not harm a third police officer accompanying the two officers. 'As he was not on the wanted list, we allowed him to return to the barracks, having first disarmed him.'[17] During the summer, three long-time Republican opponents, District Inspector Swanzy, Head Constable Cahill, and Head Constable Clarke, were transferred out of town for their own protection. The assassinations accelerated RIC resignations in Cork, and intimidated many constables.

For the most part, the 'old' RIC (Irish constables with long service) and the IRA seemed to have a 'live and let live' policy in Cork city. A policeman would often be safe as long as he showed no hostility towards local Volunteers. Numerous constables were held up and disarmed by Volunteers in 1920–1, yet left unharmed.[18] Attacks on police patrols were frequently planned for a specific result, such as seizing arms or 'clearing' an area from RIC oversight. This strategy largely succeeded, and by the middle of 1921, city police were penned into just three barracks and unable to patrol except in large numbers.

The IRA showed its focus during the abduction of Detective Thomas Ryan in November 1920 (see Chapter Three for details). Thinking Ryan was a British military intelligence officer, the Volunteers kidnapped Ryan while he walked from mass with fellow police Detective Carroll. Though Ryan's assailants recognized Detective Carroll, they left him alone. When the IRA discovered Ryan's true identity, he was released unharmed. Ryan was later wounded during the attempted assassination of Detective Malliff, who had been accused of using 'aggressive tactics' against IRA prisoners. (Ryan appears to have been shot solely because he was walking with Maliff at the time of the shooting.) Detective Maliff, though severely wounded, survived but was transferred out of the city. (See Chapter Three.) In March 1921, IRA Volunteers killed Constable Sterland, an Auxiliary Cadet they accused of acting as an intelligence officer in the city.[19] The British Army's Irish Command pointed out the obvious. 'The extremists are particularly sensitive to any attempt at special detective work or secret service on the part of the authorities, and any individuals suspected of being employed in such a capacity are at once marked down for assassination.'[20]

The IRA's assassination campaign apparently reduced the Cork city RIC to passivity. City Volunteer Raymond Kennedy recalled:

'there were the old police who were thinking of their pensions and they were just inactive.'[21] Florrie O'Donoghue told Ernie O'Malley:

> The RIC knew some of our men, and when they were arrested they didn't pass on their information up to the British. Police let go our men who were caught after curfew. One RIC who often saw me moving about Cork and who knew me, never reported that he had seen me. They were scared.[22]

The August 1920 City Hall raid should be seen in this light. The British Army captured the Cork No. 1 Brigade's senior leadership, including Volunteers who had been active in the city for years. However, the military only identified Lord Mayor MacSwiney, and subsequently released the other IRA officers. Local police were either unwilling to name the prisoners, or were never asked to do so. Following their arrest in the spring of 1921, prominent Brigade officers Seán Culhane, Dan Donovan, and Mick Murphy remained unidentified for their participation in specific shootings in the city, though some constables must have known them.[23] (Murphy successfully maintained his alias, despite his local fame as a hurler.) Captain Douglas Wimberly (serving in Cobh with the Second Battalion, Cameron Highlanders Regiment) wrote of the Cork RIC: 'they would no longer identify suspicious rebels we produced before them, knowing that to do so meant revenge, and generally death later for them ...'[24] Florrie O'Donoghue wrote to his wife in June 1921: 'The men on whom he depended for identification purposes – the old RIC – are almost wiped out, and large areas now exist in which he has nobody to identify prisoners taken.'[25]

MILITARY INTELLIGENCE IN CORK CITY

The British Army's Sixth Division tried to fill the intelligence vacuum left by Cork's defeated RIC. Two army battalions patrolled the city (Second Battalion, Oxford and Buckinghamshire Light Infantry Regiment, known as the Ox and Bucks; and the Second Battalion, Royal Hampshire Regiment). Each battalion appointed one intelligence officer to oversee local information gathering and analysis.[26] These two battalion intelligence officers later reported to an Army captain responsible for intelligence in the city. In addition, the Sixth Division intelligence staff commanded by Captain Kelly worked out of Victoria Barracks, as did the Seventeenth Infantry Brigade's small intelligence team. (The Seventeenth Brigade, one of three brigades in the Sixth Division, was responsible for the county Cork area.) All told, the strength of the combined intelligence staffs in Cork city numbered eight officers, three clerks, and a photographer.[27]

The size of the Sixth Division intelligence staff was typical of British infantry divisions during this period.[28] However, in an unconventional war that required the generation of prompt, actionable intelligence (rather than mere analysis), that small size was inadequate. For a comparison, during the guerrilla phase of the Anglo-Boer War, the British Army assigned 132 officers and 2,320 enlisted men to intelligence duties, and also formed native scouts into a Corps of Guides.[29] A similar ramp-up of military intelligence personnel never occurred in Ireland. The Sixth Division's small staff was responsible for an area far beyond Cork city, including the entire province of Munster, which constituted the heart of the Irish rebellion. Future Field Marshal Bernard Montgomery, the Brigade Major of Cork's Seventeenth Brigade, complained that general staff duties 'became somewhat arduous owing to the large area of a Brigade to look after, and the number of units it had to deal with. In the Seventeenth Brigade, we had at one time nine battalions, and the work was frightfully hard ... it was really too much.'[30]

Military intelligence officers organized their own network of informers and agents, often recruited and maintained by the division staff. In addition, each of the division's battalions and detachments generated large numbers of prisoners, reports, and leads, which must have severely taxed the small division team. Though helpful to local efforts, division and brigade intelligence personnel were overstretched, leaving Cork city's three battalion intelligence officers largely on their own. It appears, therefore, that the British Army seriously undermanned its intelligence operation in Cork.

Cooperation between military intelligence and the RIC did occur in Cork. The British Army claimed there was 'excellent liaison' in the city.[31] The IRA informer Pat Margetts agreed: 'There was very close cooperation between the RIC and the military in Cork.'[32] That relationship appears to have been informal, though joint raiding patrols were apparently common. However, the systematic and comprehensive organization of Crown force intelligence in the city remained elusive. It was not until April 1921 that the Irish Command formed the 'Cork Local Centre' to coordinate police and military intelligence efforts.[33] Reporting to the RIC Divisional Commissioner (in command of all police units in Munster), Lt Keogh (formerly of the Sixth Division intelligence staff) worked as an intelligence liaison between the two forces. However, the military and police relationship remained dysfunctional.[34] The Army complained of the local centres: 'They would have achieved even more had they been given clear and definite instructions as to their duties and had senior police officers had any conception as to what intelligence meant.'[35] Captured IRA documents were funnelled to either the RIC or the division intelligence staff, depending on the nature of the material. The incongruent system, reported the Army, resulted in 'loss of efficiency, duplication of work and complications in almost every way'.[36] Historian Eunan O'Halpin regarded cooperation between various British intelligence agencies in Ireland as essentially flawed. 'Coordination with other bodies seems to have been inadequate, due partly to mutual rivalry and partly to mistrust of the police.'[37]

British intelligence did score some notable victories against the Cork city Volunteers. As previously mentioned, 'the murder gang' killed seven local Volunteers during four weeks in November and December, and a number of local arms dumps were uncovered in January 1921. Some senior IRA officers were arrested in 1921, resulting in a reorganization of the city's command structure. Brigade officer Matt Ryan was jailed in March, and city Active Service Unit commander Tom Crofts was arrested in April. May saw the capture of ASU leaders Peter Donovan and Seán Twomey, and the later arrest of city commander Dan 'Sandow' Donovan and Brigade intelligence officer Seán Culhane in a random round-up. Mick Murphy, who succeeded Donovan as 'OC Cork City', was captured along with a number of his staff officers after a raid on a battalion meeting in June 1921.[38] However, these Crown force successes did not change the city's military situation, and June saw some of the most intense IRA activity of the entire conflict.

Though better organized in 1921 than 1920, military intelligence efforts proved only sporadically effective. Auxiliary Cadet commander Brigadier-General Crozier simply dismissed the Army's efforts. 'The "secret service" (under the Army) was no secret service but a mere gang of agents provocateurs and the like.'[39] Sixth Division commander General Strickland criticized his Intelligence staff in late 1920. 'Intelligence Officers must be on the move and put themselves in a position to collect information, plenty of which is now available. It is not to be found in the office.'[40]

Following Strickland's instructions, Sixth Division intelligence officers tried to gather information outside their offices. General Macready, commander of British Army forces in Ireland, wrote: 'As soon as the rebels began to attack and molest the troops, there was no dearth of volunteers for Intelligence work, and when in the summer of 1920, authority was obtained from the War Office to enlarge and improve the entire organization, little difficulty was found in obtaining keen volunteers who were well acquainted with the localities in which they were stationed.'[41] Unfortunately, according to Florrie O'Donoghue, those officers 'showed a boy scout mentality, and a complete absence of any sense of reality of the situation which then existed.'[42]

The Irish experiences of future Major General Sir Kenneth Strong seems typical of the enthusiastic if amateur Army intelligence specialists.[43] Strong started his long spy career as a detachment intelligence officer in Ireland. (He later headed Allied intelligence in General Eisenhower's European headquarters during World War II.) Strong recalled that as a subaltern in county Offaly he received little intelligence training and was given only £5 per month to pay his informants. He reported: 'I never to my knowledge managed to capture a single Sinn Feiner of any importance ... They had, they had said, been in our net, but because of our ignorance or the unwillingness of witnesses to identify them for fear of reprisals, we had let them go.' Strong's method of meeting with agents seemed especially foolhardy. 'To get to a rendezvous, I would disguise myself usually as the owner of a small donkey cart, but my accent was against me and I had several narrow escapes.'

Similar boldness proved fatal in the Cork No. 1 Brigade area. IRA officer Martin Corry, operating in the city suburbs, remembered two such British officers, 'who were dressed like tramps. They were foolish enough to go into a house to look to see if there were any names on the door [in accordance with Martial Law restrictions].'[44] The officers were arrested and shot. As mentioned in Chapter Two, the Royal Artillery officers, Lts Brown and Rutherford, were captured and executed after moving around Macroom disguised as tourists. Captain Thompson, the Manchester Regiment intelligence officer assassinated in November 1920, travelled to work on the same road at an identical time each day, making him an easy mark for Volunteer gunmen. In 1921, Major Compton-Smith, a highly regarded intelligence officer with the Welsh Fusiliers, was captured while visiting Blarney posed as a fisherman.[45] Florrie O'Donoghue interrogated Compton-Smith shortly before his execution by the IRA.[46]

From something he let drop I was under the impression that the army men of the SS [Secret Service] thought that intelligence could really be organized and that either Kelly of the 6th Division was not competent enough, or that he was not making sufficient effort to organize himself. The British really thought they could organize an intelligence system. They had not learned the difficulties or they certainly did not know their own weakness. Compton-Smith thought either Kelly was fooling them or that he was incompetent. As a result they may have organized Loyalists.[47]

STRICKLAND'S CALL FOR HELP

Ultimately, the success of British intelligence depended on information from local civilians. During two newspaper interviews in January 1921, General Strickland appealed to Cork loyalists for such assistance.[48] Strickland also approached individual Unionists. 'One day,' recalled Cork Unionist Olga Pyne Clarke, 'he stamped into my father's office and in his extremely rude, brusque manner said, "Look here, Clarke, you are trusted by both sides: it's your duty to give me information".'[49]

More obvious requests were apparent earlier. In September 1920, unknown persons slipped leaflets under doors and into letterboxes throughout a Cork city district. The notices asked for information about attacks on police, and offered cash rewards and instructions on how to submit the intelligence. An appalled 'Cork Moderate' complained in a letter to the *Cork Constitution*: 'It is difficult to conceive of anything more clumsy or ill-advised ... If it is meant as a serious matter to remedy the evil complained of, then, God help us.'[50]

A Sixth Division draft memo shows that local loyalists did come forward with information. The memo also reiterates the dangers of such acts.[51]

1. A question which is coming into prominence and regarding which some policy is required is the safeguarding, and if necessary, transfer to England of loyal inhabitants who for various reasons have incurred the displeasure of the IRA and are therefore unable to reside in their homes.

2. Most of the people concerned come under the following headings:
    a. Those who have given information.
    b. Those who have given evidence.
    c. Those who on account of their loyalty have already been

attacked by the rebels, or are likely to be if they remain in their homes.

At present Class (a.) are re-compensed out of a special intelligence fund and transferred to England.

There is no proof the military organised Cork loyalists into a formal intelligence group, such as 'The Anti-Sinn Fein Society'. There is evidence that loyalists living in county Cork earlier formed a unit called the 'Irish Coast Intelligence Corps'. (See Chapter Two.) A similar formation would be expected in Cork city during 1920–1. Loyal citizens found themselves caught in a brutal guerrilla campaign against the forces of the British Crown. The military government beseeched Cork's inhabitants for assistance in beating back the Republican menace. The city contained a large pro-British population, including thousands of Unionists and ex-servicemen. It would be surprising if no one answered British pleas for help. However, if such a group did form, it contributed little to the Crown forces' efforts in Cork. As the previous chapters have shown, the British were unable to maintain their successful operations of November 1920 through January 1921.

BRITISH FOCUS ON SINN FEIN

The Sixth Division's official history describes just three specific triumphs by its intelligence department in Cork city during 1920–1. The victories mentioned are the City Hall raid in August 1920, the killing of six IRA Volunteers at Clogheen in March 1921, and an effort to discredit Lord Mayor Donal 'Og' Ó'Callaghan in late 1920. The first two episodes have been explored, and civilian informers cannot claim credit in either case. (The City Hall raid resulted from an IRA message captured in the mail, while the Clogheen killings stemmed from information provided by an IRA Volunteer.) The O'Callaghan case will be reviewed because it reveals the ignorance of British military intelligence during the period.

Donal 'Óg' O'Callaghan succeeded Terence MacSwiney as Cork's Lord Mayor after the latter's death on hunger strike in October 1920. O'Callaghan helped organize the pre-Rising Volunteers in Cork, but following 1916 he moved into a political role. After dropping out of IRA activities, O'Callaghan became a prominent member of Sinn Féin, and was elected Alderman and eventually Lord Mayor.

However, in the aftermath of MacSwiney's death, British intelligence officers believed O'Callaghan would assume command of the Cork No. 1 Brigade, and schemed to rid themselves of the 'extreme' leader.[52] Their idea was to discredit O'Callaghan by portraying him as a British spy, clearing the way for a less militant officer to take charge of the Brigade. In fact, O'Callaghan was a moderate Republican committed to the political side of the independence struggle. On the other hand, MacSwiney's logical successor, Brigade Vice Commander Seán O'Hegarty, was a strong proponent of physical force, and a skilled and ruthless military leader. Either the British dramatically misread both O'Hegarty and O'Callaghan, or they were entirely ignorant of the two men's outlooks and standings in Cork's Volunteer movement. Either way, the military intelligence officers displayed a remarkable lack of knowledge about their opponents.

In order to derail O'Callaghan's promotion, the British Army 'arranged that a letter would be sent through the ordinary post, and that this letter would include a request for money to reward one of these people for information he had supplied ... O'Callaghan had to get out of the country at short notice to save his own skin.' While O'Callaghan did covertly leave Cork during this period to join a Sinn Féin publicity tour in America, the IRA did not doubt his intentions. In April 1921, Michael Collins wrote to Florrie O'Donoghue about a similar British disinformation effort. 'Furthermore, it would look as if this information was a trap, and the matter might be looked up. I have come across many things like this, and down at your end you will remember the letter about the present Lord Mayor of Cork.'[53] Regardless, the British Army claimed success in the O'Callaghan case, which illustrates a consistent self-promotion in its post-conflict reports, and the failure (even a year later) to recognize the strategic blunder of working to replace moderate Donal O'Callaghan with militant Seán O'Hegarty.

The attempt to discredit Lord Mayor O'Callaghan underlines the misdirected focus of British intelligence. Historian Eunan O'Halpin believes the Crown could not differentiate Sinn Féin from the Volunteers. 'Instead, Sinn Féin was treated as a hostile and subversive organization, indistinguishable from the IRA.'[54] Florrie O'Donoghue recalled:

> In Cork City all attention had been directed towards Terence MacSwiney and Tomás MacCurtain. They had been working, but after 1918 or 1919, a new set of officers sprang up. [Seán] O'Hegarty,

myself, [and] Dan Donovan were looked upon as small fries by the RIC. They seemed to concentrate on the TDs and members of Sinn Fein. Of course Sinn Fein was a composite organization in the minds of the British. It was supposed to cover all our activities – IRA, IRB, etc.[55]

Evidence from Cork city supports O'Halpin's and O'Donoghue's assertion. According to Siobhan Creedon Lankford, her husband Seamus Lankford was a Sinn Fein activist unaffiliated with the IRA, but yet found himself a regular target for the British 'murder gang'.[56] Seamus Lankford worked at the Cork Workhouse with Pat Higgins, a former Volunteer leader who resigned from the Brigade leadership in February 1918 and transitioned into the political sphere.[57] Like Seamus Lankford, Pat Higgins was also hunted by British forces.[58] Numerous Sinn Fein elected officials were the source of similar unwanted attention. Alderman Stockley miraculously escaped assassination following the shooting of RIC District Inspector MacDonagh in March 1920.[59] Alderman Seán Sullivan, a former leader of the Cork Volunteers who resigned his IRA post in late 1918 (after opposing armed attacks on police),[60] was likewise targeted for assassination the same week.[61] Sinn Féin Alderman Coughlan saw his house invaded twice, once hours after the Dillon's Cross Ambush, the same night the British 'murder gang' killed two Volunteers in their beds across town. Liam de Róiste, a Sinn Féin TD, was the subject of a failed assassination attempt in March 1921, which resulted in the death of a Catholic priest in his home.[62] J.J. Walsh, the city's other Sinn Féin TD, spent 1920 'on the run' and 1921 in prison.[63] In March 1921, British soldiers raided the home of Cork Alderman John O'Riordan and charged him with possession of arms and ammunition, and arrested Alderman Alfred O'Rahilly around the same time.[64] Alderman Tadg Barry, another former Volunteer leader who had moved to Sinn Féin, was arrested in early 1921 and killed by a British sentry at Ballykinlar Prison Camp during the Truce Period.[65] As reported above, British intelligence officers arranged an elaborate ruse to undermine Lord Mayor O'Callaghan.

Although they were important spokesmen for Irish independence aspirations and symbols of popular Republican support in the city, Cork's Sinn Féin leaders remained largely irrelevant to the IRA military campaign of 1920–1. The British wasted their resources tracking Sinn Féin activists, and would have produced better results by focusing on the IRA. Such a poor tactical decision illustrates the inability of British Intelligence officers to ascertain, analyse, and understand their opponents. The concentration on Sinn Féin likely resulted from the Crown forces failure to identify Volunteer leaders in the city. This again underlines the scarcity of quality information about IRA activities in Cork.

Throughout 1920 and 1921, the Crown forces made only limited inroads against the Volunteer organization in the city. Although a number of local IRA leaders were captured, key Brigade officers escaped arrest throughout the conflict. Brigade commander Seán O'Hegarty, Adjutant Florrie O'Donoghue, Quartermaster Joe O'Connor, and ASU O/C Pa Murray operated for three years in Cork without being jailed. (O'Hegarty and O'Connor were briefly imprisoned during the City Hall raid, but were released without being identified.) Following their return to the city, former prisoners (and brigade leaders) Seán MacSwiney and Connie Neenan resumed their covert activities without detection.[66] At least thirty Volunteers worked fulltime on IRA duties in Cork at the time of the July Truce.[67] British military intelligence seemed unable to determine exactly whom it was fighting in Cork city in 1920–1.

A post-conflict British Army intelligence review reveals military ignorance about the Cork IRA. The authors' display a rough understanding of the IRA organization, accurately reporting its two-battalion structure in the city, the withdrawal of Brigade Headquarters to Ballyvourney in February 1921, and the appointment of an officer in command of all city IRA forces.[68] However, the report includes some glaring mistakes. It claims that the city IRA Active Service Unit was a 'murder gang' divided into three sections.[69] Two of these sections were allegedly 'broken up', while the third was destroyed at Kerry Pike. This inaccurately represents the IRA Active Service Unit (composed of a dozen fulltime Volunteers, maintained as a force until the July Truce), dismisses the fighting function of the city's companies and battalions, and misidentifies the duties of the Kerry Pike victims, who had served with the brigade flying column outside the city since January 1921. The report further claims the city's two battalions had 'ceased to function' by July 1921.[70] However, this was not the case. While hard-pressed in March and April, the city IRA had counterattacked, and undertook five major ambushes in June (see Chapter Four for details). City commander Pa Murray reported that by that time the British had yielded much of the city to his Volunteers, forcing him to deploy his guerrillas in the suburbs in order to engage Crown forces.[71] Despite claims to the contrary, by the time of the Truce in July 1921 the British were no closer to defeating the IRA in Cork city than they had been a year earlier. The military report illustrates a problematic British mindset, identified by Colonel French in an earlier intelligence lecture. 'We did not look at the situation sufficiently from the enemy's point of view ... We were out of sympathy with his aspirations and despised his methods.'[72]

STALEMATE

The military situation in Cork at the time of the July 1921 Truce should be considered a draw. The IRA operated with relative impunity in much of the city, and the threat of ambush prevented the British from patrolling in small and nimble groups. On the other hand, constant British dragnets made it dangerous for Volunteers to move about town, and the IRA's poorly-armed street fighters proved incapable of ejecting Crown forces from their strong local bases.

This stalemate had different implications for each side. To the Volunteers, survival equalled success. West Cork's Tom Barry wrote about his flying column: 'The very existence of such a column of armed men, even if it never struck a blow, was a continuous challenge to the enemy.'[73] Barry's point extends to Ireland as a whole, including Cork city. As long as the city Volunteers stayed intact as a fighting force, they were an implied threat to British loyalists and those local civilians 'who would stand aloof either through indifference or fear'.[74] The British Administration could not function while that IRA menace remained. The Crown forces were entrusted with returning peace and order to the city. However, a military deadlock guaranteed continued instability in Cork. The Crown's rule of law could only be enforced after a clear and outright British victory over the Volunteers.

Britain's inability to destroy the IRA in Cork city must be interpreted as a victory for the guerrillas. As Eunan O'Halpin wrote: 'The IRA had won by not being defeated.'[75] The survival of the Cork city IRA is even more remarkable when considering the extreme disparity of the opposing forces in terms of numbers, arms, training, and treasury. Ineffective British intelligence operations bear the blame for the Crown force failure in the city. As will be shown in the next chapter, IRA intelligence proved decisive in the local rebellion.

SUMMARY

British efforts in the city were undone by the lack of accurate information about the Volunteers. The Crown forces only achieved a
coherent intelligence organization late in the conflict, and even then
their operations were hindered by duplicate efforts and inefficiency.
The small staff assigned to military intelligence duties in Victoria
Barracks shows the British Army's lack of emphasis on information
gathering and analysis. Military officers working in and near the city
were mostly amateurs without special training, and their inexperi-
ence was apparent. Crown force appeals for help from Cork's sizable
loyal population did not yield significant returns. British intelligence
leaders failed to understand their opponents and concentrated on
Sinn Féin activists instead of IRA fighters

While reviewing Britain's intelligence performance in Ireland
during 1916–21, secret service historian Christopher Andrews titled
his chapter 'The Irish Debacle'. That harsh heading seems fitting
when describing Crown force intelligence efforts in Cork city during
1920–1.

NOTES

1 Hart, *British Intelligence in Ireland*, p. 66.
2 Sturgis, p. 4.
3 Ibid, pp. 61, 75, 93–4. Sturgis claimed that five staff members committed suicide
   during the 1920–1 period. See Sturgis, p. 180.
4 Ibid, p. 90.
5 Ibid, pp. 75–6.
6 Reported by Sturgis, p. 90; Anderson to Sturgis, quoted by the editor, p. 250.
7 Ibid., p. 19.
8 Ibid., p. 42.
9 'Colonel C.N. French, Hampshire Regiment, "General Lecture on Intelligence",
   Synopsis of Eleven Lectures Delivered before an Intelligence Conference,
   October 1921,' 7/16, Major-General Charles Howard Foulkes Papers, Harte
   Centre for Military Archives, Kings College, London. The Hampshire
   Regiment's Second Battalion was stationed in Cork.
10 OC Sixth Division to GHQ Ireland, 13 May 1920, Strickland Papers, IWM.
11 De Róiste Diary, 29 May 1920.
12 O'Donoghue in the O'Malley Notebooks.
13 In July 1920, the RIC complained about the police boycott in Cork city. See
   Outrages Against Police, week ending 1 August 1920, CO 904/149, PRO. The
   police also reported RIC boycott notices posted outside every Catholic church
   in the city in August 1920. See Outrages Against Police, week ending 15 August
   1920, CO 904/149. Almost the entire jury pool of 200 local citizens failed to
   appear at the July Summer Assizes. See the *Cork Constitution,* 20 July 1920.

14 O'Donoghue, *Florence and Josephine O'Donoghue's War of Independence*, p. 85.

15 Ibid, p. 86. Ferris was transferred to Belfast, promoted to District Inspector, and wounded by the IRA in May 1921 for his participation in unofficial reprisals. See the *Cork Constitution*, 28 September 1920; and Jim McDermott *Northern Ireland Divisions* (Belfast: BTP Publications, 2001), pp. 50, 77, and 80.

16 During the raid of 22 November 1917, police wrecked the Sinn Féin office and put five Republicans in hospital. District Inspector Swanzy led the police party. Both Garvey and Harrington were identified by witnesses, and the latter's 'brutal conduct deserves special mention'. See a witness statement signed by ten victims dated 28 November 1917, Ms. 31,148, NLI.

17 Pa Murray BMH Statement. According to police reports, while Murray's men did not kill the third constable, they did shoot him in the leg. See Outrages Against Police, 12 May 1920, CO 904/147.

18 For examples, see Constables Leahy and Camden (Outrages Against Police, 28 June 1920, CO 904/148); unnamed Auxiliary Cadet (18 November 1920, CO 904/149); Constable Skelton (week ending 19 January 1921, CO 904/150); and Constable Connor (4 March 1921, CO 904).

19 Robert Aherne BMH Statement; Mick Murphy BMH Statement.

20 *Sinn Féin and the Irish Volunteers*, p. 12, booklet released by the Irish Command, copy in the Strickland Papers, IWM.

21 Raymond Kennedy in the O'Malley Notebooks.

22 O'Donoghue in the O'Malley Notebooks.

23 See Seán Culhane's and Mick Murphy's BMH Statements. Donovan and Murphy were very prominent G.A.A. players, which should have made them known to police. Donovan had also marched openly in uniform with the Brigade leadership contingent during Tomás MacCurtain's funeral procession.

24 William Sheehan *British Voices From the Irish War of Independence 1918–1921* (Cork: Collins Press, 2005), pp. 178–9. In World War II, Wimberly commanded the Fifty-first Highland Division at the Battle of El Alamein, and retired from the British Army as a Major General.

25 O'Donoghue Letters, dated 17 June 1921, Ms. 31,176.

26 Hart, *British Intelligence in Ireland*, p. 40.

27 The 6th Division official history lists the combined strength of the Division Intelligence staff and the Seventeenth Brigade intelligence staff as five officers, three clerks, and a photographer. See the *History of the 6th Division in Ireland*, p. 66. The Irish Command's intelligence report stated that two battalion intelligence officers were posted in an ad-hoc city intelligence office, and they reported to a Captain in charge of the city. (See Hart, *British Intelligence in Ireland*, p. 40.) Those three officers, combined with the division and brigade intelligence staffs, total eight officers, plus the three clerks and photographer at Victoria Barracks.

28 See the U.S. Army Command and General Staff School *Notes on British, Dominion, and Indian Armed Forces* (Fort Leavenworth, KS: U.S. Army Command and General Staff School, 1945), pp. 32, 37. This Anglo-American military liaison reference book details British unit designations, breakdowns, and staff compliments. (Courtesy Col. Mario G. Paolini Military History Library, San Francisco, CA.)

29 Peter Gudgin *Military Intelligence, The British Story* (London: Arms & Armour Press, 1982), p. 37.

30 Montgomery letter to A.E. Percival dated 14 October 1923, provided in Sheehan, p. 149.

31 Hart, *British Intelligence in Ireland*, p. 40.

32 Pat Margetts in the O'Malley Notebooks.
33 Hart, *British Intelligence in Ireland*, p. 41.
34 British intelligence historian Keith Jeffrey wrote: 'The British Intelligence effort in Ireland from 1919 to 1921 was crippled by a lack of coherence and centralized direction.' See Jeffrey 'British Military Intelligence Following World War One', in K.G. Robertson *British and American Approaches to Intelligence* (London: MacMillan, 1988), p. 74.
35 Hart, *British Intelligence in Ireland*, p. 27.
36 Ibid., p 30.
37 Eunan O'Halpin 'British Intelligence in Ireland', in Christopher Andrews and David Dilks (eds.) *The Missing Dimension, Governments and Intelligence Communities in the 20th Century* (London: MacMillan Publishers, 1984), p. 76.
38 Mick Murphy BMH Statement; *Cork Examiner*, 14 June 1921.
39 FP Crozier *Ireland Forever* (Bath: Cedric Chivers Ltd, 1971), p. 90.
40 General Strickland to all OCTs, 24 December 1920, A/0341, DDA, NLI.
41 Macready *Annals of an Active Life* (London: Hutchinson, 1924), Vol. II, p. 462.
42 O'Donoghue, *No Other Law*, p. 118.
43 Kenneth Strong *Intelligence at the Top, the Recollections of an Intelligence Officer* (London: Cassell and Company, 1968), p. 1.
44 Martin Corry in the O'Malley Notebooks.
45 Cork Quarterly Session, *Cork Constitution*, 17 October 1921.
46 O'Donoghue in the O'Malley Notebooks.
47 I would not read too much into O'Donoghue's qualification '...they *may have* organized the loyalists'. (My italics.) Ernie O'Malley roughly transcribed his interviews, and was hardly a stenographer. He typically summarized his subject's thoughts, and provided specific quotes to support those themes, sometimes inserting them without prior context. O'Donoghue mentioned a loyalist spy group in Cork elsewhere in his interview with O'Malley, and inferred the same in his memoir (O'Donoghue, *Florence and Josephine O'Donoghue's War of Independence*, p. 84).
48 *Cork Constitution*, 18 January 1921; *Manchester Guardian*, reprinted in the *Cork Constitution*, 24 January 1921.
49 Olga Pyne Clark, p. 51.
50 *Cork Constitution*, 18 September 1920.
51 Undated draft memo, Strickland Papers, IWM.
52 *History of the 6th Division in Ireland*, p. 49.
53 Collins to O'Donoghue, 14 April 1921, Ms. 31,192, NLI.
54 See O'Halpin, 'British Intelligence in Ireland', p. 70. British documents and reports from the period use the terms 'Sinn Féin' and 'IRA' interchangeably.
55 O'Donoghue in the O'Malley Notebooks.
56 Lankford, p. 258.
57 O'Donoghue, *Florence and Josephine O'Donoghue's War of Independence*, p. 40.
58 Lankford, pp. 256–62.
59 *Cork Examiner*, 19 March 1920.
60 O'Sullivan, commander of the city's Second Battalion, opposed the Brigade's use of pistols during the escape of Denis MacNeilus from Cork Gaol in November 1918, and later resigned after he refused to attack an RIC barracks in Ballygarvan on 2 January 1920. See O'Donoghue, *Florence and Josephine O'Donoghue's War of Independence*, pp. 51, 81–2.
61 Tomás MacCurtain Inquest, CO 904/113.
62 De Róiste Diary, 15 May 1921.

63 J.J. Walsh *Recollections of an Irish Rebel* (Tralee: Kerryman Press, 1944), pp. 47–52.

64 *Cork Constitution*, 11 March 1921.

65 Cork No. 1 Brigade Casualty Roll, CPM.

66 MacSwiney escaped from Spike Island Prison in March 1921, along with Limerick IRA leader Tomás Malone. The Cork No. 1 Brigade arranged the jailbreak, communicated the plan to the prisoners, and sent a powerboat to pick the fugitives from a work detail outside the camp gate. See O'Donoghue (ed.), *Sworn to Be Free, A Complete Book of IRA Jailbreaks, 1918–1921* (Tralee: Anvil Books, 1971), p. 133; and Malone's account in MacEoin, pp. 94–7.

67 Fulltime Volunteers included the Brigade Staff, Intelligence Staff, and the Active Service Unit. There were likely far more fulltime Volunteers active in the city during this period.

68 Hart, *British Intelligence in Ireland*, pp. 39–40.

69 Ibid., p. 40.

70 Ibid., p. 41.

71 Pa Murray BMH Statement.

72 Col. French Intelligence lecture, Foulkes Papers, Harte Centre for Military Archives.

73 Barry, p. 23.

74 O'Donoghue, *Florence and Josephine O'Donoghue's War of Independence*, p. 83.

75 O'Halpin 'British Intelligence in Ireland', p. 70.

CHAPTER SEVEN

IRA Intelligence in Cork

The previous chapters showed that Cork's Crown forces appealed for assistance from the loyal population and recruited civilian informers in the city. The Cork city IRA shot a number of suspected civilian informants in 1920–1. The Volunteers claimed some of these victims were involved in a British spy ring it termed the 'Anti-Sinn Féin Society'. Case by case examinations have shown that it is impossible to determine the guilt of many of the suspected spies. However, an analysis of IRA intelligence efforts will answer the essential question posed by Republican testimonies: Were the city IRA forces capable of identifying and locating civilian informers?

FLORRIE O'DONOGHUE AND IRA INTELLIGENCE IN CORK CITY

Brigade Intelligence Officer Florence (Florrie) O'Donoghue was the most important figure in the Cork city IRA's intelligence operation. Born in Rathmore, Co. Kerry in 1895, O'Donoghue moved to Cork in 1910 to serve an apprenticeship in a drapery shop. Initially apolitical, O'Donoghue was inspired by the Easter Rising to join the Irish Volunteers in late 1916. Brigade leaders Tomás MacCurtain and Seán O'Hegarty recognized O'Donoghue's potential and promoted him rapidly, first to Brigade Communications Officer, and subsequently Brigade Adjutant in late 1917.[1] In 1919, O'Donoghue foresaw the importance of information gathering and assumed the additional post of Brigade Intelligence Officer. A shrewd and effective officer, O'Donoghue became one of the IRA's most highly regarded leaders. David Nelligan, an IRA double agent working for the British secret service, rated O'Donoghue, 'amongst the best intelligence officers in the Volunteers'.[2] Irish Lt General Michael Costello referred to him as 'the extraordinarily able and successful IRA intelligence officer in Cork'.[3] 'Shrewd, calm, and capable,' wrote West

Cork's Tom Barry, 'I rated him as one of the best ten officers I met during my membership of the IRA. An "all round" officer, his specialty was intelligence, and he can be bracketed justly with Michael Collins, the Director of Intelligence, as the outstanding IO [intelligence officer] in Ireland.'[4] In May 1922, O'Donoghue was elected to the IRA Executive (Anti-Treaty) with the fifth highest vote tally, and became the Anti-Treaty IRA's acting Adjutant General.[5] The May 'Army Unification Agreement' saw him nominated first as IRA Director of Intelligence, and later Adjutant-General.[6] O'Donoghue's papers (which, along with Ernie O'Malley's, are a cornerstone of Anglo-Irish war studies) reveal a careful and meticulous mind. Through him, IRA intelligence in Cork took shape.

DEVELOPMENT OF INTELLIGENCE IN CORK

O'Donoghue recalled that his interest in military intelligence grew gradually. In late 1918, O'Donoghue planned the Cork Gaol escape of IRA Volunteer Denis MacNeilus, following the latter's arrest for shooting a Cork policeman. The successful jailbreak sparked some profound questions in the inexperienced O'Donoghue.

> We were completely ignorant of the enemy, except in the most general and fragmentary way. We never made any attempt to study closely his organization, routine, morale, equipment, and personnel. Was there any reason why we should continue to remain in so dense a state of ignorance? We thought not. Out of these ideas our intelligence service was born; or rather I should say, was born locally, because [Michael] Collins was developing similar ideas in Dublin, though we did not know it then.[7]

By the beginning of 1920, O'Donoghue's operation began to take shape.

> Partly as the result of the MacNeilus and Ballyquirk incidents, and partly out of our ignorance of enemy organization and sources of strength, I became more and more impressed by the need for putting the collection and evaluation of information on some organized basis. We had then nothing more than a few individual men in the General Post Office who brought up an occasional copy of the police message in cipher – messages that we were not always able to decode. I thought we needed a basic organization in every Company and Battalion, with men specially detailed to study the area and its possibilities from the

Intelligence point of view, as well as a wide development of such sources as Post Offices and Telephone Exchanges.[8]

It was not until after March 1920, that O'Donoghue corresponded regularly with Michael Collins in Dublin. The two began to share information and methods which proved beneficial to them both.

> Collins and I, each without the knowledge of the other, were trying to build up something similar, but with this difference. I put down a basic organization in the Companies and Battalions but had made no progress in the espionage aspect at that stage, where he had practically no basic organization, but had made very considerable progress on the more valuable espionage aspect. Working in Dublin, and with contacts in London, his opportunities in this regard were much more extensive than mine. Out of the Quinlisk case [*February 1920*] there arose a comparing of notes and a mutual co-operation and close contact that proved valuable.[9]

(O'Donoghue soon made up for his 'espionage' deficiency in a spectacular way, which will be discussed below.)

In an article in the Irish military journal *An Cosantóir*, O'Donoghue credited the IRA's military intelligence success to three factors.

> This efficiency was due to neither chance nor to the exclusive abilities of one man. It was due to three things: First, to a keen appreciation on the part of GHQ at the time of the value of Intelligence; Second, to the efficient organization and exploitation of sources of information; and, Third, to the fact that every member of the Defence forces at that time – and to a large extent every loyal citizen also – regarded it as a paramount and personal duty, promptly and at all times, to pass on to those in authority every item of enemy information that resulted from his constant watchfulness. And of these three contributory sources, the last was by far most important.[10]

Evidence largely supports O'Donoghue's assertions in relation to the situation in Cork during this period.

IRA GHQ AND INTELLIGENCE

IRA General Headquarters stressed the importance of intelligence early in the Anglo-Irish conflict. The Volunteer magazine *An tÓglach* encouraged IRA units in this area in January 1920.

There is one branch of service which we possess a great superiority over the enemy – intelligence ... It is a vital service, and one on which our strength largely depends. No effort should be spared to make this department of our work as efficient as possible. Every individual Volunteer should co-operate in this work, both during his hours of active service and his hours of leisure. No information bearing on the strength, resources, machinery, and intentions of the enemy should be neglected.[11]

Three months later, the journal again underlined this area: 'One of the most important branches of our work at present time is the proper organization of our own Intelligence department.'[12] In December 1920, IRA Director of Intelligence Michael Collins wrote to all IRA Brigade Intelligence officers to stress and outline the Volunteer intelligence organization.[13] O'Donoghue transmitted these instructions (with some of his own edits) to Cork No. 1 Brigade Battalion commanders.

COLLABORATION BETWEEN MICHAEL COLLINS AND FLORRIE O'DONOGHUE

By mid-1920, O'Donoghue was in almost daily contact with Michael Collins.[14] Some of their communications survive in O'Donoghue's papers in the National Library. They reveal the nature of IRA intelligence during the period. As O'Donoghue mentions above, collaboration between Dublin and Cork did not occur until March 1920. While Collins' fabled network was strong in Dublin, initially the 'Big Fellow' was somewhat ignorant of affairs in Cork.

The Quinlisk case reveals the early lack of coordination between Cork and Dublin. As mentioned in Chapter Four, Timothy Quinlisk had been employed by British authorities to track down Michael Collins in Dublin. Unsuccessful in Dublin, Quinlisk moved to Cork after GHQ intelligence officers told Quinlisk that Collins had relocated there. Remarkably, Collins' staff neglected to inform the Cork No. 1 Brigade of their ruse, and the Corkmen had to unravel Quinlisk's covert mission on their own.[15] While coordination between Dublin and Cork improved after this incident, Collins still showed ignorance about events and conditions in the city. For example, five months following Tomás MacCurtain's assassination, Collins asked O'Donoghue: 'Are you looking for a man named Head

Constable Cahill? Do you know anything of him?'[16] If Collins had read a Cork newspaper, he would have known Cahill's identity, since the policeman had figured very prominently in the MacCurtain Inquest.[17]

Contrary to popular depictions, Collins was not a Smiley-like spymaster, micro-managing intelligence networks throughout Ireland. His value lay in his superb Dublin organization, which penetrated the headquarters of Britain's military and civilian administrations in Ireland. Outside of Dublin, Collins effectively organized and distributed information from around the country, and encouraged intelligence efforts in areas he knew required attention.

As the conflict progressed, Collins gained greater understanding of events in Cork through his correspondence with O'Donoghue. With similar reports flowing to him from different country units, Collins drew a general picture of national and regional developments, which enabled him to channel relevant information from one area of Ireland to another. The MacCurtain assassination case illustrates his function. During the summer of 1920, the Cork No. 1 Brigade requested Collins' assistance in locating District Inspector Swanzy, who it believed arranged Tomás MacCurtain's killing.[18] O'Donoghue told Collins that his Cork intelligence subordinate had discovered Swanzy's luggage being mailed to Lisburn, County Antrim. Using that information, Collins contacted one of his agents, an RIC sergeant stationed in Belfast.[19] After the police informant located Swanzy in Lisburn, Collins ordered IRA Volunteers in Belfast to place Swanzy under observation. When the Cork No. 1 Brigade sent two Cork Volunteers to Lisburn to assassinate Swanzy, Collins put them in touch with the IRA's Belfast Brigade. The combined group then killed Swanzy as he left Sunday services.

Other communications show Collins using his contacts to help intelligence efforts in Cork. He told O'Donoghue in 1920: 'a Miss Scannell, formerly of Bandon, more recently in Dublin, has been transferred to the Telegraph Office Cork ... She is very easily approached and will be anxious to help.'[20] In another instance Collins wrote: 'A sergeant late of County Meath promoted Head Constable, Neary, is at present in Macroom. Some of our friends should get in touch with him and say he was directed to do so through Headquarters, by Boylan, Dunboyne.'[21] Collins likewise introduced O'Donoghue to a Cork RIC clerk who agreed to pass on police communications.[22] A captured letter detailing the hiring of a Dublin Castle spy was also channelled to Cork. (It read: 'I beg to confirm your appointment on the terms mentioned by me on that occasion, and your pay at £1 per diem, will date as from the 19th inst. Will you please go to Cork directly.')[23] Collins initially encouraged Florrie O'Donoghue's efforts in Cork, then subsequently assisted him by providing valuable information from Collins' contacts throughout Ireland.

Collins most important service was the passing of RIC cipher keys to Cork,[24] which enabled O'Donoghue's network to decode secret police messages sent by telegraph or post. (Terence MacSwiney was convicted in 1920 for possession of one such cipher key.) IRA organization of sympathetic Cork Post and Telegraph Office personnel made government communications vulnerable. According to O'Donoghue: 'Brigade intelligence had organized a number of employees into a team for copying coded RIC messages passing through the telegraph department, and transmitting copies to the Brigade.'[25] This gave the IRA access to sensitive RIC communications in Cork. The case of the spy Timothy Quinlisk again illustrates the IRA's advantage. The Brigade intercepted and deciphered a routine telegram from Dublin Castle to the RIC headquarters in Cork. The message told Cork police to expect a letter the next day from the RIC Special Branch to a police spy operating in the city. The following morning O'Donoghue intercepted the covert message through the crude method of holding up the police messenger. The letter revealed Quinlisk's position as a police agent, providing the IRA with ample evidence to shoot him as a British spy.[26]

Besides police codes, IRA General Headquarters also provided financial assistance to the Cork No. 1 Brigade intelligence operation. The aid mainly concerned the formation of a permanent 'Brigade Intelligence Squad'. In early 1921, O'Donoghue selected and trained six intelligence officers for fulltime service in the city. Bob Aherne, Gavin Fitzgerald, Denis Hegarty, Mick Kenny, John O'Brien, and Frank Mahoney (head of the unit) moved about town on 'permanent observation', living off a stipend of £25 for their upkeep.[27] O'Donoghue stated that Dublin funded his office with a weekly draft of £35.[28] It should be noted that the money was not used to pay informers. O'Donoghue wrote: 'It is so common a practice in other countries to buy information that I had better say I never had one single penny to disburse for Intelligence purposes during the whole of the Tan War, and that no single individual of the thousands who helped in this work expected any payment.'[29] Bob Aherne recalled that he was awarded an additional £1 per week for operating costs.

'The extra £1 allowance was given to cover my expenses when in the company of British military and Black and Tans whom I met in public houses and hotels in Cork City ... I need hardly add that the allowance was quite insufficient for the purpose at hand.'[30] O'Donoghue remarked later: 'In fact we never had any real money ... Never surely was a fight for freedom financed as this one.'[31]

This financial support, while minimal, is significant, since it would appear to be the most pronounced GHQ funding of any IRA unit outside of Dublin. Intelligence was the only department in the Cork No. 1 Brigade to receive monetary assistance, leaving, for example, the twelve-man City Active Service Unit to fend for itself. O'Donoghue, Brigade OC Seán O'Hegarty, and Brigade Quartermaster Joe O'Connor also received £3 per week from GHQ for living expenses.[32] According to O'Donoghue: 'we were glad of this, for while a man has dependants in a city, his family needed the money.'[33] The financial assistance to Cork was rarely seen elsewhere during the War of Independence (leading to some resentment of GHQ),[34] and it revealed the close connection between Cork and Dublin. The funding of the Brigade's intelligence department also illustrates the importance IRA GHQ placed on information gathering in Cork city.

'EFFICIENT ORGANISATION AND EXPLOITATION OF SOURCES OF INFORMATION'

The Cork No. 1 Brigade used a number of different methods to gather intelligence in Cork city in 1920–1. IRA personnel monitored letters and telegrams, tapped telephone lines, observed British police barracks and military posts, and followed known British intelligence operatives. Brigade intelligence officers relied on information coming from civilian employees of the Crown forces; sympathetic members of the police and military; employees in key businesses in the city, such as hotels and the railway; local Volunteers and Cumann na mBann members; and the thousands of IRA supporters in the city.

IRA MONITORING OF THE MAIL, TELEGRAPH, AND TELEPHONE

The Cork mail system was a centre of IRA intelligence-gathering. The communications hub for mail and telegraph messages throughout Munster, the Cork General Post Office proved vulnerable to IRA infiltration. A number of the city's early Republican leaders emerged from the Cork GPO, including city TD J.J. Walsh, Sinn Féin co-founder P.S. O'Hegarty, and Brigade O/C Seán O'Hegarty (brother of P.S.) In early 1916, Seán O'Hegarty recruited an entire IRB circle from GPO employees.[35] Florrie O'Donoghue eventually organized Republican postal workers into special sections that intercepted RIC mail and telegrams (as well as other suspicious messages), and forwarded them to IRA intelligence officers for deciphering (when necessary), analysis, and action.[36] When O'Donoghue established a fake identity for himself in mid-1920, he used IRA postal workers to stamp envelopes addressed to his fictitious name.[37] The work of IRA operatives in the Cork city GPO is underlined in a tribute to postal worker Ernie Sorenson upon his receipt of the War of Independence Service Medal. 'Seemingly you worked for one Government and was [sic] paid by another ... This applies to civil servants who synchronosingly utilized inner knowledge and information to advance the cause of the Republic.'[38]

British authorities recognized the IRA strength in Ireland's mail system. 'The postal services, it should be noted,' remarked a Dublin Castle spokesperson, 'are officials in the pay and service of the British Government, but they are not true to their employer.'[39] According to the British Army's Sixth Division, 'All methods of communication, except wireless telegraph, were more or less at the mercy of a population who were actively or passively hostile, and 99 per cent of the staff who dealt with telegrams and telephone calls were themselves ardent rebels.'[40] RIC Chief of Intelligence Sir Ormond Winter complained: 'The postal and telegraph systems were manifestly corrupt ... [and] led to the necessity of conducting all correspondence either by courier or aerial mail, which frequently caused delay and handicapped the transmission of intelligence.'[41]

In Cork, the IRA claimed to control local mail. Bob Aherne reported: 'From early 1919 onwards, raids on mails were of very frequent occurrence in our district, postmen being held up when delivering the mail. Letters addressed to military, police personnel, or known loyalists were examined and passed on to the Battalion Intelligence Officer. These raids often resulted in the obtaining of valuable information relating to the movements of enemy secret service agents who were then becoming very active in Cork.'[42] According to Florrie O'Donoghue: 'Mails were a potential source of information to both sides. Our raids upon them, which earlier had been somewhat indiscriminate, were now under complete control, and were made with a specific objective in view.'[43] However, the IRA was not above conducting massive postal raids late in the conflict, such as 24 April 1921, when Volunteers held up forty postmen across Cork city and confiscated their mailbags.[44]

Local citizens were aware of the IRA's postal monitoring. In a letter to an Irish newspaper, a Cork Unionist wrote of the IRA: 'They open and examine my letters, so this will be sent by hand to be posted in England.'[45] In a message to General Strickland, another Cork loyalist explained: 'I did not write my name or address lest my letter would be opened and I would be a marked man.'[46] On at least one occasion, British intelligence officers sent disinformation through the Cork Post Office, assuming its contents would be discovered and shared with the IRA. (The Donal 'Óg' O'Callaghan case, mentioned in the previous chapter.) The message was intercepted, though O'Donoghue did not fall for the trick.[47]

The IRA also tapped phone lines in Cork city. The tapping appeared to have started in late 1920 and continued throughout the conflict. Police reported the theft of equipment from the Telephone Exchange in the Cork GPO during the autumn of 1920, including the disappearance of a portable phone set in November.[48] City Volunteer Con Lane included in his list of IRA activities in 1920–1, '… tapping telephones, capturing instruments from P.O. [*Post Office*] officials …'[49] Michael Collins inquired about the telephone monitoring, asking O'Donoghue, 'how are you getting on with the tapping at night?'[50] The British Army's Sixth Division cautioned officers in its Seventeenth Brigade (headquartered in Cork city) about telephone calls, 'A careless conversation may lead to disastrous results.'[51] City Volunteer leader Connie Neenan recalled the identification of a civilian spy through a panicked phone call to the British Army's Sixth Division Intelligence officer Captain Kelly. Neenan claimed the phone operator duly noted the conversation and the parties involved, and gave the information to the IRA. The suspected informer (Seán O'Callaghan) was abducted and killed by the Volunteers.[52] According to O'Donoghue, the IRA operation included a 24-hour tapping station, which ensured coverage in the city.[53]

IRA INTELLIGENCE CONTACTS IN CORK CITY

Human intelligence sources varied in Cork city, but valuable contacts could be found among RIC and British Army personnel. Brigade

Vice-Commander Michael Leahy of Cobh received a message from a District Inspector following his arrest in the August City Hall raid. The police informer told Leahy: 'There's not an RIC man in East Cork who will give him away.' The District Inspector also warned Leahy of a local woman who was 'talking too much'.[54] In Cork city, three police officers stationed at Union Quay Barracks, Constables MacNamara, Kelly, and Sinnot, passed information to the IRA until their dismissal in October 1920.[55] (Kelly and MacNamara subsequently joined the Sinn Féin fundraising circuit in America.) Sympathetic RIC County Inspector's Clerk, William Costello proved an even more valuable IRA contact. Michael Collins put Costello in touch with Florrie O'Donoghue, and Costello provided him with key information from the city's police headquarters. (In early 1921, after Costello's promotion to Special Crimes Sergeant and transfer to county Kerry, O'Donoghue connected Costello with Kerry No. 1 Brigade intelligence officer Tim Kennedy.)[56] Another important IRA operative in the city was Pat Margetts, an Irish soldier serving in the Highland's Regiment, stationed in Victoria Barracks.[57] A Republican sympathizer, Margetts sent sensitive information to the Cork city IRA through its reliable operative Nora Wallace. Margetts also served as a communication conduit to captured Volunteers imprisoned in the Barracks. There were other helpful soldiers, such as the unnamed Army sentry who scouted for the IRA party trying to storm the Cork Gaol in March 1921.[58]

Republican moles within British Army ranks concerned Sixth Division commander General Strickland. In an order from June 1920, Strickland '... wanted to point out that we have a number of very undesirable characters in the Ranks who are in close touch with the Sinn Féin movement, and do not even refrain from selling arms, etc.'[59] In late 1920, Sixth Division Headquarters asked its commanders: 'Are there any Irishmen now serving in your command who you consider should be transferred outside Ireland in view of the present political situation?'[60] The British Army's General Headquarters Ireland later referred to applicants '... for the transfer of soldiers out of Ireland owing to such soldiers having tendencies for Sinn Féin'.[61]

Cork's Crown forces were even more vulnerable to leakage of information by its civilian employees. Sixth Division Headquarters warned, 'Servants, orderlies etc. overhear scraps of conversation and gossip…This information leaks out.'[62] In hindsight, the problem was clear to the Sixth Division.

One of the great difficulties which the army had to compete during all
this period was the necessity for employing a considerable amount of
local civilian labour for essential services, such as mechanical transport, clerical work, etc. However carefully these people were selected,
there were bound to be a certain number of cases of treachery.[63]

British concerns were justified in Cork city. For example, Cork
No. 1 Brigade Transportation Officer Jim Grey and two IRA
colleagues serviced British Army vehicles through their auto
mechanic garage, located just outside Victoria Barracks. In fact the
business was a front for IRA activities.[64] City First Battalion commander Dan Donovan told his nephew of various Republicans
working for the British, including General Strickland's maid, and
half a dozen Volunteers employed in Victoria Barracks as painters
and carpenters.[65] Concern over internal security extended to the top
of the British Military Government in Cork. After meeting with a
Cork loyalist who provided information, Strickland wrote about the
encounter in his diary, but upon reflection scratched out the
informer's name.[66] Apparently Strickland recognized that not even
his own diary was secure.

Clerks working at military bases offered the IRA the best access to
sensitive British information. IRA Volunteer Jack Kilty passed infor-
mation from Royal Navy Admiralty Headquarters at the
Haulbowline Naval Base.[67] Two more Victoria Barracks clerks
provided critical intelligence to the IRA. One operative was Con
Conroy, an IRA officer and Royal Navy veteran, employed as a clerk
in the Garrison Adjutant's office.[68] (City IRA leader Dan Healy places
Conroy in the position of 'confidential secretary to the O/C, 17th
Infantry Brigade'.)[69] According to IRA agent Josephine Brown
O'Donoghue (who will be discussed below), Conroy lasted only a
month before his identity was uncovered.[70] However, it would appear
that Conroy survived a few months, probably the entire autumn,
until he was forced to go on the run in January. (IRA documents
captured in the Bowles Farm raid in Clogheen gave away Conroy. A
few weeks later Conroy was captured at Rahinisky House, along
with Seán MacSwiney and other city Volunteers.) During his time at
Victoria Barracks, IRA sources credited Conroy with providing
information that enabled city Volunteers to ambush a British Army
lorry in Barrack Street in October 1920. He also gave the Brigade the
travel details of the three British Army officers killed at Waterfall in
November 1920. Conroy's arrest left the IRA with a single high-level

contact in Victoria Barracks. However, she proved to be one of the most important IRA intelligence sources of the entire conflict.

CODENAME 'G'

The story of Josephine McCoy Brown O'Donoghue is certainly dramatic.[71] Raised in Cork, the daughter of an RIC Head Constable, she trained as a clerk and typist before emigrating to Wales to work as a solicitor's secretary. There she married Coleridge Marchment (who changed his surname from Brown to Marchment after declaring bankruptcy). The couple produced two sons, Reggie and Gerald, and lived near Cardiff. After Coleridge was conscripted into the British Army, Josephine moved into the Cardiff home of her in-laws, the Brown family. Josephine was unhappy with the Browns, believing the family to be strongly anti-Catholic and domineering in their relationship with her oldest son Reggie. Seeking an escape in late 1916, she returned with her infant son Gerald to Cork city, and lodged with her sister at the McCoy home on Rockboro Terrace, Blackrock Road, Cork. (Her parents had both died by this time.) The Brown family convinced Josephine to leave Reggie with them in Cardiff while she established herself in Ireland.

A few months after arriving in Cork, Josephine asked the Browns to send Reggie to her, but they refused. The situation grew more complicated when her husband Coleridge was killed in the Passchendaele Offensive (Third Ypres) in late October 1917. Only then did she realize that the Browns had no intention of giving up young Reggie. Josephine eventually sued for custody of the child, but a London court awarded guardianship to the Brown family. The trial was decided after the judge ordered the five-year-old Reggie to take the stand, and the boy asked to remain with the Browns. Heartbroken, Josephine returned to Cork and her new position at Victoria Barracks.

Shortly after arriving in Cork, Josephine found a clerical position in Victoria Barracks. A few months later, Mrs Brown (as she was later called in newspapers) transferred to the Sixth Division typist pool, and was subsequently promoted forewoman over the staff of twenty-five clerks and typists. This proved to be a very sensitive position, placing her in control of written material produced by the Sixth Division headquarters staff. All unit reports, instructions from Dublin and London, and operational orders passed through her hands. She even took charge of the Division Sergeant-Major's office in his absence. The headquarters posting was key, since the Sixth Division controlled British Army units in counties Cork, Kerry, Limerick, Tipperary, and Waterford. After Martial Law was declared in December 1920, the region's military government was likewise administered from Victoria Barracks. The IRA could not have found a better- positioned civilian in all of Munster to assist them.

Sympathetic with the Sinn Féin independence campaign, Josephine first offered her services to the IRA during the summer of 1919, while she vacationed in Youghal, Co. Cork. Using a contact in the Youghal IRA, she passed a few messages to Republican prisoners in Victoria Barracks, but the Volunteers did not press her for further assistance. A couple of months later, after receiving an abusive letter from the Brown family (they frequently requested her financial assistance for their upkeep of Reggie), Josephine sought comfort in the Holy Trinity Church in Cork. She eventually told her story to a Capuchin priest at the church, who turned out to be the zealous Republican, Father Dominic O'Connor. Father Dominic, the brother of Brigade Quartermaster Joe O'Connor, also served as Cork No. 1 Brigade Chaplain. He quickly put Josephine in contact with Florrie O'Donoghue. After a single meeting, O'Dongohue recognized the importance of Josephine's sensitive position. She agreed to share privileged documents with O'Donoghue, and the two arranged information exchanges. With her identity known only to Florrie O'Donoghue, Brigade Commander Seán O'Hegarty, and Brigade Quartermaster Joe O'Connor, Mrs Brown took the code-name 'G' (the initial of her son Gerald) and became a prized IRA spy.

Josephine described her activities during two years of IRA service:

> Current documents, particularly those relating to the Intelligence section of the Division, were of course of primary value. When it was possible to bring out copies of them I did so. When it was not possible, I made shorthand notes to whatever extent time and opportunity permitted. Documents of which a number of copies were made as normal routine were less difficult to procure, and over the whole period I brought out hundreds of these. At other times it seemed to me that nothing less than the original document itself would be credible, and I had to take the risk of bringing it out and getting it back into file the next day. On other occasions material actually made up for the post was taken by me and subsequently put back in the post after it had been opened, read, and resealed by Florrie. As well as bringing out documents and notes, I was of course able to give him up to date

information about the composition and personnel of the different sections of the Division Staff, the location and strength of formations, transfers of officers, and many other matters.[72]

Mrs Brown's spying was partially motivated by her desire to regain custody of her son Reggie. She asked for assistance in the matter, and in late 1920 Florrie O'Donoghue collaborated with Michael Collins to abduct the child in Cardiff, Wales. In November, O'Donoghue travelled to England and used Collins' contacts with the IRA in Britain to arrange the kidnapping. On 2 December, O'Donoghue and Cork city Volunteer Jack Cody marched into the Brown house and took the child at gunpoint. Reggie was eventually smuggled to Cork and housed with Josephine's sister in Youghal. Though British officials suspected a leak in headquarters, they focused on the wrong employees, even throwing one of them in jail.[73] Mrs Brown successfully forwarded information to the IRA for the duration of the conflict. (O'Donoghue and Mrs Brown later fell in love and were secretly married in April 1921.)

Florrie O'Donoghue paid tribute to his wife's contributions in his Liam Lynch biography, *No Other Law*:

> Cork No. 1 Brigade had established a most valuable contact at British 6th Division Headquarters, a lady who has not been persuaded to abandon the anonymity of the pseudonym 'G' under which she operated. From this source came much material of value, not alone to the local brigade but to the whole Army, a fact to which Michael Collins paid frequent tribute. There was at all times, a regular and reasonably speedy exchange of information between the three Cork Brigades and between each of them and the Director of Intelligence. When necessary, on a particular matter, daily communication was maintained. There were cases in which communications issued by Major-General Strickland did not reach his Brigade Commanders more than a day before they were in the hands of the IRA Brigade Commanders opposing them. There was a case, in May 1921 in which a document issued from British 6th Division Headquarters, transmitted to the Cork No. 1 Brigade by their operator there, was circulated, in part, and with some observations, to the Brigade Commandants of the 1st Southern Division. A copy of the circular was captured by the British, again issued with their observations, and a new circular once more came into our hands, this whole series of incidents taking place within a week.[74]

O'Donoghue gave IRA historian Ernie O'Malley another example of Mrs Brown's effectiveness.

At the end of the Tan War,' wrote O'Malley, 'Florrie and a number of officers got out of town every night. They used to go separately to a small cottage so as not to draw attention to themselves. They were, however, observed. An ex-British officer noticed one or some of them, and he gave information. Florrie's wife, Strickland's secretary, saw this note but had no time. She tried to memorize it. Later, she got hold of the note and brought it out with her as evidence. The man was arrested, court-martialled and shot before nightfall. The document was returned the next day. That shook the daylights out of the British.[75]

The suspected informer here is probably Francis McMahon, who was abducted outside the Cork War Pensions Office in May. Major G.B. O'Connor is another possibility, though the timing of O'Connor's killing (the day of the Truce, when O'Donoghue was stationed on the Cork/Kerry border) makes McMahon the most likely victim.

Sensitive British military documents captured by the IRA testify to Mrs Brown's effectiveness. Michael Collins' correspondence with Florrie O'Donoghue indicates the high quality of information flowing from Cork.[76] In March 1921, Collins wrote: 'Thanks for the minutes of the Conference held by enemy on the 15th.' On 5 April he offered, 'many thanks for the copy of [*Captain*] Kelly's letter. As you say, it is a pity we cannot publish the thing complete.' Two weeks later, Collins scribbled: 'Thanks for the note regarding Strickland's recommendation.' O'Donoghue's collection of captured documents includes a list of the Sixth Division chain of command; its troop displacements and supply requirements; routine orders concerning troop movements; and at least one 'Sixth Division Weekly Intelligence Summary', which O'Donoghue reprinted in *No Other Law*.[77] The variety of sensitive documents in the IRA's possession illustrates the effectiveness of its intelligence operations. O'Donoghue recalled: 'There was a definite leakage of information. The British kept trying to close the gaps but they stayed open for us.'[78]

It seems likely that Mrs Brown passed on information about civilian informers in Cork. IRA intelligence officer Bob Aherne alluded to her later, when explaining his detection of local informers in the city. 'As a result of information contained in letters captured by us in raids on postmen delivering the mail, or from constant observations on barracks, *or from an IRA contact employed as confidential secretary to a high military officer in Victoria (now Collins) Barracks, Cork*, the identity of these suspected spies was established and the facts reported to the brigade which directed the action to be taken.'[79] [italics mine.]

A final aspect of the Josephine Brown case concerns the inability of the British military to detect her espionage. Victoria Barracks personnel were aware of Mrs Brown's custody battle, as she had received compassionate leave to attend the trial in 1918. Reggie's abduction was covered extensively in Cork newspapers, and Josephine reported the matter to General Strickland after her 'notification'. Newspaper reports clearly identified the kidnappers as armed Irishmen. Despite the Volunteers' attempts to cover their tracks, Mrs Brown was the obvious suspect in the case and Scotland Yard detectives subsequently investigated her in Cork. It is difficult to understand how British intelligence officers neglected to connect the Reggie Brown abduction to the IRA. Their failure is even more remarkable once it became clear that there was a security leak in Victoria Barracks. The only explanation is that the officers could not fathom a betrayal by a competent young woman from a strongly loyal background. The episode is yet another example of the poor performance by British Army intelligence specialists in Cork.

Josephine Brown's position must be taken into account when considering IRA intelligence efforts in Cork city. Through her the IRA breached the Sixth Division Headquarters security at its highest level. The Volunteers had access to the most sensitive British Army documents, including those relating to military intelligence. We can assume that any reports naming or even concerning specific civilian informers would have been shared with the IRA. She could also identify British Army personnel working on intelligence (adding suspicion to the military officers killed at Waterfall), as well as any civilians indiscreet enough to enter Victoria Barracks to offer information. Her presence gave the IRA the capability to root out civilian informers operating in the city.

'A PARAMOUNT AND PERSONAL DUTY TO PASS ON EVERY ITEM OF
ENEMY INFORMATION'

O'Donoghue believed the most important factor in the success of IRA intelligence was the observation of suspicious British activities by local Republicans. Through the effective organization of the city Volunteers, information was quickly funnelled to IRA intelligence officers for analysis. The operation relied on the active assistance of grassroots IRA Volunteers, other local Republicans, and an extensive network of sympathizers in the Cork population.

Throughout 1920, O'Donoghue organized the Cork city IRA forces into a coherent intelligence structure. In late 1920, the Brigade ordered the two city Battalions to appoint a special lieutenant in charge of intelligence.[80] Company intelligence officers were likewise selected for service in the city. The Brigade commanded: 'All Company Captains in your area will appoint four men (more if the area requires it) to act under the Battalion Lieutenant for Intelligence.' A total of sixteen companies comprised the two city Battalions, and those accounted for every one of the city's neighbourhoods. No part of the city escaped potential IRA observation. If the city battalions did indeed assign four intelligence officers per company, that would mean sixty-four Volunteers assumed observation duties at the company level. By adding the two city battalion intelligence officers, and the six-man Brigade Intelligence Squad, the total number of city Volunteers working on intelligence grows to seventy-two. By contrast, the combined strength of British Army military intelligence staffs operating at Victoria Barracks appears to have numbered twelve, with only three officers focused solely on the city.[81] This disparity shows the heavy emphasis the IRA placed on information gathering in Cork.

The structure, methods, and concepts of the IRA's intelligence network in Cork can be found in an extraordinary Brigade order lodged in O'Donoghue's papers. Although the document is long and detailed, it indicates the thoroughness and efficiency urged by the Brigade Intelligence Officer.

> November 22, 1920
> Cork No. 1 Brigade Headquarters
> To all Battalion O/Cs:
> It is beyond question that the Intelligence Service is of supreme importance, and it is the duty of every Volunteer Commander to see that the lead which we secured in this matter against the enemy is properly maintained. The objectives of the Intelligence Service are:
> 1. To discover the intention of the enemy. In the present conflict this intention is political as well as military.
> 2. To keep in touch with, observe, and report at once the movements of enemy agents seeking information:
>   a. In your own area.
>   b. In moving from or to your area.
> 3. To keep under constant observation all enemy bases. It must not be

possible for any enemy party to move out from their base without the knowledge of our local intelligence branch.

No. 1 is the concern of every Volunteer and even of every citizen. Conversations of every representative in clubs, in their homes, their movements, etc. will indicate enemy intention and will be reported to the immediate superior officer ...

No. 2 is of more direct important consequence of the individual Volunteer. In this respect every Volunteer must always be on the alert. Every stranger in a locality must be kept under observation and his movements carefully noted. Every suspicious individual must immediately be reported to the officer in charge of the area, and if necessary held in custody until instructions have been obtained. Look out for English accents. The index number on motor cars should be noted and compared with lists taken by adjoining districts. In this regard the numbers of motor cars of Division Commissioners, County Inspectors, District Inspectors, and Officers commanding troops, should be known to all Volunteers, who will consequently be able to recognize those vehicles directly when they are seen. A Crossley tender conveying a murder gang passes your road, later on you hear of some Irish citizen being brutally murdered. If you have taken the number of that tender you may be able to deal with it the next time you see it. Get photos of local enemy forces ...

Post Offices:

Special attention must be paid to these. The staff of each office or suboffice in your area should be carefully viewed, and those willing to assist in the Intelligence Department carefully selected and kept in constant touch with. Even the smallest office must not be overlooked, as there are scraps of information about the enemy to be picked up even in these, and it is in the assemblage of these scraps that results will be obtained. This Branch of Service must be worked with ceaseless energy, care, and discretion.

A reliable person in each PO should constantly be on the lookout for letters addressed to firms in England or Dublin – that is any address or firm with which people do not generally deal ...

Telephone and telegram messages ... All messages sent by enemy police, soldiers, or agents, should be copied and recorded...

The register number of every motor car and lorry in your area should be noted and a record kept.

... The names and ranks of all officers (enemy) in your area should be known to you, as well as their residences, personal appearance, and general habits. Changes in personnel of enemy organizations should be notified to Brigade Director of Information, and names of successors forwarded.

If the Intelligence Service is to be of benefit to you and to the entire organization, no detail can be neglected, nothing which observation can command must be unknown to you. Until you have collected all possible information about the enemy, you will not be able to deal with him effectively, or give proper protection to our own people.

As from Friday, December 10, monthly Battalion reports to be forwarded. This circular should then be destroyed.

Brigade Information Officer[82]

Considering the emphasis on personal observation, one must take into account the sheer number of Volunteers available for surveillance in the city. Cork city IRA forces totalled around 2000 Volunteers in 1921.[83] (The Cork No. 1 Brigade boasted a total roll of 7400 Volunteers, which made it the largest in Ireland.)[84] In 1920–1, Cork was a relatively small city of about 77,000 people.[85] That means that one in every thirty-five Cork citizens was a Volunteer. Such a ratio indicates that the IRA enjoyed sufficient manpower to keep the city under observation.

The composition of the IRA in Cork extended its reach throughout the city. With a membership drawn primarily from Cork's lower and middle classes, Volunteers could be found in shops, factories, hotels, banks, schools, and commercial offices.[86] No facet of Cork's civic life escaped connection to the Volunteer network. Bob Aherne of the Brigade Intelligence staff described his initial efforts as 'D' Company intelligence officer. 'Certain men employed in public houses, hotels, railways, on the docks, and in business houses, were nominated by me to report anything, no matter how trivial it might appear, which related to enemy activity or personnel.'[87] City commander Dan Donovan remembered '... terrific scouting on the streets of Cork. Unarmed men ready to work'.[88] One low-ranking Volunteer recalled: 'The great majority of us rank and filers were given such undemanding if essential jobs as the gathering of more or less useless information.'[89] Bob Aherne did not believe this information was useless, and emphasised the critical role played by these ordinary city Volunteers.

> I would, however, like to pay a tribute to the many unknown non-ranking IRA men who, through their vigilance and their unselfish devotion to duty of a monotonous but highly important, and often dangerous, nature, made possible the excellent intelligence service which was a feature of the Cork No. 1 Brigade in the fight for freedom.[90]

Added to the various IRA Volunteers working throughout the city were the Fianna boy scouts, and ten local branches of Cumann na mBan, led by the formidable Mary MacSwiney (sister of Brigade commander Terence).[91] The national leadership of each organization sought to utilize its members in Volunteer intelligence gathering efforts. By late 1920, the Cumann was reorganized to partner with existing IRA companies, in order to better provide assistance in such areas as intelligence.[92] The information gathering of Republican women and boys, though largely undocumented, must have significantly contributed to the IRA campaign. An anonymous Cork loyalist complained of the local situation in January 1921. 'The Sinn Féin boy and girl scouts are everywhere, watching the people and listening to them when they happen to converse in the streets.'[93]

Besides observing the homes of Crown forces, the IRA focused on city locations frequented by British personnel. O'Donoghue wrote: 'It became evident that certain places were of special importance because of the facilities they offered to the enemy. Hotels and clubs were obvious examples. The project to establish valuable contacts in each of these places had made considerable progress by mid 1920.'[94] IRA veteran Connie Neenan boasted: 'We had staff in every hotel. You could not enter Cork at the time without us knowing all the details about you.'[95] One such contact was Edward Fitzgerald, a waiter in the Cork Conservative Club, the bastion of Unionism in Cork city.[96] First Battalion intelligence officer Seán Culhane recalled: 'General Strickland and his staff went there. If a new officer showed his nose in there, Fitz, if he was of high rank, would let me know at once and he passed on conversations which led us to avoid trouble.'[97] Fitzgerald figured prominently in the assassination of RIC Divisional Commissioner Smyth in July 1920 (the commander of the RIC in Munster). The waiter notified the IRA of Smyth's presence in the club, admitted Volunteer gunmen through a side door, and pointed out Smyth in the smoking room.[98]

The Cork Rail Station served as another centre of Volunteer intelligence efforts.[99] The Volunteers monitored British Army train traffic and incoming passengers, and frequently destroyed military stores in the Cork rail yard. Bob Aherne recalled, 'In this we were helped by railway employees, porters, shunters, engine drivers and others, many of whom were themselves members of the IRA, or, if not actually members, were sympathetic.'[100] The presence of IRA contacts in the railway system was considered essential for local operations. When Florrie O'Donoghue became aware of the replacement of Volunteer staff at the Cork station in July 1921, he appealed to IRA Chief of Staff Richard Mulcahy for assistance.

Herewith is a copy of a report regarding employment of ex-soldiers on the Great Southern and Western Railway received from IO Cork No. 1. Apart from the glaring injustices of the Company's actions, you will readily understand the importance of our having reliable men in the goods stores, especially at Cork. The number of men there is very much reduced of late to arrests, dismissals, etc., and it seems essential that some action be taken against the Company.[101]

City Volunteers also closely scrutinized the movements of the British Army intelligence staff in the city. Dan Donovan recalled: 'we were watching their intelligence officers.'[1,2] Some of the IRA attention had deadly intentions. Connie Neenan reported the unsuccessful operation by two Cork city Volunteers to shoot British intelligence officer Lt Hammond at his home outside London.[103] Pa Murray recorded multiple failed attempts to assassinate Sixth Division intelligence commander Captain Kelly.[104] Bob Aherne recalled that Kelly remained a top target for the city's intelligence squad. 'One of the most important jobs assigned to me was to get some information as to the whereabouts of a British officer, Captain Kelly ... We had a photo of Kelly ... I watched for him outside the barracks, inside public houses, hotels, and everywhere I though he might be seen. This went on for months.'[105] In a similar fashion, IRA officer Bob Langford tracked a group of four intelligence officers, including the elusive Lt Keogh, to a Cork Opera box. However, the July Truce announcement upset the IRA's intended assassination of the officers.[106]

Surviving Brigade documents provide glimpses of the IRA's efforts in the city. A report details Captain Kelly's background and family antecedents.[107] A Union Barracks motor pool roster lists drivers, car registration numbers, and the distinguishing characteristics of vehicles.[108] A notebook provides manpower strengths in RIC barracks across the city.[109] A roll states the names and addresses of thirty British Army brigade and division staff officers (including two Brigadier Generals) living outside Victoria Barracks.[110] Names and ranks of military intelligence staff officers in the city are likewise listed.[111]

An English journalist visiting Cork in May 1921 provides an outsider's view of the IRA's covert intelligence war:

Cork City is – or until lately was – full of spies, and one speedily found that to be a stray Englishman bent upon an apparently aimless mission was to be almost invariably mistaken for a Government agent. Nor is it an overpleasant sensation to find yourself watched at times through the lace curtains of the hotel windows or to realize that walking up a crowded street, you are being followed by a hungry-looking individual in brown. The most undesirable place to visit in such circumstance is the Victoria Barracks, and for prudence sake one is apt to return to one's hotel by a circuitous route. Sinn Féin intelligence is exceedingly keen, and it soon dawns upon one that most plain-clothes visitors to the barracks are objects of peculiar interest to the various groups of young men who lounge at street corners in that vicinity.[112]

Florrie O'Donoghue gave a frightening example of the IRA's vigilance during a lecture he gave to Irish Army officers during the Emergency.[113] O'Donoghue described his discreet visits to the confidential RIC informant William Costello (mentioned above). The careful policeman would deal only with O'Donoghue, and only in Costello's Cork home. Whenever Costello had new information, O'Donoghue dutifully slipped into Costello's house after Curfew. Within a few weeks of O'Donoghue's first visit, an IRA company officer asked O'Donoghue for permission to shoot a civilian spy secretly meeting with a police officer. O'Donoghue checked the constable's address and discovered that it was Costello's home and he himself was the subject of the pending execution. Local Volunteers had carefully watched Costello for over a year, and they quickly detected O'Donoghue's nocturnal visits. Fortunately for O'Donoghue, the Volunteers followed Brigade protocol and did not attempt any unilateral action.

CIVILIAN SUPPORT OF THE IRA IN CORK

An essential component of IRA intelligence was the active support of the citizens of Cork city. Unfortunately, civilian assistance is extremely difficult to quantify or document. It remains a critical issue: How many city residents supported the IRA during the War of Independence? No observer will ever be able to precisely determine the extent of cooperation between the IRA and Cork's population. IRA veterans did testify to the aid they received locally.

Florrie O'Dongohue later wrote: 'One thing they [the British] lacked which the IRA had in generous measure – the co-operation of the people – and without it they were blind and impotent.'[114] Dan Donovan recalled: 'Cork city was very Republican.'[115] The city indeed was among the most generous districts in Ireland in terms of subscriptions to the Dáil National Loan in 1920,[116] and unlike the rest of Ireland, Dáil Court attendance in Cork did not decline in 1921.[117] Returns from the 1918 General Election show strong Republican support in the city.

Table Six: Cork City 1918 General Election

Candidate	Party	Votes
Walsh	Sinn Féin	20,801
De Róiste	Sinn Féin	20,506
Talbot-Crosbie	Nationalist	7,480
Sullivan	Nationalist	7,162
Williams	Unionist	2,519
Farrington	Unionist	2,254

Source: Cork Constitution, 16/12/18
NOTE: Returns are for two parliamentary seats.

Family and friendship networks among Cork's 2,000 Volunteers should also be considered. For every Volunteer in Cork, there was a parent, sibling, or close friend willing to protect them. Such connections cannot be underestimated. For a significant portion of Cork's population, the Anglo-Irish fight in Cork was a personal affair. Cork city's exasperated RIC County Inspector reported of the IRA in March 1921: 'They can find food and comfort in any one of hundreds of houses, the occupiers of which will do everything in their power to shelter them from police.'[118]

Traumatic civic events in 1920 likely increased Republican support. The assassination of Lord Mayor Tomás MacCurtain raised condemnations from across Cork's political and social spectrum.[119] His funeral attracted over 100,000 mourners, a figure surpassing the city's total population.[120] Hunger strikes by Terence MacSwiney in London and local IRA members in Cork Gaol (which resulted in the death of city Volunteer Joseph Murphy) likewise generated large protests in the city. Appeals for clemency for the IRA prisoners came from such diverse bodies as nine former Lord Mayors of Cork, veterans of the Irish Guards Regiment in Cork, and 200 RIC pensioners living in Munster.[121] An estimated 100,000 Cork citizens watched Lord Mayor Terence MacSwiney's funeral procession.

The burning of Cork city centre (including the destruction of the City Hall and Carnegie Library) could only have fuelled resentment of the Crown forces' military occupation. Trigger-happy British soldiers likewise added to the anger. At least seventeen Cork civilians unaffiliated with the IRA were killed by British gunfire in 1920–1, typically by curfew patrols.[122] Raids on local households were also rampant during this period. The *Irish Bulletin* reported seventy raids in Cork city on a single day in November 1920.[123] Random shootings, executions of IRA prisoners, and arson attacks on local businesses by Crown forces contributed to a volatile situation. Bitterness towards the British is evident even in one of the IRA's most vocal opponents, Catholic Bishop Daniel Cohalan. After Auxiliary Cadets killed a Catholic priest in West Cork, Cohalan received a condolence message from the RIC Inspector-General. Cohalan responded: 'I should accept the sympathy from the Inspector-General of the old RIC. The verbal sympathy of the Inspector-General whose men are murdering my people and have burned my city I cannot accept or convey to the relatives of the murdered Canon Magner.'[124]

The British recognized Cork's pro-Republican population. Colonel French of the Hampshire Regiment (stationed in the city) told an Army conference: 'five sixths of the population is either actively or passively opposed to us.'[125] The Sixth Division Official History referred to the 'evil population of Cork',[126] and 'a population who were actively or passively hostile'.[127] The Irish Command later remarked of Cork city: 'The inhabitants are mainly of the lower orders and were on the whole bitterly opposed to the Crown forces, the proportion of loyal persons being very small.'[128] Major Bernard Montgomery, stationed in Cork's Victoria Barracks during 1921–2, recalled, 'I believe I regarded all civilians as "Shinners"'.[129] Major Percival, who operated with the Essex Regiment in West Cork, later corrected a misimpression among fellow army officers. 'The rebel campaign in Ireland was a national movement backed by a large proportion of the population and was not conducted by a few hired assassins as was often supposed.'[130]

Indicative of local cooperation was a lack of arrests among the city's IRA leadership. Despite Cork's small size, prominent Brigade leaders moved about the town with ease until early 1921. Much of the local population would have recognized the Brigade Staff, since they marched as a uniformed contingent during Tomás MacCurtain's funeral procession in March 1920. Seán Culhane recalled: 'We used to walk the streets of the town, Seán Hegarty, Florrie O'Donoghue, Mick Murphy, etc.'[131] Dan Donovan (finally picked up in a random street search in Cork in May) escaped arrest for most of the conflict despite the fact: '...I was a good footballer and was known to half the population of Cork.'[132] Mick Murphy was a renowned hurler routinely seen by thousands of GAA spectators, yet he was not caught until June 1921. By the time of the Truce, Cork city still hosted a thirteen-person Brigade staff,[133] the six-man intelligence staff, and the twelve-man Active Service Unit. Their survival indicates that much of Cork's population willingly sheltered wanted men, or at least turned a blind eye to their underground activities. City Volunteer Eamonn Enright's memory seems accurate. 'The people were very good during the Tan War.'[134]

IRA operations continued throughout 1921, despite the presence of 2000 British troops in the city. The Volunteers used Wallace's Newspaper Shop on New Brunswick Street as Brigade headquarters from 1917 until the British Army closed it in May 1921.[135] Local munitions factories produced home-made bombs and ammunition until the Truce.[136] The Brigade intelligence office, disguised as a small trading firm in a commercial building, was never detected.[137] Arms finds declined after a January peak. As Tables Two and Three show, IRA activity remained high. By June 1921, IRA attacks had chased British patrols out of many of the city's neighbourhoods.[138] The Volunteers could only have sustained their guerrilla war through the active or tacit support of the local population.

The IRA intelligence network was respected by the Crown forces. The British Army's General Headquarters remarked of wider IRA efforts: 'their intelligence service is good.'[139] Major A.E. Percival (later Lt General), an intelligence officer stationed in West Cork, wrote: 'The IRA Intelligence Service was, of course, easy owing to the majority of the population being friendly, but nevertheless it reached a very high standard of efficiency, and every movement and often every intended movement, of the Crown Forces was known; information was passed about in an uncanny sort of way without any organisation being apparent on the surface.[140] Cork's Sixth Division Headquarters warned the Seventeenth Infantry Brigade (operating in the city), 'The rebel spy system is so organised that a person must never be asked to state the source of information, or name the person from whom it was obtained.'[141] Officers were cautioned: 'the rebel spy system is so well organised that a careless telephone conversation may lead to disastrous results.'[142] Soldiers were ordered to be on their guard, and 'officers must realize that rebel spies are everywhere'.[143] British General Headquarters warned: 'the slightest slackness is detected and leads to attack.'[144]

The British did score some successes against the city's IRA. They uncovered a series of arms dumps in early 1921, though they were unable to sustain their momentum in this key area. Empowered to detain suspects without trial, the Crown forces captured numerous IRA officers throughout 1921, which forced a reorganization of the city's Volunteer structure.[145] (Most actions were now carried out by the city Active Service Unit, supported by individual companies. The Brigade Headquarters had also relocated to the mountains near Ballyvourney, and an 'O/C City' was appointed to command all IRA forces in Cork.) British dragnets netted some of the city's senior IRA leaders, including Dan Donovan, Mick Murphy, and Tom Crofts. However, the IRA simply replaced these officers from its deep reservoir of Volunteers. Writing in June 1921 from his Ballyvourney hideout, Florrie O'Donoghue dismissed the capture of Volunteers, reporting: 'We have more men than we can possibly utilize.'[146] Major ambushes in Cork city in June 1921 showed the continued tenacity and unyielding strength of the IRA. By the time of the July Truce, the Crown forces still had not found a way to seriously hamper its Republican foes.

In the spring of 1921, Liam de Róiste gave a believable description of Cork's secret intelligence war.

> People talk much about spies and informers these days, as in so many cases it seems Crown forces have very definite information. But they must surely be credited with having a well-organized system of obtaining information now, and with having some intelligence. People also overlook the fact that the IRA have also displayed organization in obtaining information, sometimes of a surprising nature. I would assume as natural that it is easy enough in the circumstances of this conflict to obtain information on one side or another.[147]

SUMMARY

Under the leadership of Florrie O'Donoghue, the IRA in Cork city developed a sophisticated intelligence network. With assistance from IRA GHQ, O'Donoghue set up a permanent brigade intelligence staff, and received relevant information from Michael Collins' contacts throughout Ireland. Intelligence officers were appointed in the city's neighbourhoods, and ordinary Volunteers were ordered to gather information. O'Donoghue deployed special teams to monitor local mail, telegrams, and telephones. Sympathizers in the police and military, as well as IRA operatives working for the British as civilian employees, provided additional assistance. Josephine Brown gave O'Donoghue access to the most sensitive information flowing from Victoria Barracks. Throughout the city, thousands of Volunteers, Cumann members, Fianna boy scouts, and ordinary supporters observed British sympathizers and personnel. Key local institutions, such as hotels, ports, clubs, and train stations were likewise monitored. The Volunteers relied on a largely sympathetic civilian population for additional information. This advanced intelligence network enabled the IRA to survive the conflict intact in Cork.

The IRA proved adept at intelligence in Cork. The success of the Volunteer spy network must be considered when considering the detection and execution of civilian informers in the city.

NOTES

1 Biographical information can be found in O'Donoghue, *Florence and Josephine O'Donoghue's War of Independence*, pp. 8–42.
2 Nelligan, p. 68.
3 Barry, p. X–XI.
4 Barry, p. 158.
5 O'Donoghue, *No Other Law*, p. 224.
6 Ibid, p. 243.
7 O'Donoghue, *Florence and Josephine O'Donoghue's War of Independence*, p. 56.
8 Ibid.
9 Ibid, p. 68.
10 O'Donoghue, 'We Need Trained Guerrilla Fighters', *An Cosantóir*, p. 395, Vol. III, No. 5, May 1943. O'Donoghue edited the journal while serving as Intelligence Officer in the Irish Army's Southern Division during the Emergency period. Showing his continued military intelligence acumen, during this period O'Donoghue uncovered German and American spy networks in his command area.
11 *An tÓglach*, Vol. II, No. 5, 15 January 1920, CPM.
12 *An tÓglach*, Vol. II, No. 9, 15 April 1920, CPM.
13 Collins Memo, Ms. 31,202, NLI.
14 O'Donoghue in the O'Malley Notebooks, UCD. Some of the correspondence can be found in Ms. 31,192, NLI, and it indicates such a frequency of contact.
15 O'Donoghue, *Florence and Josephine O'Donoghue's War of Independence*, p. 68.
16 Collins to O'Donoghue, 25 August 1920, Ms. 31,192, NLI.
17 'Tomás MacCurtain Inquest Report', CO 904/47, PRO. Cahill's name likewise can be found repeatedly in the *Cork Constitution* and *Cork Examiner* newspaper coverage of the inquest.
18 O'Donoghue notes for an unpublished article on the assassination, Ms. 31,313.
19 O'Donoghue notes, Ms. 31,313; Seán Culhane in the O'Malley Notebooks,

UCD; Seán Culhane BMH Statement.
20 Collins to O'Donoghue, 11 October 1920, Ms. 31,192, NLI.
21 Collins to O'Donoghue, 20 July 1920, Ms. 31,192, NLI.
22 O'Donoghue in the O'Malley Notebooks.
23 Letter to London from Captain Carpenter, Ms. 31,223, NLI.
24 O'Donoghue Intelligence Lecture, Ms. 31,443, NLI
25 O'Donoghue, *Tomás MacCurtain*, p. 64.
26 Beaslai, pp. 392–5; O'Donoghue, *Tomás MacCurtain*, p. 164; O'Donoghue, *Florence and Josephine O'Donoghue's War of Independence*, pp. 68–9.
27 Robert Aherne BMH Statement; Intelligence Squad listed by O'Donoghue, Ms. 31,401; Collins to O'Donoghue, 8 March 1921, Ms. 31,192, NLI; O'Donoghue in the O'Malley Notebooks.
28 O'Donoghue in the O'Malley Notebooks.
29 O'Donoghue, *Florence and Josephine O'Donoghue's War of Independence*, p. 69.
30 Robert Aherne BMH Statement.
31 O'Donoghue, *Florence and Josephine O'Donoghue's War of Independence*, p. 69.
32 O'Donoghue in the O'Malley Notebooks; O'Donoghue, *Florence and Josephine O'Donoghue's War of Independence*, p. 69.
33 O'Donoghue in the O'Malley Notebooks.
34 O'Malley, p. 329.
35 Statement of Fred Murray in Moirin Chavesse, *Terence MacSwiney*, (Dublin: Clonmore and Reynolds, 1961), p. 199.
36 O'Donoghue Intelligence Lecture, Ms. 31,443, NLI.
37 O'Donoghue, *Florence and Josephine O'Donoghue's War of Independence*, p. 99.
38 C.C. O'Riordan's 1967 Tribute to Sorenson, L 1968:17, CPM.
39 Dublin Castle press release, 18 November 1920, British Government in Ireland Publicity Department, CO 904/168.
40 *History of the 6th Division in Ireland*, p. 49.
41 Hart, *British Intelligence in Ireland*, p. 75.
42 Robert Aherne BMH Statement.
43 O'Donoghue, *No Other Law*, p. 89.
44 *Cork Constitution*, 25 April 1921.
45 Letter to the *Church Times*, reprinted in the *Weekly Summary*, 11 February 1921.
46 Letter to General Strickland from 'An Anonymous Loyalist', 24 January 1921, Strickland Papers, IWM.
47 *History of the 6th Division in Ireland*, p. 49; Michael Collins to O'Donoghue, 14 April 1921, Ms. 31,192, NLI.
48 CI Report for Cork City and East Riding, December 1920, CO 904/113. Also, in late September armed men (presumably Volunteers) raided the Cork Post Office and took away telephone equipment. See the *Cork Constitution*, 29 September 1920.
49 Pension Statement of C. Lane, C Company, Second Battalion, Cork No. 1 Brigade, L 1991:152, CPM.
50 Collins to O'Donoghue, 19 March 1921, Ms. 31,192, NLI.
51 Order Number G/S 19/20/1, *Summary of Important Instructions to 17th Infantry Brigade from HQ 6th Division*, Strickland Papers, IWM.
52 Connie Neenan in the O'Malley Notebooks, UCD.
53 O'Donoghue Intelligence Lecture, Ms. 31,443, NLI.
54 Michael Leahy in the O'Malley Notebooks.

55   Gaughan, pp. 167–8. Michael Kelly and John MacNamara were RIC union organizers, and played a role in the 'Listowel Mutiny', which culminated in the assassination of District Commissioner Smyth in the Cork Conservative Club.
56   O'Donoghue Intelligence Lecture, Ms. 31,443; O'Donoghue in the O'Malley Notebooks; Dwyer, *Tans, Terror and Troubles,* p. 261.
57   Stan Barry in the O'Malley Notebooks, UCD; Pat Margetts in the O'Malley Notebooks.
58   Dan Donovan letter to Florrie O'Donoghue, 27 September 1958, Ms. 31,293, NLI.
59   Brigade Major to All Officers Commanding, 30 June 1920, A/0341, DDA. (That fear of weapons sales was grounded in reality. Florrie O'Donoghue recalled that in 1919. 'Odd weapons and small supplies of ammunition were coming in through the crews of trading vessels. Almost the only other source of supply was purchase from individual soldiers.' He proceeded to tell the story of three deserting Connaught Rangers, whose rifles he bought for £6, along with a pair of civilian outfits for each soldier. See O'Donoghue, *Florence and Josephine O'Donoghue's War of Independence,* p. 80. Pa Murray also recalled British soldiers from Cork being 'an easy mark for the purchase of arms', in 1917, until authorities banned them from bringing their weapons home while on leave. See Murray's BMH Statement.
60   Staff Captain 6th Division to All Officers Commanding, 9 November 1920, A/0341, DDA.
61   GHQ Ireland to OC 6th Division, 12 June 1920, Ibid.
62   GS 18/20/1, 'Summary of Important Instructions to the 17th Brigade'.
63   *History of the Sixth Division in Ireland,* p. 59.
64   O'Donoghue, *Florence and Josephine O'Donoghue's War of Independence,* pp. 77–9.
65   Donal Donovan Interview.
66   General Strickland Diary, 20 January 1921, Strickland Papers.
67   Seamus Fitzgerald, 'East Cork Activities – 1920', p. 364; Mick Leahy in the O'Malley Notebooks.
68   *Cork Constitution,* 27 January 1921, 24 February 1921; Daniel Healy BMH Statement; R. Langford Pension Statement, CAI; Mick Murphy in the O'Malley Notebooks; Mick Murphy BMH Statement.
69   Dan Healy BMH Statement.
70   O'Donoghue, *Florence and Josephine O'Donoghue's War of Independence,* p. 120.
71   For details see chapters six and seven in O'Donoghue, *Florence and Josephine O'Donoghue's War of Independence.*
72   O'Donoghue, *Florence and Josephine O'Donoghue's War of Independence,* p. 120.
73   Florence O'Donoghue in the O'Malley Notebooks; Josephine McCoy O'Donoghue in O'Donoghue, *Florence and Josephine O'Donoghue's War of Independence,* p. 120.
74   O'Donoghue, *No Other Law,* p. 111.
75   O'Donoghue in the O'Malley Notebooks, UCD. A similar story appears in *Rebel Cork's Fighting Story,* p. 24. It referred to a retired Army officer who gave Captain Kelly 'accurate information of the movements of the Brigade Staff to their billets outside the city. The message fell into the hands of the Brigade intelligence organization, and that night the writer of it was executed'.
76   The following correspondence from Collins to O'Donoghue can be found in Ms. 31,192, NLI.
77   Ms. 31,223, NLI; O'Donoghue, *No Other Law,* p. 171 and Appendix One.

Excerpts from other Sixth Division documents can be found in *An tÓglach*, Vol. 111, No. 1, 15 March 1921; Cork No. 2 Brigade Order, 2 February 1921, refers to 6th Division training procedures, Lankford Papers, UI69/24, CAI; and IRA GHQ Director of Training Memo #2 1921, quotes Strickland's January Training Report, Lankford Papers.

78 O'Donoghue in the O'Malley Notebooks.

79 Robert Aherne BMH Statement. Con Conroy could also have been the source.

80 Cork No. 1 Brigade Order, 23 December 1920, Ms. 31,202, NLI.

81 See Chapter Six for details.

82 Cork No. 1 Brigade Order, 22 December 1920, Ms. 31,202, NLI.

83 *Rebel Cork's Fighting Story*, p. 9; Dan Donovan in O'Malley Notebooks.

84 First Southern Division Strength Report for July 1921, Ms. 31,216, NLI; O'Donoghue, *No Other Law*, p. 155; O'Donoghue and Seán O'Hegarty letter to Papal Nuncio, Ms. 31,268.

85 The 1911 Census counts the population at 76,000, while the 1926 Census lists 77,000. See the 1911 and 1926 Census of Population, Cork City Library.

86 Peter Hart, 'Class Community, and the Irish Republican Army in Cork, 1917–1923', in O'Flanagan and Buttimer.

87 Robert Aherne BMH Statement.

88 Dan Donovan in the O'Malley Notebooks.

89 Seán O'Faolain, *Vive Moi* (London: Rubert Hart Davis, 1965), p. 137. Two of Cork's noted authors from the post-revolutionary period, Seán O'Faolain and Frank O'Connor, both served with the city IRA during the Anglo-Irish War. Neither were officers or on 'fulltime active service', yet their experiences were typical of ordinary Volunteers. O'Faolain, being three years O'Connor's senior, appeared to have been the more active of the two. In a conversation with Ernie O'Malley, Volunteer Seán Daly remembered O'Faolain as 'a bit of a dreamer.'

90 Robert Aherne BMH Statement.

91 Lil Conlon *Cumann na mBan and the Women of Ireland*, (Kilkenny: Kilkenny Press, 1969).

92 At its Annual Convention in October 1920, the Cumann na mBann passed a resolution ordering, 'That Cumann include detective work and the acquiring of information about the enemy among its activities.' In February 1921, Fianna Eireann leaders remarked, 'Intelligence work must be included in the programme of training.' These document excerpts are found in the Foulkes Papers, 7/24, Harte Center for Military Archvies.

93 Anonymous loyalist letter to General Strickland, 10 February 1921, Strickland Papers, IWM.

94 O'Donoghue 1964 draft and notes for a proposed article on the assassination of Divisional Commissioner Smyth, Ms. 31,312, NLI.

95 MacEoin, p. 240.

96 Seán Culhane in the O'Malley Notebooks; Seán Culhane BMH Statement; Dan Healy BMH Statement; and O'Donoghue in the O'Malley Notebooks.

97 Seán Culhane in the O'Malley Notebooks.

98 Seán Culhane in the O'Malley Notebooks; Culhane's BMH Statement; Pa Murray's BMH Statement.

99 Volunteers Seán Healy and Charlie Daly (who was killed by British soldiers in the Blackpool Railway Tunnel) both worked at the station. Seán Culhane recalled that he tracked District Inspector Swanzy to Lisburn through an examination of his bags being mailed to his new location, made possible by a Volunteer staffing the station luggage department. See his BMH Statement.

100 Robert Aherne BMH Statement.

101 From IO First Southern Division to CS GHQ, 2 July 1921, Mulcahy Papers,

P/17A/20, UCD.

102 Dan Donovan in the O'Malley Notebooks.

103 Connie Neenan in the O'Malley Notebooks. I have not found another record of this attempt, though there is evidence of multiple visits to London by Cork Volunteers in 1920 and 1921.

104 Pa Murray BMH Statement; Pa Murray in the O'Malley Notebooks. Ernie O'Malley visited with Cork No. 1 Brigade officers in 1921, and reported: 'Kelly, one of their intelligence officers was badly wanted by the Cork men.' See O'Malley, p. 308.

105 Robert Aherne BMH Statement. Biographical details about Captain Kelly can be found in Florrie O'Donoghue's papers, Ms. 31,192.

106 Langford Pension Statement, CAI.

107 Dated 10 February 1921, Ms. 31,192, NLI. The Brigade also distributed photos of Captain Kelly. See the BMH Statements of Robert Aherne and Pa Murray.

108 Found in S. Lankford Papers, CAI.

109 Ms. 31,183, NLI.

110 Ms. 31,227, NLI. Again, this list shows that the IRA did not randomly kill British personnel or civilian supporters in Cork city. If it meant to terrorize the population, these officers would be an excellent starting point. As the Brigade Intelligence circular points out, British officers lived openly throughout Cork.

111 Listed as such separate from the above list, Ms. 31, 227, NLI.

112 *Cork County Eagle and Advertiser*, 21 May 1921.

113 O'Donoghue Military Intelligence Lecture, Ms. 31,443. Costello is not named in the lecture, but was identified by O'Donoghue in a conversation with Ernie O'Malley. See O'Donoghue in the O'Malley notebooks.

114 O'Donoghue, *No Other Law*, p. 49.

115 Dan Donovan in the O'Malley Notebooks.

116 Joost Augusteijn, *From Public Defiance to Guerrilla Warfare* (Dublin: Irish Academic Press, 1996), p. 64.

117 Ibid., p. 237.

118 CI Report for Cork City and East Riding, March 1921, CO 904/114.

119 Condolence and condemnation resolutions were passed by the following local bodies: Ancient Order of Hibernians, Cork Branch; Cork City and County Unionist Association; Cork Athletic Grounds; Cork Branch of Irish Commercial Travellers; Cork Chamber of Commerce; Cork District Trades and Labour Council; Cork Federation of Discharged and Demobilized Soldiers and Sailors; Cork Harbour Commission; Cork Hebrew Organization; Cork Medical Association; Cork Municipal Officers and Staff; Cork Pig Buyers; Cork Post Office Clerks; Cork School of Commerce; Cork Zionist Association; Munster GAA; Parnell Guards Fife and Drum Band; and University College Cork Students. See the *Cork Examiner*, 22–24 March 1920.

120 For local reactions to the killing and reports of MacCurtain's funeral, see the *Cork Constitution* and the *Cork Examiner* for the week of 20–27 March 1920.

121 For the former mayors, see the *Cork Constitution*, 15 September 1920; the ex-Guardsmen in the *Cork Constitution*, 23 September 1920; and the RIC pensioners in the *Cork Constitution*, 13 September 1920.

122 James Burke (*Cork Weekly News*, 18 July 1920); William McGrath (*Cork Weekly News*, 18 July 1920); James Coleman (*Cork Examiner*, 18 November 1920); Carl Johansen (*Cork Examiner*, 3 December 1920); Finbarr Darcy (*Cork Constitution*, 6 January 1921); Gerald Prigg (*Cork Constitution*, 17 January 1921); Patrick O'Sullivan (*Cork Constitution*, 6 February 1921);

Michael Murray (*Cork Constitution,* 6 March 1921); James Mullane (*Cork Constitution,* 21 March 1921); John Healy (*Cork Weekly News,* 29 March 1921); Patrick Sheehan (*Cork Examiner,* 16 May 1921); Father James O'Callaghan (*Cork Examiner,* 16 May 1921); Patrick Keating (*Cork Examiner,* 23 May 1921); Thomas O'Keefe (*Cork Constitution,* 5 June 1921); Seán Lucey (*Cork Examiner,* 13 June 1921); Michael Leahy (*Cork Examiner,* 20 June 1921); and William Horgan (*Cork Constitution,* 29 June 1921). There are likely more on this list. Many other civilians were wounded during the same period. No members of the police or military were charged or convicted for any of these killings.

123 The raids took place on 22 November 1920. See the *Irish Bulletin,* 27 November 1920.

124 *Irish Times,* 17 December 1920.

125 Army conference lecture summary, 7/16, Foulkes Papers, Harte Center for Military Archives.

126 *History of the 6th Division in Ireland,* p. 45.

127 Ibid, p. 49.

128 Hart, *British Intelligence in Ireland, 1920–1921,* p. 39.

129 Sheehan, p. 151.

130 Percival military lecture, in Sheehan, p. 100.

131 Seán Culhane in the O'Malley Notebooks.

132 Dan Donovan in the O'Malley Notebooks. Donovan and Culhane were arrested in a British sweep, after the military cordoned off an entire Cork neighbourhood and arrested any non-residents found in a house. Neither was identified while in prison. See Culhane's BMH Statement.

133 Ms. 31,401, NLI.

134 Eamonn Enright in the O'Malley Notebooks.

135 O'Donoghue *Tomás MacCurtain,* p. 149; Mick Murphy BLM Statement; *Cork Constitution,* 18 May 1921.

136 Locations listed in the Brigade Casualty Rolls, CPM; O'Donoghue *No Other Law,* p. 165; *Rebel Cork's Fighting Story,* p. 24.

137 O'Donoghue, *Florence and Josephine O'Donoghue's War of Independence,* pp. 99–100; Pa Murray BMH Statement.

138 Pa Murray BMH Statement.

139 *Sinn Féin and the Irish Volunteers,* booklet by Staff, General Headquarters Ireland, Strickland Papers, IWM.

140 From Percival's lecture on guerilla warfare, provided in Sheehan, p. 93. During the Second World War, Percival gained infamy in Singapore after he surrendered his 80,000 troops to a numerically inferior Japanese force, in the worst British military defeat in its history. During his Irish service, West Cork Republicans (most notably Tom Barry), accused Percival and his Essex Regiment troops of brutality. Though a flawed officer, Percival grasped guerrilla warfare better than his colleagues, and championed the innovative tactic of sending small, mobile British columns into the country for weeks at a time. IRA leader Seán Moylan believed that had Percival's idea been adapted throughout the country, it 'would in a month have made it impossible for the IRA to exist as it did'.

141 *Summary of Important Instructions to the 17th Infantry Brigade from HQ 6th Division,* GS 12/106, Strickland Papers, IWM.

142 Ibid., Order dated 30 June 1921, IWM.

143 Ibid.

144 *Sinn Féin and the Irish Volunteers,* IWM

145 See Pa Murray in the O'Malley Notebooks; Pa Murray's BMH Statement;

Daniel Healy's BMH Statement; and Bob Aherne's BMH Statement.
146 O'Donoghue Letter, 16 June 1921, Ms. 31,176, NLI.
147 De Róiste Diary, 11 April 1921.

CHAPTER EIGHT

A Theory

Any analysis of the IRA's executions of Cork civilians in November 1920 and February 1921 depends on the recollections of IRA veterans. Their evidence provides a critical context to these shootings, especially in regards to the supposed members of the Anti-Sinn Féin Society.

IRA TESTIMONY

Ernie O'Malley gathered most of the relevant Cork city IRA statements about thirty years after events there. A senior IRA leader from 1919–23, O'Malley held arguably the finest fighting record in the Volunteer movement, which gave him tremendous prestige in IRA circles. O'Malley's Cork subjects displayed remarkable candour during their interviews, offering blood-chilling anecdotes that frequently contradicted the 'official' Republican version of the war, then in vogue. In the O'Malley Notebooks, one does not always find chivalrous freedom fighters engaged in a clean war. We also hear of young men making mistakes, killing in cold blood, and living a nightmarish existence. The veterans' testimonies give every indication of honesty. At least eight of them, including some of the IRA's senior leaders in Cork, describe a pro-British civilian intelligence network in the city.[1] There is little reason to believe these former Volunteers would have deliberately told O'Malley such consistent fabrications. Either a pro-British civilian spy group operated in Cork, or else the IRA veterans were utterly ignorant about the true situation in the city during 1920–1.

Connie Neenan gave O'Malley conflicting evidence concerning the shooting of suspected civilian informers. As we saw in Chapter Three, Neenan was locked in a British prison for most of the period surrounding these killings. However, he returned to Cork at the end of February 1921 and succeeded Mick Murphy as commander of the city's Second Battalion, the area where many of the IRA assassinations occurred. He told O'Malley:

> The Anti-Sinn Féin Society was mostly composed of Protestants who were running businesses in the City. Beale was the first to be caught. Pat Collins, a brother-in-law of mine, Jerry Keating, and Jack Hogan caught Beale off Abbey Street at 3 o'clock at night, but their guns wouldn't go off ... They tracked Beale for half a mile. They searched Beale, finding a list of the Anti-Sinn Féin group on him, and a cheque for £1000. They killed Beale and left him on the outskirts ... There was a father and son on the list, Blemens in Blackrock who worked at Woodford Bourne. Then there was a manager for Thompson the Baker, Reilly, and others, but one escaped, Tilson, who was one of the owners of Bade Co. He cut his throat on the way to London. They were linked as well. The Blemens had a good pair of shoes on them and the lads took the shoes off them ... We did not know the British had organised the youngsters in the Y.M.C.A. to track our men. They were mostly from good families. It was then, only five months after the murder of Tomás MacCurtain that we learned that a kid of 15 tracked him home that night, but the kids confessed their tracking and they were killed. We thought that stopped their Y.M.C.A. organisation. Tom Downing, a Catholic who lived in our parish, who worked as a clerk in the post office, disappeared one night, September 1920. He had something to do with the Anti-Sinn Féin group. O'Callaghan who was in our parish phoned Captain Kelly, and Kelly replied: 'You damned fool. Come by and see me.' He was sending information into the Victoria Barracks. A girl in the telephone exchange told us and Callaghan was shot that day.[2]

There are many glaring mistakes in Neenan's testimony. Beale was not the first member of this supposed group shot. James Blemens, Frederick Blemens, and Alfred Reilly all preceded Charles Beale. James Blemens lived on Blackrock Road, rather than the city suburb of Blackrock. He did not work for Woodford Bourne, but was a horticulture and bee-keeping instructor. Charles Beale, rather than Blemens, worked for Woodford Bourne. Tom Downing was not killed until December 1920, three months after September. However, despite all his errors, Neenan provides a number of accurate details about the November and February shootings. He recalls: 'A manager of Woodford Bourne ... a manager of Thompson the Baker, Reilly ... Tilson ... he cut his throat on a train to London ... a kid of fifteen ...' Neenan seems to be repeating a story he heard earlier, but has confused some of its characters.

'THE MOST OPEN-SPOKEN YOUNG FELLOW'

Despite Connie Neenan's muddled identifications, a vague but coherent chronology explains the IRA's discovery of a pro-British intelligence group in the city. In a conversation with author Uinseann MacEoin, Connie Neenan claimed that in September 1920, 'we laid a trap and caught this clerk in the main post office. He was the channel through which the notes were passed'.[3] The Cork mails also figured in city Volunteer Eamonn Enright's recollection. 'Some of the big businessmen had managed the Anti-Sinn Féin Society. They were Unionists and Protestants. Three of them were shot after a raid on the mails. A manager of Woodford Bourne was shot.'[4]

The initial victim here could have been Sean O'Callaghan, abducted on 15 September, and executed as an informer a few days later.[5] However, the testimony of two Third Battalion IRA intelligence officers complicates the picture. In a Bureau of Military History Statement, Tim O'Keefe and Joe Aherne recalled the following incident from their vantage point in Ballincollig, a few miles from Cork city.

> About the end of the summer, 1920, a raid for mails was made at Waterfall, which resulted in the capture of a letter from Nagle, a local postman, to a man by the name of O'Sullivan, an ex-British soldier. They arrested Nagle, who gave all information, also a photo of O'Sullivan and details of the place in Cork City where he was to meet with him. Leo [*Murphy, OC Third Battalion*] and some others went there instead of Nagle and shot him dead. Later Nagle was also tried and also shot.[6]

The only recorded civilian execution in 'the end of the summer, 1920' was Sean O'Callaghan, abducted and secretly shot in the middle of September. It is possible the Ballincollig officers O'Keefe and Aherne mistook 'O'Sullivan' for Sean O'Callaghan. Perhaps they confused the dates, and their O'Sullivan was either William Sullivan (killed 14 February 1921); Michael Finbarr O'Sullivan (killed 20 February 1921); or Christy O'Sullivan (killed 26 May 1921). However, an intriguing incident occurred on 24 September, nine days after Sean O'Callaghan was kidnapped. The *Cork Constitution* reported that some armed civilians, 'apparently Volunteers', abducted an unidentified man in front of the Cork General Post Office, and took him away in an automobile.[7] No further mention of this incident nor the victim can be found. If this person was executed by the IRA and also named 'O'Sullivan', then a neat chronology intersects with the Ballincollig Volunteers' statement. As Connie Neenan recalled, 'in September 1920', the IRA did indeed 'set a trap' and kidnap someone in front of 'the main post office'. This all occurred after a 'raid on the mails', as Eamon Enright remembered. According to this theory, the interrogation of Nagle the postman by the Ballincollig IRA set off a chain reaction culminating in the execution of the 'Anti-Sinn Féin Society' leadership in February 1921. Unfortunately, while this hypothesis is plausible it remains unproven.

Regardless of whether it was through an informer named O'Callaghan or O'Sullivan, it seems clear that the city IRA first became aware of the 'Anti-Sinn Féin Society' in September 1920. How then did the Volunteers discover the group's composition? Two important IRA veterans claim it was an unfortunate teenager named Parsons who helped them to identify the group members.

Mick Murphy's testimony is again vital to this theory. Like Neenan, Murphy should be approached with care. His talks with Ernie O'Malley and to the Bureau of Military History include exaggerations and overstatements. However, Murphy's version corresponds with the local events of 1920–1. The most compelling part of his testimony relates to the discovery of the civilian group.

> Parsons was shot. He was the most open-spoken young fellow that I ever met in my life. He gave us all their names and he told us their meeting place, the Y.M.C.A. And he told us they used to meet in a house in Rockboro Road and that a Mrs Brown lived next door. It was Blemens' house they met in. A father, son and daughter lived there. Mrs Brown was in touch with Florrie O'Donoghue, and she told Florrie about them. We got into the back and we saw them and we heard them. And they were shot, one by one, and in groups.[8]

There is no record of a young man named Parsons disappearing in Cork in 1920–1. There was a William Edward Parsons born in Cork city in 1906,[9] which would make him 14 at the time of Murphy's purported encounter. No record of his death, nor a listing of him as missing, can be found.[10] However, a key Volunteer does support Murphy's version. Martin Corry (a future Fianna Fáil TD) operated in the city suburbs and acted as 'Chief Executioner' for the Cork No. 1 Brigade.[11] Corry recalled:

> Parsons was a spy from the Junior Ring of the Young Men's Christian Association. He was a lad of 16 years and he had a limp. They were paid £5 a week and they received a bonus when men were captured as a result of their efforts. £60 he received for the lad who was shot in the railway tunnel. He had a kind of a limp.[12]

Corry is the third IRA leader to describe the execution of a teenage informant working out of the Y.M.C.A, and the second to use the name Parsons, which leads to the conclusion that such a person did exist.

While Martin Corry supports Murphy's claims about Parsons, Corry undermines the teenager's supposed role in the Anti-Sinn Féin Society. Corry's recollection that Parsons helped track 'the lad who was shot in the railway tunnel' is most likely a reference to Volunteer Charlie Daly, who was killed by British operatives in the Blackpool Railway Tunnel. Unfortunately for Mick Murphy, that incident took place on 1 March 1921,[13] weeks after the supposed Anti-Sinn Féin Society executions. Either Murphy's or Corry's memory is at fault here.[14]

The entire exercise would appear fruitless except for a key detail in Murphy's narrative. Murphy stated: 'He [Parsons] said they used to meet in a house in Rockboro Road and that a Mrs Brown lived next door. It was Blemens' house they met in … Mrs Brown was in touch with Florrie O'Donoghue, and she told us about them. We got into the back and we saw them and we heard them. And they were shot one by one, and in groups.'

There is no Rockboro Road in Cork. However, there is a Rockboro Terrace, which is a series of five homes lying on the Blackrock Road.[15] The IRA intelligence agent Mrs Josephine McCoy Brown lived at Number 2, Rockboro Terrace.[16] As Murphy claimed, Mrs Brown was most definitely 'in contact with Florrie O'Donoghue'.

According to newspaper accounts, James Blemens was abducted from his home on Blackrock Road. James Blemens and his son Frederick actually lived at Number 1, Braemer, in a short lane of two connected houses lying on Blackrock Road.[17] Number 2 Rockboro Terrace adjoins Number 1 Braemer. In fact, Frederick Blemens' backyard laid only a few metres from Josephine Brown's Rockboro Terrace residence. Like young Parsons allegedly said, Mrs Brown lived next door.

The physical proximity of Josephine Brown to James and Frederick Blemens strengthens Murphy's statement. Mrs Brown was a prized IRA intelligence source who could be relied on to report any suspicious activities by her neighbours. Her home provided easy access to the Blemens' backyard, which is consistent with Murphy's claim. It is believable, therefore, that Mrs Brown alerted O'Donoghue to a mysterious meeting of her next-door neighbours, and that O'Donoghue and Murphy observed a meeting of loyal Cork citizens who were gathering intelligence for the Crown forces in Cork. This information enabled the Cork city IRA to identify various members of this group, the bulk of whom were later exiled or executed.

CHRONOLOGY

The discovery of the pro-British spy group apparently occurred in September 1920. Over the next few months, Cork City Volunteer intelligence officers gathered additional information about the group's make-up, some of it coming through the observation of a meeting in the Blemens' home in October or November. With the accumulated evidence in hand, the IRA suddenly struck this group in February 1921.

Ballyvourney volunteer James Minighan gave his own version of events in February.

> Word came out to the Joker [Seán O'Hegarty] that certain members of the Anti-Sinn Féin Society were implicated in tracking down our men and Seán sent my sister to Cork with a verbal message, for he would not write anything down on paper if he could avoid it. She was told to tell Florrie O'Donoghue that Beale, Baker and White were to be shot at once.[18]

At that time Seán O'Hegarty resided with the Brigade flying column near Ballyvourney,[19] which is consistent with Minighan's claims of his location and his need to send a courier into the city. Minighan includes the interesting recollection that 'certain members of the Anti-Sinn Féin Society were implicated'. Is it possible that the IRA knew the identities of this group of civilian enemies and only shot those it considered a direct threat? That would explain why some alleged informers were expelled from the city while others were assassinated. It would also indicate a firmer IRA grasp of the situation in Cork than previously believed.

Paddy O'Reilly, an IRA officer in the Brigade's Fifth Youghal Battalion, told Ernie O'Malley about a related incident in his battalion area. 'Information from Brigade HQ notified him of a ring of spies called "Anti-Sinn Féin" and ordered him to shoot the Ring Leader, and order two others to leave the country. This was done and the ring leader was shot, 25/3/21.'[20] Mr J. Cathart, a managing director of Paisley and Company, was shot in his Youghal home on the evening of 25 March.[21] A sign reading 'Convicted Spy – Spies and Informers Beware' was left on his body. A few hours later, Auxiliary Cadets hung a board inscribed with the word 'Revenge' on a tree in his garden, to warn locals to expect reprisals for Cathart's killing. A body of police dressed in mufti subsequently marched in his funeral procession.[22] Both these acts indicate a police connection to Cathart, which adds to suspicion that he was in fact a civilian spy.

Florrie O'Donoghue told Ernie O'Malley that there was a Unionist intelligence group operating in Cork city, composed of members of the Freemason Society.

> It looked as if the 6th Division felt the RIC were not really effective or that their own intelligence was not getting results so they organized this group thoughtfully. They knew these people and their psychology. The greatest part of Freemason strength was concentrated in Cork City and scattered in Cork. From time to time one of these was shot as evidence piled up, five or six in all. That finished them as an intelligence force.'[23]

Five civilian victims fall into the category of prominent Protestants. They are: James Blemens, Frederick Blemens, Alfred Reilly, Charles Beale, and James Cathart. This number matches O'Donoghue's figure. However, it is by no means certain if the group referred to by O'Donoghue was in fact the Anti-Sinn Féin Society.

So what happened in Cork city? Was there an Anti-Sinn Féin Society? Or was this group an invention of paranoid Volunteers to justify their assassination of political opponents?

THE 'ANTI-SINN FÉIN SOCIETY' THEORY

An explanation does mesh with the available evidence of events in Cork city during 1920–1921. By the summer of 1920, paid police spies were active in the city, but regarded as ineffective by the IRA. However, in September 1920 the Volunteers became aware of a

small organization of patriotic pro-British civilians providing intelligence to the Crown forces in Cork city. The IRA detected a group
member (either Sean O'Callaghan, or 'O'Sullivan' who worked with
the Ballincollig postman Nagle), probably through an incriminating
letter seized in an IRA mail raid. The Volunteers then kidnapped,
interrogated, and executed this informant. The episode prompted
the Cork city IRA to search for other civilians in this group, which
they called 'The Anti-Sinn Féin Society'.

Around the same time, Cork Volunteers picked up the youth
Parsons for shadowing IRA members. Parsons gave the IRA more
specific information about the civilian spy group, including its meeting place at the Blemens home on Blackrock Road. Josephine Brown
may have reported strange happenings at the same location. One
night Mick Murphy and Florrie O'Donoghue climbed into the
Blemens' yard and observed a meeting of the network. With additional evidence in hand, the IRA picked up two suspected informers,
Frederick and James Blemens. Probing for a possible link, At the
same time, while investigating a possible link, the Volunteers decided
to interrogate and execute two other known police informers, Tom
Downing and George Horgan.

Following the November executions, the IRA may have accumulated more information about the city's pro-British spy network. By
January, the Crown forces seemed to possess better intelligence
about local IRA efforts, and conducted a series of successful raids for
arms and Volunteers. British intimidation of Cork residents through
Martial Law restrictions and reprisals may have yielded additional
information about IRA activities. Faced with an evolving situation,
the IRA decided to strike against known civilian spies in the city. An
intercepted letter from Charles Beale to a British military officer may
have triggered the purge. The Volunteers targetted a number of
previously identified paid police spies, as well as the leaders of the
'Anti-Sinn Féin' group of loyal Crown subjects providing information to the British. Less important members of this network were
ordered out of the country at the same time. For the rest of the
conflict, informers were shot on a case-by-case basis, as their activities were revealed to the IRA.

The 'Anti-Sinn Féin' group did not directly participate in the
threats and arson that occurred in Cork city during the last months
of 1920. Those were conducted by Crown forces, most likely
Auxiliary Cadets, who used the 'Anti-Sinn Féin' moniker to cover
their reprisal warnings and blazes in the city. So why did the IRA call

the local group of civilian informants the 'Anti-Sinn Féin Society'? One explanation is the Volunteers associated the civilian intelligence network with the 'Anti-Sinn Féin' attacks of this period, perhaps because the pro-British civilians identified the Republican victims. The IRA did detect the espionage group the same time as the city's first unofficial reprisal in September 1920. It is also possible the Volunteers used the name as a convenient pseudonym for this type of local enemy, since the phrase was appearing in local newspapers during the same period. They had done something similar with the term 'murder gang', which was commonly used by the British, and then adapted by the IRA to describe certain groups of Crown forces operating against them in a particular fashion. Regardless, it seems the IRA veterans used the 'Anti-Sinn Féin Society' phrase to refer to a civilian spying group, rather than the arsonists who were active in late 1920.

This 'Anti-Sinn Féin Society' theory relies heavily on Republican sources who had a motive to justify their assassinations of fellow citizens. It also conflicts with British police and military claims that local civilians executed by the IRA were almost entirely innocent of 'spying'. British and Irish explanations clearly contradict each other. However, like the IRA, police and British Army authors had their own motivations to alter the record. Their performance in 1920–1921 ranged from inadequate to incompetent. They had proved unable to defeat a part-time army of amateurs in the third-largest city in Ireland. British official histories and reports of the period display little self-criticism or honesty about the poor results achieved in Cork. Like IRA recollections, British denials about these victims cannot be accepted uncritically.

One of these two competing versions of events is essentially correct. To accept the British explanation, one must assume that the IRA's intelligence network provided false information resulting in the erroneous execution of twenty-six innocents. However, such IRA ineptitutde is not believable when considering the strength of IRA intelligence in Cork city.

The Volunteers had the means to identify their civilian enemies. Through a well-organized intelligence apparatus, the IRA kept the city under close watch. Thousands of Republican activists and sympathizers observed their fellow citizens. British communications were intercepted. IRA spies penetrated the police and military head-quarters. British intelligence officers were kept under surveillance. Information was collected and analyzed in a timely fashion.

There is little evidence pointing to a sectarian campaign of intimidation or reprisal against the city's Protestant Unionist population. The IRA likewise did not attempt to purge the city of ex-soldiers. Republican motivations in these cases seem to have been legitimate. The Volunteers believed they shot informers operating in conjunction with the city's Crown forces.

Considering the strength of the IRA intelligence network in Cork city, it seems that in most cases, the IRA probably correctly executed people who were passing information to the Crown forces. The Volunteers also likely made some mistakes, though there is simply not enough evidence to clearly identify their innocent victims.

SUMMARY

IRA Veterans consistently claimed that a secret group of Unionist civilians provided information in Cork. British sources disgree with these accounts, but provide few specifics or evidence about these cases. The Volunteers' version is the most plausible because of the extensive and successful IRA intelligence network in Cork. By and large, the IRA likely executed the 'right' people in 1920–1, though it seems probable that some mistakes were also made. Unfortunately, this study cannot draw more specific conclusions about what occurred in Cork city during the Irish War of Independence.

NOTES

1 See Stan Barry, Martin Corry, Eamonn Enright, James Minighan, Mick Murphy, Florrie O'Donoghue, Connie Neenan, and Paddy O'Reilly in the O'Malley Notebooks.
2 Connie Neenan in the O'Malley Notebooks.
3 MacEoin, p 239
4 Eamonn Enright in the O'Malley Notebooks.
5 For details, see Minister of Defence correspondence in 1922 relating to O'Callaghan's kidnapping and execution, A/0535, MA.
6 Tim O'Keefe's and Joe Aherne's story can be read in the combined BMH Statement of five leaders of the Third Battalion, Cork No. 1 Brigade (WS 810), National Archives.
7 *Cork Constitution*, 25 September 1921.
8 Mick Murphy in the O'Malley Notebooks.
9 Index of Birth and Death Certificates, Church of Latter Day Saints Archive, Cork.
10 A Joseph Parsons resided on High Street in Cork in 1914, and he may or may not have been related to young Parsons. See Guys Cork Directory, 1914.

11 Mick Leahy in the O'Malley Notebooks.
12 Martin Corry in the O'Malley Notebooks.
13 *Cork Examiner*, 2 March 1921.
14 Ernie O'Malley's transcription skills are another possible culprit.
15 Guy's Cork Directory 1920, Local History Collection, Cork City Library.
16 O'Donoghue, *Florence and Josephine O'Donoghue's War of Independence*, pp. 111, 113–14, 134.
17 Guy's Cork Directory 1914, Guy's Cork Directory 1920.
18 Jerry Minighan in the O'Malley Notebooks.
19 O'Hegarty was then preparing the column's Coolavokig Ambush.
20 Paddy O'Reilly in the O'Malley Notebooks.
21 *Cork Constitution*, 26 March 1921.
22 *Cork Constitution*, 29 March 1921.
23 Florrie O'Donoghue in the O'Malley Notebooks.

CHAPTER NINE

Conclusions

During the War of Independence, the Cork No. 1 Brigade was known within the IRA for shooting informers first and asking questions later. Ernie O'Malley recalled of its Brigade commander:'Seán Hegarty had the name of being not very particular about evidence, but that might be talk.'[1] In 1921, Florrie O'Donoghue heard a similar sentiment voiced by IRA GHQ. He protested to IRA Chief of Staff Richard Mulcahy: 'I think GHQ has somehow got the idea that in the Cork Brigades, especially Cork No. 1, men are being shot as spies more or less on suspicion.' He pointed out: 'Instead of this, as I'm aware myself, the greatest care is taken in every case to have the case fully proved and beyond all doubt. The men shot in most cases have admitted their guilt before being executed.'[2] Forty years later he spoke of his 'personal moral responsibility' in these cases, and wrote: 'Frequently we deferred action over and over again where there was reasonable doubt; in most of these cases we never took any action at all.'[3] Cork IRA intelligence officer Seán Culhane agreed. 'We were careful that before a spy was shot it had to be a definite case of spying.'[4]

The IRA in county Cork did shoot innocent men as 'informers' during 1920–1. The Cork No. 2 Brigade executed a blameless traveller after forcing him to sign a false confession that he gave away the Clonmult flying column.[5] The Cork No. 1 Brigade's Third Battalion appeared to have shot a tramp for no other reason than his entering Ballincollig Barracks to inquire about work.[6] Brigade Vice-Commander Mick Leahy, who operated in Cobh's Fourth Battalion area, reported another disturbing incident. After arresting a former schoolmate, Leahy ultimately killed the man, not for spying, but rather because sensitive parts of the local IRA operation had been revealed to the prisoner during his detention. 'He had to be executed for by this time he knew too much, too many people, too many houses and byways.'[7] Almost certainly there were other mistakes in the Cork No. 1 Brigade, and most likely one or more of these occurred in Cork city.

There is no conclusive evidence that a pro-British civilian intelligence group called the 'Anti-Sinn Féin Society' operated in Cork in 1920–1. However, IRA veterans consistently claimed that such a group did exist, and that a number of its members (James and Frederick Blemens, Alfred Reilly, Charles Beale, and James Cathart) were executed as a result. It is plausible that such a network existed in Cork. The 'Irish Coast Intelligence Corps' was organized in a similar fashion. General Strickland appealed to Cork Unionists for this kind of assistance. It is certain that the Crown forces needed such a formation. Local conditions in late 1920 were ripe for a handful of the city's thousands of Unionists to band together to defend the Crown against incessant Republican attacks. Such a development would be expected in the War of Independence context. Unfortunately, the most compelling evidence of the 'Anti-Sinn Féin Society' group comes from former Republican guerrillas.

In addition to members of the 'Anti-Sinn Féin Society', IRA veterans claim they shot numerous police spies operating individually in the city. Overall, there is strong circumstantial evidence implicating some of the IRA's victims. In others there is not.

Police or military ties to the victims have been established in eleven cases (Timothy Quinlisk, Tom Downing, George Horgan, Michael Walsh, William Mohally, Michael O'Sullivan, Daniel McDonnell, Cornelius Sheehan, J. Cathart, W.J. Nolan, and James Bagley). The IRA offered unsubstantiated explanations in the case of seven other civilian victims (Fred Blemens, James Blemens, Alfred Reilly, Charles Beale, Seán O'Callaghan, William Sullivan, and John O'Leary). In thirteen cases, no obvious connection with the Crown forces or IRA explanation for the assault is forthcoming (John Good, T.J. Poland, Thomas Goulding, James Flynn, Denis Donovan, Stephen O'Callaghan, Edward Hawkins, Daniel Hawkins, John Sherlock, Francis McMahon, John Lynch, Christy O'Sullivan and Major G.B. O'Connor).

This study has shown that the Crown forces recruited informers in Cork city and received some information about IRA activities, most notably from late 1920 to early 1921. The British scored some significant successes against the IRA, including the uncovering of a major arms dump in Clogheen, the shooting of numerous Volunteers in the city, the arrests of some senior Brigade leaders, and the killing of six members of the Brigade flying column at Kerry

Pike. However, the Crown forces were ultimately unable to defeat the IRA in Cork city, and British intelligence efforts were found to be lacking. Boycotted and suffering through a campaign of selective assassination, the RIC became largely ineffective in the city. The Crown forces proved vulnerable to double agents and infiltration from Republican operatives on their civilian staffs. Most notably, the IRA agent Josephine McCoy Brown O'Donoghue gained access to the most sensitive material in the British Army headquarters at Victoria Barracks. As a result, one must assume that the IRA was privy to every British report concerning intelligence or civilian informers in Cork. The profound implications of this security breach must be considered when addressing the discovery of civilian informers in the city.

Cork city IRA forces fought the British throughout the war's duration. Levels of violence against Crown forces did not abate in 1921. Though it suffered setbacks in late 1920 and early 1921, the Volunteers reorganized and rallied in the city. Their efforts were greatly assisted by the Cork No. 1 Brigade intelligence service. Using hundreds of Volunteers and civilian assistants, the Brigade kept British forces and suspected civilian opponents under constant observation. Mail, telegraphs, and telephones were monitored for useful information. A largely sympathetic population could be counted on for support. In local hotels, pubs, and the railway stations, IRA operatives observed British movements. Fulltime intelligence officers analyzed information to identify problems and opportunities.

The IRA's greatest strength in Cork city was its intelligence network. Available evidence shows that it functioned well and was organized in a professional manner. Republican claims regarding civilian informers in Cork city must be seen through the prism of the IRA's intelligence capability. Did the IRA have the means to identify its civilian enemies? This study has shown that the answer is yes.

There is little indication that the IRA deliberately targeted ex-soldiers or Unionists as part of a general terror campaign, or as reprisals for Republican defeats. The Volunteers believed their victims were guilty of spying in 1920–1.

Available British sources contradict the IRA version of events. Police reports and official military histories do not admit to any British informers losing their lives in Cork city during the conflict. These claims, however, seem dubious in the wake of clear evidence to the contrary in a number of cases (most notably Timothy Quinlisk, Michael Walsh, Daniel McDonnell, Cornelius Sheehan, and James Bagley). The authors of the official histories had a motivation to downplay their poor performance, and understate British failures during the conflict. They also do not take into account the compartmentalized intelligence efforts by the RIC, Auxiliary Cadets, British Army, and MI5 in Cork city.

Without a doubt, the Crown forces lost some of their civilian informers to the IRA in Cork during 1920–1. However, the true number remains unclear. At this stage it is impossible to assemble a comprehensive dossier for every suspected civilian informant in Cork. One must assume that due to the sensitivities regarding this subject, certain records about informers were either destroyed or never kept. Any contemporary IRA documentation about these cases was eliminated to prevent incriminating evidence from falling into British hands. From the British perspective, to even begin such a study one would need to review every report, private diary, and notebook of every policeman, military officer, and government agent who served in Cork city. Those records, however, do not exist. No oral history project was ever undertaken to gather relevant information from a Crown force viewpoint. The candid memories of British personnel in the city have been lost to history.

It is probable that the IRA successfully identified many civilian informers working in the city. Scattered memories, occasional reports, and contemporary documentation indicate local events, patterns, and causes. Some important details have emerged from the opening of the Bureau of Military History, and others may be found in the Military Pension Archive, which is expected to become available in the near future. However, even with this new material, uncertainties surround numerous individual cases. Unfortunately, the deaths of some suspected informers in Cork city are clouded in confusion and mired by conflicting explanations from British and Irish sources. The nature of espionage ensures that many questions go unanswered.

They will remain so.

This study shows that when considering spies, informers, and the 'Anti-Sinn Féin Society' in Cork city during 1920–1, historians may suspect the truth, but they will never be sure of it.

NOTES

1   O'Malley, p. 309.
2   O'Donoghue to R. Mulcahy, 24 June 1921, P17A/20, Mulcahy Papers, UCD.
3   O'Donoghue, *Florence and Josephine O'Donoghue's War of Independence*, p. 84.
4   Seán Culhane in the O'Malley Notebooks.
5   Ms. 31,249, NLI.
6   *Cork County Eagle and County Advertiser,* 9 July 1921.
7   Mick Leahy in the O'Malley Notebooks.

Bibliography

PRIMARY SOURCES

Cork

Cork Archives Institute
Seamus Fitzgerald Papers
Donal Hales Papers
Robert Hales Papers
Robert Langford Papers
Siobhan Lankford Papers
Liam de Roiste Diaries

Cork City Library
Census for the City of Cork, Census of the Population Reports
Cork Chamber of Commerce and Shipping Annual Reports, 1919–1922
Guys Cork Directory

Cork Public Museum
Tomas MacCurtain Papers
Terence MacSwiney Papers
Sean O'Hegarty Papers

University College Cork
Alfred Rahilly Papers
Public Records Office, London, British in Ireland Series (Microfilm)

Dublin

National Library of Ireland
F.S. Bourke Collection
Department of Defence Archives (Microfilm)
Frank Gallagher Papers

Joseph McGarrity Papers
J.J. O'Connell Papers
Florence O'Donoghue Papers
James O'Donovan Papers

University College Dublin
Richard Mulcahy Papers
Ernie O'Malley Papers
Ernie O'Malley Notebooks (included with papers): Interviews with
  Stan Barry, Charlie Brown, Mick Burke, Dan Corkery, Martin
  Corry, Tom Crofts, Sean Culhane, Sean Daly, Dan 'Sandow'
  Donovan, Eamonn Enright, Seamus Fitzgerald, Dan Healy, Sean
  Hendrick, Ray Kennedy, Michael Leahy, Pat Margetts, James
  Minighan, Mick Murphy, Seamus Murphy, Patrick 'Pa' Murray,
  Connie Neenan, Florence O'Donoghue, Paddy O'Reilly, George
  Power, Connor Reilly, Mick O'Sullivan.

Military Archives (Cathal Brugha Barracks)
Bureau of Military History – Statements of Robert Aherne, Seàn
  Culhane, Dan Donovan, Daniel Healy, Mick Murphy, Patrick
  Murray, Florence O'Donoghue.
Department of Defence Correspondence Relating to Disappearances
  in Cork City
'Executions by IRA'
'British Casualties, Military'
Statement of Captain O'Dwyer

LONDON

Imperial War Museum
Gen. E.P. Strickland Papers – *History of the 6th Division in Ireland*,
  official history covering 1919–1921, written by the division staff;
  *Summary of Important Orders to the 17th Infantry Brigade from
  HQ 6th Division*, a booklet prepared by brigade staff; *Sinn* Féin
  and the Irish Volunteers, booklet prepared by the General
  Headquarters staff of the Irish Command; Miscellaneous corre-
  spondence and material relating to Strickland in Ireland
  1920–1921; Strickland Diaries.
Lt Gen. Sir Hugh Jeaudwine Papers
Lt Gen. A.E. Percival Papers

Kings College, Liddell Hart Centre for Military Archives
Papers of Maj. Gen. Howard Foulkes

INTERVIEWS/CORRESPONDENCE

Seán O'Callaghan
Dr Margaret O'Donoghue
Dan O'Donovan
Donal O'Donovan
Seán O'Regan
Father Patrick Twohig
Pat Whooley

NEWSPAPERS AND PERIODICALS

An Cosantóir
An tÓglac
An tOglac (1961–1971)
Cork Constitution
Cork County Eagle and Munster Advertiser
Cork Examiner
Cork Weekly News
Freeman's Journal
Irish Bulletin
Irish Times
New York Times
Old Ireland
Skibbereen Star
Sinn Féiner
South Wales Echo
Times of London
Weekly Summary
Western Bulletin
Wolfe Tone Annual

PAMPHLETS

American Commission on the Conditions in Ireland Interim Report, (London, Hardin & Moore Ltd, 1921)
Evidence on Conditions in Ireland, (Washington DC: American Commission on Conditions in Ireland, 1921)
Who Burnt Cork City? (Dublin: Irish Labour and Trade Union Congress, 1921)

SELECT BIBILIOGRAPHY

Abbott, Richard, *Police Casualties in Ireland 1919–1922*, (Cork: Mercier Press, 2000).

Andrew, Christopher, *Secret Service, The Making of the British Intelligence Community* (London: Heinemenn, 1985).

Andrews, C.S., *Dublin Made Me* (Dublin: Mercier Press, 1969).

Augusteijn, Joost, *From Public Defiance to Guerrilla Warfare* (Dublin: Irish Academic Press, 1996)

—(ed.) *The Irish Revolution 1913–1923* (New York: Palgrave, 2002).

Barry, Tom, *Guerilla Days in Ireland* (Boulder, CO: Roberts Rinehart Publishers, 1995).

Beaslai, Piaras, *Michael Collins and the Making of a New Ireland, Vol. I* (Dublin: Phoenix Publishing Company, 1926).

Bell, J. Bowyer, *The Secret Army* (New Brunswick, NJ: Transaction Publishers, 1997).

Borgonovo, John 'Informers, Intelligence, and the "Anti-Sinn Féin Society": The Anglo-Irish Conflict in Cork City, 1920–1921', MA Thesis, University College Cork, 1998.

—(ed.) *Florence and Josephine O'Donoghue's War of Independence, 'A Destiny that Shapes Our Ends'* (Dublin: Irish Academic Press, 2006).

Bowden, T., 'The Irish Underground and the War of Independence, 1919–1921', *Journal of Contemporary History*, VIII, No. 2, (1973).

Boyce, D. George, *Nationalism in Ireland* (London: Routledge, 1985).

—*The Irish Question and British Politics, 1868–1996* (London: MacMillan, 1996)

Boyle, John F. and de Burca, Pádraig, *Free State or Republic* (Dublin: University College Press, 2002).

Brewer, John D., *The Royal Irish Constabulary: An Oral History* (Belfast: Institute of Irish Studies, Queens University, 1990).

Buttimer, Cornelius and O'Flanagan, Patrick (eds), *Cork: History and Society, Interdisciplinary Essays on the History of an Irish County* (Dublin: Geography Publications, 1993).

Callwell, C.E., *Field-Marshal Sir Henry Wilson: His Life and Diaries* (London: Cassell, 1927).

Campbell, Colm, *Emergency Law in Ireland, 1918–1924* (Oxford: Oxford University Press, 1994).

Chavasse, Moirin, *Terence MacSwiney* (Dublin: Clonmore and Reynolds, 1961).

Choiller, Brendan MacGiolla, *Intelligence Notes, 1913-1916* (Dublin: State Paper Office, 1966).

Clarke, Olga Pyne, *She Came of Decent People* (London: Methuen, 1986).

Conlon, Lil, *Cumann na mBan and the Women of Ireland, 1913–1925* (Kilkenny: Kilkenny People Press, 1969).

Coogan, Tim Pat, *The Man Who Made Ireland, The Life and Death of Michael Collins* (Niwot, CO: Roberts Rhinehart, 1992).

Costello, Francis J., *Enduring the Most, The Life and Death of Terence MacSwiney* (Dingle: Brandon Books, 1995).

—*The Irish Revolution and Its Aftermath* (Dublin: Irish Academic Press, 2003).

Crozier, Brig. General F.P., *Ireland Forever* (Bath: Cedric Chivers, 1971).

—*Word to Gandhi* (London: Williams and Norgate, 1927).

Curran, Joseph, 'Decline and Fall of the IRB,' *Eire/Ireland*, Winter, (1975) pps. 14–23.

—*The Birth of the Irish Free State* (Alabama: University of Alabama Press, 1980).

D'Alton, Ian, 'Keeping Faith: An Evocation of the Cork Protestant Character 1820-1920' in *Cork History and Society* (Dublin: Geography Publication, 1993).

Dangerfield, George, *The Damnable Question, A Study in Anglo-Irish Relations* (Boston: Little, Brown and Company, 1976).

Deasy, Liam, *Towards Ireland Free* (Cork: Royal Carbery Books, 1992).

Doherty, Gabriel and Keogh, Dermot (eds), *Michael Collins and the Making of the Irish State* (Cork: Mercier Press, 1998).

Dwyer, T. Ryle, *Michael Collins, The Man Who Won the War* (Cork: Mercier press, 1990)

—*Tans, Terror and Troubles, Kerry's Real Fighting Story 1913–23* (Cork: Mercier Press, 2001).

Fallon, Charlotte Mary, *Soul on Fire, The Biography of Mary MacSwiney* (Cork: Mercier press, 1986).

Fitzgerald, Seamus, 'East Cork Activities', *Capuchin Annual*, 1970.

Fitzpatrick, David, *Politics and Irish Life 1913–21: Provincial Experiences of War and Revolution* (Dublin: Gill and MacMillan, 1977).

—(ed.) *Revolution in Ireland?* (Dublin: Trinity History Workshop,

Trinity College Dublin, 1990)

—'"Unofficial Emmisaries": British Army Boxers in the Irish Free State, 1926', *Irish Historical Studies*, XXX, No. 118 (November 1996).

Garvin, Tom, *The Evolution of Irish Nationalist Politics* (Dublin: Gill and MacMillan, 1981).

—*Nationalist Revolutionaries in Ireland 1858–1928* (Oxford: Clarendon Press, 1987).

—*1922: The Birth of Irish Democracy* (Dublin: Gill and Macmillan, 1996).

Gaughan, J. Anthony, *The Memoirs of Constable Jeremiah Mee* (Dublin: Anvil Books, 1975).

Griffith, Kenneth and O'Grady, Timothy, *Curious Journey, An Oral History of Ireland's Unfinished Revolution* (Cork: Mercier Press, 1998).

Gudgin, Peter, *Military Intelligence, the British Story* (London: Arms & Armour Press, 1982).

Hamilton, Nigel, *Monty, The Making of a General, 1887–1942* (New York: McGraw Hill Books, 1981).

Harrington, Niall, *Kerry Landing* (Dublin: Anvil Books, 1992).

Hart Peter, 'Class Community, and the Irish Republican Army in Cork, 1917–1923', in O'Flanagan and Buttimer *Cork: History and Society, Interdisciplinary Essays on the History of an Irish County* (Dublin: Geography Publications, 1993).

—'The Protestant Experience in Southern Ireland', in Richard English and Graham Walker (eds.) *Unionism in Modern Ireland* (Dublin: Gill and MacMillan, 1996).

—*The IRA and Its Enemies, Violence and Community in Cork, 1916–1923* (New York: Oxford University Press, 1998).

—(ed) *British Intelligence in Ireland, 1920-21, The Final Reports* (Cork: Cork University Press, 2002).

—*The IRA at War 1916–1923* (Oxford: Oxford University Press, 2003).

Harvey, Dan, and White, Gerry, *The Barracks, A History of Victoria/Collins Barracks, Cork* (Cork: Mercier Press, 1997).

Hopkinson, Michael, *Green Against Green: The Irish Civil War* (Dublin: Gill and MacMillan, 1988).

—(ed.) *The Last Days of Dublin Castle, the Mark Sturgis Diaries* (Dublin: Irish Academic Press, 1999).

—*The Irish War of Independence* (Dublin: Gill and MacMillan, 2002).

Jeffrey, Keith, 'British Military Intelligence Following World War One', in K.G. Robertson (ed.) *British and American Approaches to Intelligence* (London: MacMillan, 1988).

Jeffries, Henry Alan (ed.), *Cork, Historical Perspectives* (Dublin: Four Court Presses, 2004).

Kenneally, Ian, 'Reports from a "Bleeding Ireland": The Cork Examiner During the Irish War of Independence', *Journal of the Cork Historical and Archaeological Society*, Vol. 108, June 2003.

Keogh, Dermot, *Twentieth Century Ireland, Nation and State* (Dublin: Gill and Macmillan, 1994).

Keogh, Dermot and Doherty, Gabriel (eds.), *Michael Collins and the Making of the Irish State* (Cork: Mercier Press, 1998).

Leader, Naas, *Alfred O'Rahilly, Vol. II, Public Figure* (Dublin: Kingdom Books, 1989).

Lankford, Siobhan, *The Hope and the Sadness* (Cork: Tower Books, 1980).

Lee, Joseph, *Ireland 1912–1985: Politics and Society* (Cambridge: Cambridge University Press, 1989).

Lieberson, Goddard, *The Irish Uprising* (New York: CBS Records, 1968).

Macardle, Dorothy, *The Irish Republic* (Dublin: Irish Press, 1951).

MacEoin, Uinseann, *Survivors* (Dublin: Argenta Publications, 1980).

McDermott, Jim, *Northern Divisions, The Old IRA and the Belfast Pogroms 1920–22* (Belfast: Beyond the Pale Publications, 2001).

MacGiolla Choiller, Brendan (ed.), *Intelligence Notes 1913–1916* (Dublin: State Papers Office, 1966).

Macready, Gen. Sir C.F.N., *Annals of an Active Life* (London, Hutchinson, 1924).

McCoole, Sinead, *No Ordinary Women, Irish Female Activists in the Revolutionary Years 1900–1923* (Madison: University of Wisconsin Press, 2002).

McDonnell, Kathleen Keyes, *There is a Bridge at Bandon* (Dublin: Mercier Press, 1972).

Mansergh, Nicholas, *The Irish Question 1840–1921* (Toronto: University of Toronto Press, 1975).

—*Unresolved Question, The Anglo-Irish Settlement and Its Undoing, 1912–1972* (New Haven: Yale University Press, 1991).

Mitchell, Arthur, *Revolutionary Government in Ireland* (Dublin: Gill and MacMillan, 1995).

—'Alternative Government: "Exit Britannia", The Formation of the

Irish National State, 1918–1921', in Augusteijn (ed.), *The Irish Revolution, 1913–1923*, pp. 70–84.

Moylan, Sean, *Sean Moylan: In His Own Words* (Millstreet: Aubane Historical Society, 2004).

Mulcahy, Gen. Richard, 'Chief of Staff 1919', *Capuchin Annual* (1969).

Nelligan, David, *A Spy in the Castle* (Dublin: McGibbon and Kee, 1968).

Norway, Mary, *The Sinn Féin Rebellion as They Saw It* (Dublin: Irish Academic Press, 1999).

O'Brien, John, 'Population, Politics and Society in Cork, 1780–1900', in Buttimer and O'Flannagan.

O'Brien, Joseph, *William O'Brien and the Course of Irish Politics 1881–1918* (Berkeley, CA: University of California Press, 1976).

O'Broin, Leon, *Revolutionary Underground, The Story of the Irish Republican Brotherhood* (Totowa, NJ : Rowman and Littlefield, 1976).

O'Callaghan, Sean, *Execution* (London: Frederick Mueller, 1974).

O'Connor, Frank, *An Only Child* (London: MacMillan & Co., 1970).

—*Guests of the Nation* (London: MacMillan & Co., 1931).

O'Donoghue, Florence, 'We Need Trained Guerrilla Fighters', *An Cosantóir*, Vol. III, No.5, May 1943.

—*Tomas MacCurtain, Soldier and Patriot* (Tralee: Anvil Books, 1955).

—(ed) *Rebel Cork's Fighting Story* (Tralee: Anvil Books, 1961).

—'Guerrilla Warfare in Ireland,' *An Cosantóir*, Vol. XX, May 1963.

—'The Reorganization of the Irish Volunteers,' *Capuchin Annual*, 1967.

—(ed) *Sworn to Be Free, The Complete Book of IRA Jail Breaks* (Tralee: Anvil Books 1971).

—*No Other Law* (Dublin: Anvil Books, 1986).

—*Florence and Josephine O'Donoghue's War of Independence, 'A Destiny that Shapes Our Ends'* (Dublin: Irish Academic Press, 2006).

O'Faolain, Seán, *Vive Moi* (London: Rubert Hart Davis, 1965).

O'Halpin, Eunan, 'British Intelligence in Ireland, 1914–1921', in Christopher Andrew and David Dilks (eds), *The Missing Dimension: Governments and Intelligence Communities in the Twentieth Century* (London: MacMillan Publishers, 1984).

—'Aspects of Intelligence', *Irish Sword* (No. 95 & 96, 1993–1994).

—'Collins and Intelligence 1919–1923', in Doherty and Keogh, pp. 68–80.

O'Hegarty, P.S., *The Victory of Sinn Féin* (Dublin: Talbot, 1924).

—*A Short Memoir of Terence MacSwiney* (Dublin: Talbot Press, 1922).

O'Kelly, Donal, 'Ordeal By Fire – How The City Faced the Terror of 1920 and 1921', in O'Donoghue (ed.) *Rebel Cork's Fighting Story*, pp.19–25.

O'Malley, Ernie, *On Another Man's Wound* (Dublin: Anvil, 1979).

Ó Snodaigh, Padraig and Mitchell, Arthur (eds), *Irish Political Documents 1916–1949* (Dublin: Irish Academic Press, 1989).

Ó Súilleabháin, Michael, *Where the Mountainy Men Have Sown* (Dublin: Anvil, 1965).

Paine, Lauran, *Britain's Intelligence Service* (London: Richard Hale, 1979).

Russell, Liam, 'Some Activities in Cork City 1920–21', *Capuchin Annual*, 1970.

Ryan, Meda, *Tom Barry, IRA Freedom Fighter* (Cork: Mercier Press, 2003).

—*The Real Chief, Liam Lynch* (Cork: Mercier Press, 2005)

Sheehan, William, *British Voices From the Irish War of Independence 1918–1921* (Cork: Collins Press, 2005).

Strong, Maj-General Sir Kenneth, *Intelligence at the Top, The Recollections of an Intelligence Officer* (London: Cassell and Company, 1968).

Sturgis, Mark, *The Last Days of Dublin Castle, the Mark Sturgis Diaries* (Dublin: Irish Academic Press, 1999).

Townsend, Charles, *The British Campaign in Ireland 1919–1921: The Development of Political and Military Policies* (London: Oxford University Press, 1975).

Twohig, Patrick, *Blood on the Flag* (Ballincollig: Tower Books, 1996). [English Translation of Seamus Malone's *B'Fhiu An Broin*, first published in 1958.]

—*Green Tears for Hecuba* (Ballincollig: Tower Books, 1994).

Valiulis, Maryann Gialanella, *General Richard Mulcahy* (Dublin: Irish Academic Press, 1992).

Walsh, J.J., *Recollections of a Rebel* (Tralee: The Kerryman, 1944).

Winters, Sir Ormonde, *Winters Tale* (London: Richards Press, 1958).

Index